**BARRON'S
BUSINESS
LIBRARY**

Financial Management

D0286571

Second Edition

Jae K. Shim
Professor of Finance and Accounting
California State University, Long Beach

Joel G. Siegel
Professor of Finance and Accounting
Queens College of the City University of New York

BARRON'S

General editor for the first edition of Financial Management in
BARRON'S BUSINESS LIBRARY Series is George T. Friedlob,
professor in the School of Accountancy at Clemson University.

All inquiries should be addressed to:
Barron's Educational Series, Inc.
250 Wireless Boulevard
Hauppauge, New York 11788
http://www.barronseduc.com

Library of Congress Catalog Card No. 99-47469

International Standard Book No. 0-7641-1402-6

Library of Congress Cataloging-in-Publication Data

Shim, Jae K.
    Financial management / by Jae K. Shim, Joel G. Siegel. — 2nd ed.
        p.   cm. — (Barron's business library)
    Includes index.
    ISBN 0-7641-1402-6
    1. Small business—Finance. I. Siegel, Joel G. II. Title. III. Series.
HG4027.7 .S47 2000
658.15′92—dc21   99-47469

Preface

This book is written for the businessperson who must have a basic knowledge of finance to do his or her job. You may be a newly hired or recently promoted middle manager, or an entrepreneur or sole proprietor who has brilliant product ideas but no notion about financing. In any case, a knowledge of basic finance concepts is essential for you to function successfully on the job.

The goal of this book is to provide a working knowledge of the fundamentals of finance that you can apply in the real world. The financial techniques and approaches we describe can be used by any financial manager, regardless of his or her primary duties.

In *Financial Management*, we walk you through "thinking finance" and suggest strategies to help you make intelligent financial decisions and analyze their results. You will read about what you need to know, what to ask, what tools are important, what to look for, what to do, how to do it, and what to watch out for. We have tried to make this book practical, quick reading, and useful. You will learn how to appraise where you've been, where you are now, and where you're headed. We present criteria you can use to examine the performance of your operations and activities as well as to formulate realistic profit goals. Budgeting procedures and cash flow analysis are also discussed.

A basic understanding of financial information is necessary so you can evaluate the performance of your operation—are things getting better or worse? What are the possible reasons? Who is responsible? What can you do about it?

You also need to be able to analyze your company's financial statements in order to evaluate its financial health and operating performance. What has been the trend in profitability and return on investment? Will the business be able to pay its bills? How are receivables and inventory turning over?

Familiarity with tax planning strategies is essential so the company can legally minimize its taxes. We discuss sources of tax-exempt income, tax-deductible expenses, and timing income and expenses among tax years.

Budgeting is another essential topic for you to understand. In order to plan your departmental affairs properly, you need to know how to prepare a budget showing expected sales volume, sales revenue, production and manufacturing costs, operating expenses, and cash flow. The budget, which serves as a road map showing where you are to go and what you are to do, helps you to accomplish financial and operating objectives.

You also need to know what the break-even sales are to determine if a new product or proposal will cover its costs, and how to manage your assets properly to achieve the best possible return consistent with your desired risk level. We discuss ways of managing cash that help you to accelerate cash receipts and delay cash payments; how to decide whether to offer a discount for early payment and extend credit to marginal customers; and how to manage inventory.

Understanding the trade-off between risk and return is crucial. As a rule, the greater the desired rate of return, the greater the risk required to obtain it. This trade-off affects your financing and investment decisions.

As a financial manager, you will need to recognize the time value of money—the idea that a dollar is worth less the longer it takes to receive. Time value of money applications include determining the present value of receiving future cash flows, computing how much money will be in an account at a future date, and calculating interest rates, periodic payments on a loan, and the time it will take for money to grow to a specific value.

You will probably be required to make capital budgeting decisions —to select the optimum *alternative* long-term investment opportunity. Should you buy or lease? Should you sell a division or keep it? Should you manufacture product A or B? Should you expand? Capital budgeting methods that can aid you in making these decisions include determining the payback period (how long it takes to get your initial investment back) and using present value techniques that look at the discounted value in today's dollars of receiving future cash flows.

You may also be required to determine the overall cost of capital for the business. Cost of capital is basically the cost of financing, determined by taking into account the weighted-average cost of debt (interest) and cost of stock (dividends). This cost of capital is the basis for determining the discount rate used to calculate the present value of future cash flows in capital budgeting.

Strategies must be developed to find the best mix of financing for your company. Should you finance short-term or long-term? If you decide to go long-term, should you finance with debt or equity? The particular source of financing depends on the particular circumstances at the time. Further, when you merge with or acquire another business, you will need to select the most advantageous form of financing.

You may need to determine what dividend policy is best for your company, given its overall corporate objectives. The amount of dividends to be paid out depends upon many factors, such as earnings, growth rate, cash position, and opportunities for investment.

If the business is doing poorly, you must be able to take steps to improve operations and avoid business failure. Is reorganization the answer? What are the indicators of potential bankruptcy? If all else fails, you have to know the steps in liquidation.

If your company operates overseas, you must be cognizant of any special risks you face. How can you minimize political and economic exposures in foreign lands? What foreign-currency exchange-rate risk are you willing to assume?

This book includes many practical examples, applications, illustrations, guidelines, measures, rules of thumb, graphs, diagrams, and tables to aid your comprehension of the subjects discussed.

Keep this book handy in your library for easy reference throughout your professional business career. While this book does not include "all you ever wanted to know about finance," it provides a foundation on which to build your knowledge of finance and related business disciplines.

We would like to thank our wives, Chung and Roberta, for their encouragement and patience during the writing of this book. We also thank Tom Friedlob, general editor of this series, for his very valuable input and professional advice. Thanks goes to the outside anonymous reviewer for his constructive comments and suggestions. In addition, we acknowledge the excellent editorial assistance of the staff of Barron's Educational Series, which made this book possible.

Jac K. Shim, Ph.D.
Joel G. Siegel, Ph.D., CPA

Contents

Introduction

INTRODUCTION AND MAIN POINTS

Financial management is the process of planning decisions in order to maximize the owners' wealth. Financial managers have a major role in cash management, in the acquisition of funds, and in all aspects of raising and allocating financial capital, taking into account the trade-off between risk and return. Financial managers need accounting and financial information to carry out their responsibilities.

In this chapter, you will learn:
- The scope and role of finance.
- The language and decision making of finance.
- The responsibilities of financial managers.
- The relationship between accounting and finance.
- The financial and operating environment in which financial managers operate.
- The corporate forms of business organization.

GOALS OF CORPORATE FINANCE

Company goals usually include (1) stockholder wealth maximization, (2) profit maximization, (3) managerial reward maximization, (4) behavioral goals, and (5) social responsibility. Modern managerial finance theory operates on the assumption that the primary goal of the business is to maximize the wealth of its stockholders, which translates into maximizing the price of the firm's common stock. The other goals mentioned above also influence the company's policy but are less important than stock price maximization. Note that the traditional goal frequently stressed by economists—profit maximization—is not sufficient for most companies today.

PROFIT MAXIMIZATION VS. STOCKHOLDER WEALTH MAXIMIZATION

Profit maximization is basically a single-period or, at most, a short-term goal, to be achieved within one year; it is usually interpreted to mean the maximization of profits within a given period of time. A corporation may maximize its short-term profits at the expense of its long-term profitability. In contrast, stockholder wealth maximization is a long-term goal, since stockholders are interested in future as well as present profits. Wealth maximization is generally preferred because it considers (1) wealth for the long term, (2) risk or uncertainty, (3) the timing of returns, and (4) the stockholders' return. Timing of returns is important; the earlier the return is received, the better, since a quick return reduces the uncertainty about receiving the return, and the money received can be reinvested sooner. Table 1-1 summarizes the advantages and disadvantages of these two often conflicting goals.

Let us now see how profit maximization may affect wealth maximization.

EXAMPLE 1-1
Profit maximization can be achieved in the short term at the expense of the long-term goal of wealth maximization. For example, a costly investment may create losses in the short term but yield substantial profits in the long term; a company that wants to show a short-term profit may postpone major repairs or replacement even though such postponement is likely to hurt its long-term profitability.

EXAMPLE 1-2
Profit maximization, unlike wealth maximization, does not consider risk or uncertainty. Consider two products, A and B, and their projected earnings over the next five years, as shown below.

Year	Product A	Product B
1	$10,000	$11,000
2	10,000	11,000
3	10,000	11,000
4	10,000	11,000
5	10,000	11,000
	$50,000	$55,000

A profit maximization approach favors product B over product A because its total projected earnings after five years are higher. However, if product B is more risky than product A, then the decision is not as straightforward as the figures seem to indicate because of the trade-off between risk and return. Stockholders expect greater returns from investments with higher risk; they will demand a sufficiently large return to compensate for the comparatively greater level of risk of producing product B.

TABLE 1-1

PROFIT MAXIMIZATION VERSUS
STOCKHOLDER WEALTH MAXIMIZATION

Goal	Objective	Advantages	Disadvantages
Profit maximization	Large profits	1. Easy to calculate profits. 2. Easy to determine the link between financial decisions and profits.	1. Emphasizes the short term. 2. Ignores risk or uncertainty. 3. Ignores the timing of returns. 4. Requires immediate resources.
Stockholder wealth maximization	Highest market value of common stock	1. Emphasizes the long term. 2. Recognizes risk or uncertainty. 3. Recognizes the timing of returns. 4. Considers stockholders' return.	1. Offers no clear relationship between financial decisions and stock price. 2. Can lead to management anxiety and frustration.

FINANCIAL DECISIONS AND RISK-RETURN TRADE-OFF

The concept of risk-return trade-off is integral to the theory of finance. Risk refers to the variability of expected returns (sales, earnings, or cash flow) and is the probability that a financial problem will affect the company's operational performance or financial position. Typical forms of risk are economic risk, political uncertainties, and industry problems.

Risk analysis is a process of measuring and analyzing the risk associated with financial and investment decisions. It is important to consider risk in making capital investment decisions because of the large amount of capital involved and the long-term nature of the investments. Analysts must also consider the rate of return in relation to the degree of risk involved. (Return, the reward for investing, consists of current income, in the form of either periodic cash payments or capital gain (or loss) from appreciation (or depreciation) in market value.)

Proper assessment and balance of the various risk-return trade-offs available is part of creating a sound stockholder wealth maximization plan. The risk-return trade-off is discussed in Chapters 7, 10, and 12.

TIME VALUE OF MONEY

Today's dollars are not the same as tomorrow's. A dollar now is worth more than a dollar to be received later, because you can invest that dollar for a return and have more than a dollar at the specified later date. Further, receiving a dollar in the future has uncertainty attached to it; inflation might make the dollar received at a later time worth less in buying power.

Time value of money is a critical consideration in financial and investment decisions. For example, compound interest calculations can help you determine your eventual return from an investment. Discounting, or the calculation of present value, which is inversely related to compounding, is used to evaluate future cash flow associated with long-term projects; the discounted value of receiving future cash flows from a proposal is an important consideration. Time value of money has many applications in finance; for example, it can help you determine the periodic payout or interest rate on a loan or decide between leasing and buying equipment.

The time value of money is fully discussed in Chapter 6.

Let us now see why finance is important to know in order to optimally perform your responsibilities.

IMPORTANCE OF FINANCE

It's important for you to have a knowledge of finance and to know how to apply it successfully, whether you deal with production, marketing, personnel, operations, or any other aspect of corporate functioning. You should know where to look, what to ask, and where to get the answers to questions on your department or company operations. Financial knowledge aids in planning, problem solving, and decision making. Further, you must have financial and accounting knowledge in order to be able to understand the financial reports prepared by other segments of the organization.

Financial managers spend a good portion of their time planning, setting objectives, and developing efficient courses of action to achieve their objectives. As a financial manager, you may have to deal with a wide variety of plans, including production plans, financial plans, marketing plans, and personnel plans. Each of these is different, and all require some kind of financial knowledge.

Finance allows for better communication among departments. For example, the corporate budget (financial plan) communicates overall company goals to department managers so they know what is expected of them and what financial parameters exist for their operations. You must be able to identify any problems with the proposed budget before it is finalized and to make recommendations for subsequent budgets. Further, you need to be able to discuss the budget with other members of the company. Failure to understand the budget may mean failure to achieve corporate goals.

You have to present convincing information to upper management to obtain approval for activities and projects such as new product lines. Here, a knowledge of forecasting and capital budgeting (selecting the most profitable project among long-term alternatives) is essential. You must appraise your monetary and manpower requests before submitting them; if you are ill-prepared, you will create a negative impression and may well lose the chance to obtain approval of your request.

Financial knowledge is critical in a wide number of areas. You may be involved in a decision whether to use debt or equity financing and must have the knowledge to weigh the benefits and costs of each in order to meet or maintain your company's capital goals. You may be called on to analyze financial information from competitors based on their financial statements and should be able to understand and analyze such information and make intelligent financial decisions. Or you may have to plan and analyze project performance if your company invests in capital projects (property, plant, and equipment) that are tied to plans for product development, marketing, and production.

SCOPE AND ROLE OF FINANCE

In this section, we discuss the language of finance, the responsibilities of financial managers, and the relationship between accounting and finance.

The Language and Decision Making of Finance

You should master the finance vocabulary in order to comprehend financial information, to know how to utilize that information effectively, and to communicate clearly about the quantitative aspects of performance and results. Further, you must be able to express in a clear, well-thought-out manner what you need in financial terms in order to perform your job effectively.

Accounting provides financial information and includes financial accounting and managerial accounting. *Financial accounting* records the financial history of the business and involves the preparation of reports for use by external parties, such as investors and creditors. *Managerial accounting* provides financial information to be used in making decisions about the *future* of the company. Financial and managerial accounting are more fully discussed later in this chapter.

Accounting information is used by financial managers to make decisions regarding the receipt and use of funds to meet corporate objectives and to forecast future financing needs. The finance function analyzes the accounting information to improve decisions affecting the company's wealth.

Why and What of Finance

Finance involves many interrelated functions, including obtaining funds, using funds, monitoring performance, and solving current and prospective problems.

Financial managers have to know product pricing, planning, and variance analysis (comparing actual to budgeted figures). They must know how to manage assets and optimize the rate of return. They have to be familiar with budgeting, effective handling of productive assets, and the financial strengths and weaknesses of the business.

What Do Financial Managers Do?

The financial manager plays an important role in the company's goal-setting, policy determination, and financial success. Unless the business is small, no one individual handles all the financial decisions; responsibility is dispersed throughout the organization. The financial manager's responsibilities include:

■ *Financial analysis and planning*—Determining the amount of funds the company needs; a large company seeking a rapid growth rate will require more funds.

■ *Making investment decisions*—Allocating funds to specific assets (things owned by the company). The financial manager makes decisions regarding the mix and type of assets acquired and the possible modification or replacement of assets, particularly when assets are inefficient or obsolete.

■ *Making financing and capital structure decisions*—Raising funds on favorable terms, i.e., at a lower interest rate or with few restrictions. Deciding how to raise funds depends on many factors, including interest rate, cash position, and existing debt level; for example, a company with a cash-flow problem may be better off using long-term financing.

■ *Managing financial resources*—Managing cash, receivables, and inventory to accomplish higher returns without undue risk.

The financial manager affects stockholder wealth maximization by influencing:

1. Current and future earnings per share (EPS), equal to net income divided by common shares outstanding.
2. Timing, duration, and risk of earnings.
3. Dividend policy.
4. Manner of financing.

Table 1-2 presents the functions of the financial manager as defined by the Financial Executives Institute, a national organization of financial managers.

TABLE 1-2

FUNCTIONS OF THE FINANCIAL MANAGER AS DEFINED BY THE FINANCIAL EXECUTIVES INSTITUTE

A. Planning
   Long- and short-range financial and corporate planning
   Budgeting for operations and capital expenditures
   Evaluating performance
   Pricing policies and sales forecasting
   Analyzing economic factors
   Appraising acquisitions and divestment

B. Provision of Capital
   Short-term sources; cost and arrangements
   Long-term sources; cost and arrangements
   Internal generation

C. Administration of Funds
Cash management
Banking arrangements
Receipt, custody, and disbursement of company's securities
and monies
Credit and collection management
Pension monies management
Investment portfolio management

D. Accounting and Control
Establishing accounting policies
Developing and reporting accounting data
Cost accounting
Internal auditing
System and procedures
Government reporting
Reporting and interpreting results of operations to management
Comparing performance with operating plans and standards

E. Protection of Assets
Providing for insurance
Establishing sound internal controls

F. Tax Administration
Establishing tax policies and procedures
Preparing tax reports
Tax planning

G. Investor Relations
Maintaining liaison with the investment community
Counseling with analyst—public financial information

H. Evaluation and Consulting
Consulting with and advising other corporate executives on
company policies, operations, and objectives and their
effectiveness

I. Management Information Systems
Development and use of computerized facilities
Development and use of management information systems
Development and use of systems and procedures

NOTE: The size of the company and the capabilities of the various members of management determine how these responsibilities will be assigned.

CONTROLLER VERSUS TREASURER

If you are employed by a large company, the financial responsibilities are probably conducted by the controller, treasurer, and chief financial officer (financial vice-president). The activities of the controller and treasurer fall under the umbrella of finance.

There is no precise distinction between the job of the controller and treasurer, and the functions may differ slightly between organizations because of company policy and the personality of the office holder.

The controller's functions are primarily of an *internal nature* and include record keeping, tracking, and controlling the financial effects of prior and current operations. The *internal* matters of importance to the controller include financial and managerial accounting, taxes, control, and audit functions. The controller is the chief accountant and is involved in the preparation of financial statements, tax returns, the annual report, and Securities and Exchange Commission (SEC) filings. The controller's function is primarily assuring that funds are used efficiently. He or she is primarily concerned with collecting and presenting financial information. The controller usually looks at what *has* occurred rather than what should or will happen.

Many controllers are involved with management information systems and review previous, current, and emerging patterns. They report their analysis of the financial implications of decisions to top management.

The treasurer's function, in contrast, is primarily *external*. The treasurer obtains and manages the corporation's capital and is involved with creditors (e.g., bank loan officers), stockholders, investors, underwriters of equity (stock) and bond issuances, and governmental regulatory bodies (e.g., the SEC). The treasurer is responsible for managing corporate assets (e.g., accounts receivable, inventory) and debt, planning the finances and capital expenditures, obtaining funds, formulating credit policy, and managing the investment portfolio.

The treasurer concentrates on keeping the company afloat by obtaining cash to meet obligations and buying assets to achieve corporate objectives. While the controller concentrates on profitability, the treasurer emphasizes cash flow. Even though a company has been profitable, it may have a significant negative cash flow; for example, there may exist substantial long-term receivables (receivables having a maturity of greater than one year). Without adequate cash flow, even a profitable company may fail. By emphasizing cash flow, the treasurer strives to prevent bankruptcy and achieve corporate goals. The treasurer analyzes the financial statements, formulates additional data, and makes decisions based on the analysis.

The major responsibilities of controllers and treasurers are shown in Table 1-3.

The chief financial officer (financial vice-president) is involved with financial policy making and planning. He or she has financial and managerial responsibilities, supervises all phases of financial activity, and serves as the financial adviser to the board of directors.

Figure 1.1 shows an organization chart of the finance structure within a company. Note that the controller and treasurer report to the vice-president of finance.

RELATIONSHIP BETWEEN ACCOUNTING AND FINANCE

Accounting and finance have different focuses. The primary distinctions between accounting and finance involve the treatment of funds and decision making. Accounting is a necessary subfunction of finance.

The control features of the finance function are referred to as management accounting. Managerial accounting includes the preparation of reports used by management for internal decision making, such as budgeting, costing, pricing, capital budgeting, performance evaluation, break-even analysis, transfer pricing (pricing of goods or services transferred between departments), and rate-of-return analysis. Managerial accounting depends heavily on historical data obtained as part of the financial accounting function. But managerial accounting, unlike financial accounting, is future-oriented and emphasizes making the right decisions today to ensure future performance.

Managerial accounting information is important to the financial manager. For example, the break-even point analysis is useful in deciding whether to introduce a product line. Variance analysis is used to compare actual revenue and/or costs to standard revenue and/or costs for performance evaluation. Managerial accounting can help identify and suggest corrective action. Budgets provide manufacturing and marketing guidelines.

FINANCIAL AND OPERATING ENVIRONMENT

As a financial manager, you operate in the financial environment and are indirectly affected by it. In this section, we discuss financial institutions, markets, and the basic forms of business organizations.

Financial Institutions and Markets

A healthy economy depends on the efficient transfer of funds from savers to individuals, businesses, and governments who need capital. Most transfers occur through specialized financial institutions that serve as intermediaries between suppliers and users of funds.

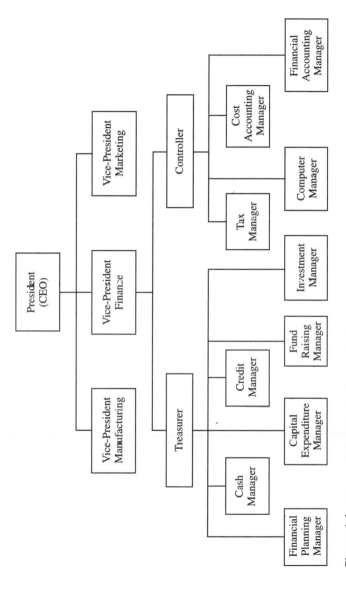

Figure 1.1 *Financial Activity Organization*

TABLE 1-3

RESPONSIBILITIES OF CONTROLLER
AND TREASURER

Controller	Treasurer
Accounting	Obtain financing
Reporting financial information	Maintaining banking relationships
Custody of records	Investing funds
Interpreting financial data	Investor relations
Budgeting	Managing cash
Controlling operations	Insuring assets
Appraising results and making recommendations	Fostering relationships with creditors and investors
Preparing taxes	Appraising credit and
Managing assets	collecting funds
Internal auditing	Deciding on the financing mix
Protecting assets	Disbursing dividends
Reporting to government bodies	Managing pension funds
Payroll	

A financial transaction results in the simultaneous creation of a financial asset and a financial liability. Financial assets include money, stock (equity ownership of a company), or debt (evidence that someone owes you a debt). Financial liabilities are monies you owe someone else, such as loans payable. The creation and transfer of such assets and liabilities constitute *financial markets*.

In the financial markets, companies demanding funds are brought together with those having surplus funds. Financial markets provide a mechanism through which the financial manager obtains funds from a wide range of sources, including financial institutions in such forms as loans, bonds, and common stocks. The financial markets are composed of money markets and capital markets. Figure 1.2 depicts the general flow of funds among financial institutions and markets.

Money markets are the markets for *short-term* debt securities (those with maturities of less than one year). Examples of money market securities include U.S. Treasury bills, commercial paper, and negotiable certificates of deposit issued by government, business, and financial institutions. Federal funds borrowings between banks, bank borrowings from the Federal Reserve Bank, and various types of repurchase

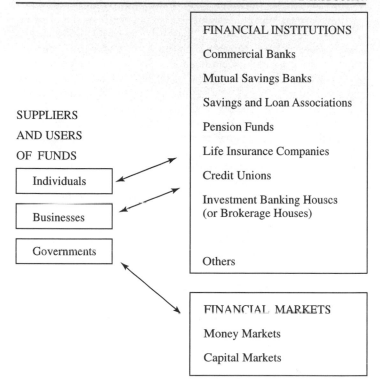

Figure 1.2 *General Flow of Funds Among Financial Institutions and Financial Markets*

agreements are also elements of the money market. These instruments have in common safety and liquidity. The money market, which operates through dealers, money center banks, and the New York Federal Reserve Bank, represents an outlet for both shortages and surpluses of liquidity, including those due to fluctuations in business.

Capital markets are the markets for *long-term* debt (that with a maturity of more than one year) and corporate stocks. The New York Stock Exchange, which handles the stocks of many large corporations, is a prime example of a capital market. The American Stock Exchange and the regional stock exchanges are other examples. In addition, securities are traded by thousands of brokers and dealers *over-the-counter,* a term used to denote all buying and selling activities in securities that do not occur on an organized stock exchange.

In the capital market, a distinction is made between the *primary market,* where new issues of securities are traded, and the *secondary market,* where previously issued securities are traded. The primary market is a source of new securities for the secondary market.

In practice, the boundaries between the money markets and capital markets are blurred, because most financial institutions deal with both kinds of financial instruments, both short and long term. In addition, revolving short-term loans become long-term loans in practice.

The financial manager has responsibility for obtaining funds and allocating them among alternative projects and specific uses, such as inventories and equipment. He or she must manage the cash flow cycle, make payments for expenses and the purchase of capital goods, and sell products and services to obtain cash inflows. In the management of cash flows, some cash is recycled and some is returned to financing sources as debt payment.

Financial market issues, including government regulation, are more fully discussed in Chapters 14 and 15.

BASIC FORMS OF BUSINESS ORGANIZATION

Finance is applicable both to economic entities such as business firms and to nonprofit organizations such as schools, governments, hospitals, churches, and so on. However, this book will focus on finance for three basic forms of business organizations. These forms are (1) the sole proprietorship, (2) the partnership, and (3) the corporation.

Sole Proprietorship

The sole proprietorship is a business owned by one individual. Of the three forms of business organizations, sole proprietorships are the greatest in number. The advantages of this form are

- No formal charter required.
- Less regulation and red tape.
- Significant tax savings.
- Minimal organizational costs.
- Profits and control not shared with others.

The disadvantages of sole proprietorship are

- Limited ability to raise large sums of money.
- Unlimited liability for the owner.
- Limited life, limited to the life of the owner.
- No tax deductions for personal and employees' health, life, or disability insurance.

Partnership

The partnership is similar to the sole proprietorship except that the business has more than one owner. Its advantages are

- Minimal organizational effort and costs.
- Fewer governmental regulations.

Its disadvantages are

- Unlimited liability for the individual partners.
- Limited ability to raise large sums of money.
- Limited life, dissolved upon the death or withdrawal of any of the partners.

There is a special form of partnership, called a *limited partnership,* where one or more partners, but not all, have limited liability up to their investment in the event of business failure. In this case,

- The general partner manages the business.
- Limited partners are not involved in daily activities. The return to limited partners is in the form of income and capital gains.
- Tax benefits are often involved.

Examples of limited partnerships are in real estate and oil and gas exploration.

Corporation

The corporation is a legal entity that exists apart from its owners, which are better known as stockholders. Ownership is evidenced by possession of shares of stock. In terms of types of businesses, the corporate form is not the greatest in number, but it is the most important in terms of total sales, assets, profits, and contribution to national income. Corporations are governed by a distinct set of state or federal laws and come in two forms: a state *C corporation* or federal *Subchapter S corporation.*

The advantages of a C corporation are

- Unlimited life.
- Limited liability for its owners, as long as there is no personal guarantee on a business-related obligation such as a bank loan or lease.
- Ease of transfer of ownership through transfer of stock.
- Ability to raise large sums of capital.

Its disadvantages are

- Difficult and costly to establish, as a formal charter is required.
- Subject to double taxation on its earnings and dividends paid to stockholders.
- Bankruptcy, even at the corporate level, does not discharge tax obligations.

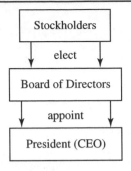

Figure 1.3 *Corporate Structure*

There are two special variations of corporation. They are a Subchapter S corporation and a limited-liability company.

Subchapter S Corporation. The Subchapter S corporation is a form of corporation whose stockholders are taxed as partners. To qualify as an S corporation, the following requirements are necessary:

▬ A corporation cannot have more than seventy-five shareholders.

▬ The owners must be individuals, estates, or certain qualified trusts.

▬ The shareholders cannot be nonresident foreigners.

▬ It must have just one class of stock (no preferred and common stock).

▬ It must properly elect Subchapter S status.

The Subchapter S corporation can distribute its income directly to shareholders and avoid the corporate income tax while enjoying the other advantages of the corporate form. *Note:* Not all states recognize Subchapter S corporations.

Limited-Liability Company. A limited-liability company (LLC) provides limited personal liability, as a corporation does. Owners, who are called members, can be other corporations. The members run the company unless they hire an outside management group. The LLC can choose whether to be taxed as a regular corporation or to pass tax liability through to members. Profits and losses can be split among members any way they choose. *Note:* The LLC rules vary by state.

The structure of a corporation is depicted in Figure 1.3.

CHAPTER PERSPECTIVE

Chapter 1 discussed the functions of finance, the environment in which finance operates, and how you fit into the corporate structure. The financial functions of the business involve record keeping, performance evaluation, variance analysis, budgeting, and utilization of resources. The financial manager must comprehend the goals, procedures, techniques, yardsticks, and functions of finance in order to perform his or her duties; a lack of knowledge of finance not only leads to incorrect analysis and decisions but also jeopardizes your future in the organization.

Without a good understanding of finance and accounting, you lack the tools needed for effective financial decision making. Decisions that make sense in terms of marketing and sales must also make financial sense; you must have the background to give sound input into the decision-making process.

Understanding Financial Statements

INTRODUCTION AND MAIN POINTS

Knowing the financial health of your company is important. Such knowledge can help you allocate resources and pinpoint areas requiring development and problems needing correction. Do you know how your company is doing financially? Is it growing or contracting? Will it be around for a long time? How profitable is your department, and what can be done to improve the profitability picture? These questions and others can be answered if you understand corporate financial statements. On the other hand, if you do not know how your company is doing financially, you cannot provide the needed financial leadership.

While Chapter 1 discussed finance from an internal perspective, this chapter looks at the key financial statements from an external viewpoint. These financial statements are the only financial information outsiders are likely to see.

In this chapter, you will learn:

■ The basic financial statements: the balance sheet, income statement, and statement of cash flows.

■ How the balance sheet portrays a company's financial position.

■ How the income statement reveals the entity's operating performance.

■ How to determine and assess a company's cash inflows and cash outflows.

■ The many types of accounts that may exist in the accounting system.

■ What the annual report is and how to read and understand its components, including the financial statements, footnotes, review of operations, auditor's report, and supplementary schedules.

■ How to read a quarterly report.

WHAT AND WHY OF FINANCIAL STATEMENTS

Financial decisions are typically based on information generated from the accounting system. Financial management, stockholders, potential investors, and creditors are concerned with how well the company is doing. The three reports generated by the accounting system and included in the company's annual report are the *balance sheet, income statement,* and *statement of cash flows.* Although the form of these financial statements may vary among different businesses or other economic units, their basic purposes do not change.

The balance sheet portrays the financial position of the organization at a particular point in time. It shows what you own (assets), how much you owe to vendors and lenders (liabilities), and what is left (assets minus liabilities, known as equity or net worth). A balance sheet freezes the action, giving the company's financial position as of a certain date. The balance sheet equation is: Assets − Liabilities = Stockholders' Equity.

The income statement, on the other hand, measures the operating performance for a specified period of time (e.g., for the year ended December 31, 20X1). If the balance sheet is a snapshot, the income statement is a motion picture. The income statement serves as the bridge between two consecutive balance sheets. Simply put, the balance sheet tells how wealthy or poor your company is, but the income statement tells you how your company did last year.

The balance sheet and the income statement tell you two different things about your company. For example, the fact the company made a big profit last year does not necessarily mean it is liquid (has the ability to meet current liabilities with current assets) or solvent (noncurrent assets are enough to meet noncurrent liabilities). (Liquidity and solvency are discussed in detail in Chapter 3.) A company may have reported a significant net income but still have a deficient net worth. In other words, to find out how your organization is doing, you need both statements. The income statement summarizes your company's operating results for the accounting period; these results are reflected in the equity (net worth) on the balance sheet. This relationship is shown in Figure 2.1.

The third basic financial statement is the statement of cash flows. This statement provides useful information about the inflows and outflows of cash that cannot be found in the balance sheet and the income statement.

MORE ON THE INCOME STATEMENT

The income statement (profit and loss statement) shows the revenue, expenses, and net income (or net loss) for a period of time. A definition of each element follows.

Revenue is the increase in capital arising from the sale of merchan-

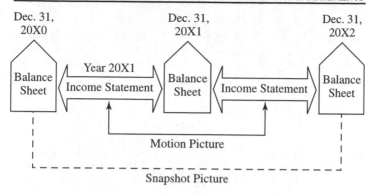

Figure 2.1 *The Balance Sheet and Income Statement*

dise or the performance of services. When revenue is earned, it results in an increase in either cash (money received) or accounts receivable (amounts owed to you by customers).

Expenses decrease capital and result from performing activities necessary to generate revenue. The expense is either equal to the cost of the goods sold or the expenditures necessary to conduct business operations (e.g., rent expense, salary expense, depreciation expense) during the period. (Depreciation is discussed in Chapter 10.)

Net income is the amount by which total revenue exceeds total expenses. The resulting profit is added to the *retained earnings* account (accumulated earnings of a company since its inception less dividends). If total expenses are greater than total revenue, a net loss results, decreasing retained earnings.

Revenue does not necessarily mean receipt of cash, and expense does not automatically imply a cash payment. Net income and net cash flow (cash receipts less cash payments) are different. For example, taking out a bank loan generates cash, but this cash is not revenue since no merchandise has been sold and no services have been provided. Further, capital has not been altered by the loan because the loan represents a liability, rather than a stockholders' investment, and must be repaid.

Each revenue and expense item has its own account. Such a system enables you to evaluate and control revenue and expense sources better and to examine the relationships among account categories.

Classified Income Statements

Although companies differ in nature and therefore the specific transactions and accounts differ from business to business, it is useful to classify the entries in financial statements into major categories. Financial statements organized in such a fashion are called classified financial statements.

In a *classified* income statement, each major revenue and expense function is listed separately to facilitate analysis. The entries in an income statement are usually classified into four major functions: revenue, cost of goods sold (cost of inventory sold), operating expenses, and other revenue or expenses. The entries in classified income statements covering different time periods are easily compared; the comparison over time of revenue sources, expense items, and the relationship between them can reveal areas that require attention and corrective action. For example, if revenue from services has been sharply declining over the past several months, you will want to know why and then take action to reverse the trend.

Revenue comprises the gross income generated by selling goods (sales) or performing services (professional fees, commission income). To determine *net* sales, gross sales are reduced by sales returns, allowances (discounts given for defective merchandise), and sales discounts.

Cost of goods sold is the cost of the merchandise or services sold. In a retail business, it is the cost of buying goods from the manufacturer; in a service business, it is the cost of the employee services rendered. For a manufacturing company, cost of goods sold is the beginning finished goods inventory plus the cost of goods manufactured minus the ending finished goods inventory.

Operating expenses are expenses incurred or resources used in generating revenue. Two types of operating expenses are selling expenses and general and administrative expenses. *Selling expenses* are costs incurred in obtaining the sale of goods or services (e.g., advertising, salesperson salaries) and in distributing the merchandise (e.g., freight paid on shipments); they relate solely to the selling function. If a sales manager is responsible for generating sales, his or her performance is judged on the relationship between promotion costs and sales obtained. *General and administrative expenses* are the costs of running the business as a whole. The salaries of the office clerical staff, administrative executive salaries, and depreciation on office equipment are examples of general and administrative expenses.

Other revenue (expenses) covers incidental sources of revenue and expense that are *nonoperating* in nature and that do not relate to the major purpose of the business. Examples are interest income, dividend income, and interest expense.

Figure 2.2 shows a classified income statement.

MORE ON THE BALANCE SHEET

The balance sheet is classified into major groups of assets and liabilities. An *asset* is something owned, such as land and automobile; a *liability* is something owed, such as loans payable and mortgage payable.

Assets

A classified balance sheet generally breaks down assets into five categories: current assets, long-term investments, property, plant, and equipment (fixed assets), intangible assets, and deferred charges. This breakdown aids in analyzing the type and liquidity of the assets held.

Current assets are assets expected to be converted into cash or used up within *one year* or the normal operating cycle of the business, whichever is greater. (The operating cycle is the time period between the purchase of inventory merchandise for resale and the transfer of inventory through sales, listed as accounts receivable, or receipt of cash. In effect, the operating cycle takes you from paying cash to receiving it.) Examples of current assets are cash, marketable securities you expect to hold for one year or less (short-term investments), accounts receivable, inventory, and prepaid expenses (expenditures that will expire within one year from the balance sheet date and that represent a prepayment for an expense that has not yet been incurred).

Long-term investments refer to investments in other companies' stocks (common or preferred) or bonds where the *intent* is to hold them for a period greater than one year. Securities are reported in the balance sheet at the lower of cost or current market value. The investment cost includes the market price of the securities when bought plus any brokerage fees you paid. If the intent is to hold a security for one year or less, it should be included in the current asset category and listed as a short-term investment (marketable securities).

Property, plant, and equipment (often called fixed assets) are assets employed in the production of goods or services that have a life greater than one year. They are *tangible,* meaning they have physical substance (you can physically see and touch them) and are actually being used in the course of business. Examples are land, buildings, machinery, and automobiles. Unlike inventory, these assets are not held for sale in the normal course of business.

Intangible assets are assets with a long-term life that lack physical substance and that arise from a right granted by the government, such

X Company

Income Statement
for the Year Ended December 31, 20XX

Revenue			
Gross Sales		$40,000	
Less: Sales Returns and Allowances	$1,000		
Sales Discounts	500	1,500	
Net Sales			$38,500
Cost of Goods Sold			
Inventory, January 1		$ 1,000	
Add: Purchases		15,000	
Cost of Goods Available for Sale		$16,000	
Less: Inventory, December 31		5,000	
Cost of Goods Sold			11,000
Gross Profit			$27,500
Operating Expenses			
Selling Expenses			
Advertising	$3,000		
Salespeople's Salaries	2,000		
Travel and Entertainment	1,000		
Depreciation on Delivery Truck	500	6,500	
General and Administrative Expenses			
Officers' Salaries	$4,000		
Depreciation	1,000		
Rent	2,000		
Insurance	1,000	8,000	
Total Operating Expenses			14,500
Operating Income			$13,000
Other Expenses (net)			
Interest Expense		$2,000	
Less: Interest Income	$ 500		
Dividend Income	1,000	1,500	
Other Expenses (net)			500
Net Income			$12,500

Figure 2.2 *A Classified Income Statement*

as patents, copyrights, and trademarks, or by another company, such as a franchise license. An example of the latter is the right (acquired by paying a fee) to open a fast-food franchise and use the name of McDonald's.

Deferred charges are certain expenditures that have already been incurred but that are deferred to the future either because they are expected to benefit future revenues or because they represent an appropriate allocation of costs to future operations. In other words, deferred charges are costs charged to an asset because future benefit exists; they are amortized to an expense in the year the related revenue is recognized and the benefit consumed in conformity with the accounting principle requiring matching of expense to revenue. Examples are plant rearrangement costs and moving costs. No cash can be realized from such assets; for example, you cannot sell deferred moving costs to anyone because no one will buy them.

Liabilities and Stockholders' Equity

Liabilities are classified as either current or noncurrent. *Current liabilities* (those due in one year or less) will be satisfied out of current assets. Examples are accounts payable (amounts owed to creditors), short-term notes payable (written evidence of loans due within one year), and accrued expense liabilities (e.g., salaries payable).

Examples of *long-term liabilities,* which have a maturity of greater than one year, are bonds payable and mortgage payable. The current portion of a long-term liability (that part that is to be paid within one year) is shown under current liabilities. For example, if $1,000 of a $10,000 mortgage is to be paid within the year, that $1,000 is listed as a current liability; the remaining $9,000 is shown under noncurrent liabilities.

The stockholders' equity section of the balance sheet consists of capital stock, paid-in capital, retained earnings, and total stockholders' equity. These are defined below.

Capital stock describes the ownership of the corporation in terms of the number of shares outstanding. Each share is assigned a par value when it is first authorized by the state in which the business is incorporated. Capital stock is presented on the balance sheet at total par value. Therefore, the capital stock account, which is at *par value,* agrees with the stock certificates (imprinted with the par value) held by stockholders. Preferred stock is listed before common stock because it receives preference should be company be liquidated.

Paid-in capital shows the amount received by the company over the par value for the stock issued. This helps keep track of the par value of issued shares and the excess over par value paid for it.

Retained earnings represent the accumulated earnings of the company since its inception less dividends declared and paid to stockholders. There is usually a surplus in this account, but a deficit may occur if the business has been operating at a loss.

Total stockholders' equity is the sum of the above categories. In a corporation, owners' equity is referred to as stockholders' equity; in a sole proprietorship or partnership, owners' equity is referred to as capital.

A classified balance sheet is presented in Figure 2.3.

STATEMENT OF CASH FLOWS

It is important to know your cash flow so that you may adequately plan your expenditures. Should you cut back on payments because of a cash problem? Where are you getting most of your cash? What products or projects are cash drains or cash cows? Is there enough money to pay bills and buy needed machinery?

A company is required to prepare a statement of cash flows in its annual report. It contains useful information for external users, such as lenders and investors, who make economic decisions about your company. The statement presents the sources and uses of cash and is a basis for cash flow analysis. In this section, we discuss what the statement of cash flows is, how it looks, and how to analyze it.

CONTENTS OF THE STATEMENT OF CASH FLOWS

The statement of cash flows classifies cash receipts and cash payments from investing activities, financing activities, and operating activities.

Investing Activities

Investing activities include the results of the purchase or sale of debt and equity securities of other entities and of fixed assets. Cash inflows from investing are comprised of (1) receipts from sales of equity and debt securities of other companies and (2) amounts received from the sale of fixed assets. Cash outflows for investing activities include (1) payments to buy equity or debt securities of other companies and (2) payments to buy fixed assets.

Financing Activities

Financing activities include the issuance of stock and the reacquisition of previously issued shares, as well as the payment of dividends to

X Company
Balance Sheet
December 31, 20XX

ASSETS
Current Assets

Cash	$3,000	
Marketable Securities	1,000	
Accounts Receivable	6,000	
Inventory	5,000	
Total Current Assets		$15,000
Long-Term Investments		
Investment in Y Company Stock		2,000
Property, Plant, and Equipment		
Land	$20,000	
Building (less accumulated depreciation)	30,000	
Machinery (less accumulated depreciation)	7,000	
Delivery Trucks (less accumulated depreciation)	5,000	
Total Property, Plant, and Equipment		62,000
Intangible Assets		
Patents (less accumulated amortization)		3,000
Deferred Charges		
Deferred Moving Costs		1,000
Total Assets		$83,000

LIABILITIES AND STOCKHOLDERS' EQUITY
Current Liabilities

Accounts Payable	$8,000	
Notes Payable (9 months)	4,000	
Accrued Expense Liabilities	2,000	
Total Current Liabilities		$14,000
Noncurrent Liabilities		
Bonds Payable		30,000
Total Liabilities		$44,000
Stockholders' Equity		
Capital Stock	$20,000	
Paid-in Capital	4,000	
Retained Earnings*	15,000	
Total Stockholders' Equity		39,000
Total Liabilities and Stockholders' Equity		$83,000

---

* A schedule of retained earnings follows:

Retained earnings—January 1	$10,000
Net income	12,500
Dividends	(7,500)
Retained earnings—December 31	$15,000

Figure 2.3 *A Sample Balance Sheet*

stockholders. Also included are debt financing and repayment. Cash inflows from financing activities are composed of funds received from the sale of stock and the incurrence of debt. Cash outflows for financing activities include (1) paying off debt, (2) repurchasing of stock, and (3) issuing dividend payments.

Operating Activities

Operating activities are connected to the manufacture and sale of goods or the rendering of services. Cash inflows from operating activities include (1) cash sales or collections on receivables arising from the initial sale of merchandise or rendering of service and (2) cash receipts from debt securities (e.g., interest income) or equity securities (e.g., dividend income) of other entities. Cash outflows for operating activities include (1) cash paid for raw material or merchandise intended for resale, (2) payments on accounts payable arising from the initial purchase of goods, (3) payments to suppliers of operating expense items (e.g., office supplies, advertising, insurance), and (4) wages.

Figure 2.4 shows an outline of the statement of cash flows.

CASH FLOW ANALYSIS

Along with financial ratio analysis (discussed in Chapter 3), cash flow analysis is a valuable tool. The cash flow statement provides information on how your company generated and used cash, that is, why cash flow increased or decreased. An analysis of the statement is helpful in appraising past performance, projecting the company's future direction, forecasting liquidity trends, and evaluating your company's ability to satisfy its debts at maturity. Because the statement lists the specific sources and uses of cash during the period, it can be used to answer the following:

- How was the expansion in plant and equipment financed?
- What use was made of net income?
- Where did you obtain funds?
- How much required capital is generated internally?
- Is the dividend policy in balance with its operating policy?
- How much debt was paid off?
- How much was received from the issuance of stock?
- How much debt financing was taken out?

The cash flow per share equals net cash flow divided by the number of shares. A high ratio is desirable because it indicates a liquid position, that is, that the company has ample cash on hand.

FORMAT OF THE STATEMENT OF
CASH FLOWS
(INDIRECT METHOD)

Net cash flow from operating activities:		
Net income	$980,000	
Adjustments for noncash expenses, revenues,		
losses, and gains included in income:		
Depreciation	20,000	
Net cash flow from operating activities		$1,000,000
Cash flows from investing activities:		
Purchase machinery	$(630,000)	
Investments in other companies' stocks	(70,000)	
Sale of land	200,000	
Net cash flows provided (used) by investing activities		(500,000)
Cash flows from financing activities:		
Issuance of common stock	$ 400,000	
Issuance of bonds payable	100,000	
Payment on long-term mortgage payable	(160,000)	
Payment of dividends	(40,000)	
Net cash provided (used) by financing activities		300,000
Net increase (decrease) in cash		$800,000
Schedule of noncash investing and financing activities:		
Issuance of preferred stock for building		$180,000
Conversion of bonds payable to common stock		100,000

Figure 2.4   *The Statement of Cash Flows*

Operating Section

An analysis of the operating section of the statement of cash flows determines the adequacy of cash flow from operating activities. For example, an operating cash outlay for refunds given to customers for deficient goods indicates a quality problem with the merchandise, while payments of penalties, fines, and lawsuit damages reveal poor management practices that result in nonbeneficial expenditures.

Investing Section

An analysis of the investing section can identify investments in other companies. These investments may lead to an attempt to assume control of another company for purposes of diversification. The analysis may also indicate a change in future direction or a change in business philosophy.

An increase in fixed assets indicates capital expansion and future growth. A contraction in business arising from the sale of fixed assets without adequate replacement is a negative sign.

Financing Section

An evaluation of the financing section reveals the company's ability to obtain financing in the money and capital markets as well as its ability to meet obligations. The financial mixture of bonds, long-term loans from banks, and equity instruments affects risk and the cost of financing. Debt financing carries greater risk because the company must generate adequate funds to pay the interest costs and to retire the obligation at maturity; thus, a very high percent of debt to equity is generally *not* advisable. The problem is acute if earnings and cash flow are declining. On the other hand, reducing long-term debt is desirable because it points to lowered risk.

The ability to obtain financing through the issuance of common stock at attractive terms (high stock price) indicates that the investing public is optimistic about the financial well-being of the business. The issuance of preferred stock may be a negative sign, since it may mean the company is having difficulty selling its common stock. Perhaps investors view the company as very risky and will invest only in preferred stock since preferred stock has a preference over common stock in the event of the company's liquidation.

Evaluate the company's ability to pay dividends. Stockholders who rely on a fixed income, such as a retired couple, may be unhappy when dividends are cut or eliminated.

PREPARING AND ANALYZING THE STATEMENT OF CASH FLOWS

In this section, we do an analysis of a hypothetical statement of cash flows, prepared from sample balance sheet and income statement figures.

EXAMPLE 2-1

X Company provides the following financial statements:

X Company
Comparative Balance Sheets
December 31
(in millions)

ASSETS	20X1	20X0
Cash	$ 40	$ 47
Accounts receivable	30	35
Prepaid expenses	4	2
Land	50	35
Building	100	80
Accumulated depreciation	(9)	(6)
Equipment	50	42
Accumulated depreciation	(11)	(7)
Total assets	$254	$228
LIABILITIES AND STOCKHOLDERS' EQUITY		
Accounts payable	$ 20	$ 16
Long-term notes payable	30	20
Common stock	100	100
Retained earnings	104	92
Total liabilities and stockholders' equity	$254	$228

X Company
Income Statement
for the Year Ended December 31, 20X1
(in millions)

Revenue		$300
Operating expenses		
(excluding depreciation)	$200	
Depreciation	7	207
Income from operations		$ 93
Income tax expense		32
Net income		$ 61

Additional information:
1. Cash dividends paid, $49.
2. The company issued long-term notes payable for cash, $10.
3. Land of $15, building of $20, and equipment of $8 were acquired for cash.

We can now prepare the statement of cash flows as follows:

X Company
Statement of Cash Flows
for the Year Ended December 31, 20X1
(in millions)

Operating activities:			
Net income			$61
Adjustments to reconcile net income to cash provided by operating activities:			
Depreciation		$ 7	
Changes in operating assets and liabilities:			
Decrease in accounts receivable		5	
Increase in prepaid items		(2)	
Increase in accounts payable		4	
Cash provided by operating activities			75
Cash flow from investing activities			
Purchase of land	($15)		
Purchase of building	(20)		
Purchase of equipment	(8)	·(43)	
Cash flow from financing activities			
Issuance of long-term notes payable	$10		
Payment of cash dividends	(49)	(39)	
Net decrease in cash			$ 7

Assume the company has a policy of paying very high dividends.

Information for 20X0 follows: Net income, $32; cash flow from operations, $20.

A financial analysis of the statement of cash flows reveals that the profitability and operating cash flow of X Company improved from 20X0 to 20X1. The company's earnings performance was good, and the $61 earnings resulted in cash inflow from operations of $75. Thus, compared to 20X0, 20X1 showed better results.

The decrease in accounts receivable may reveal better collection efforts. The increase in accounts payable is a sign that suppliers are confident they will be paid and are willing to give interest-free financing.

The acquisition of land, building, and equipment points to a growing business undertaking capital expansion. The issuance of long-term notes payable indicates that the company is financing part of its assets through debt. Stockholders will be happy with the significant dividend payout of 80.3 percent (dividends divided by net income, or $49/61). Overall, there was a decrease in cash on hand of $7, but this should not cause alarm because of the company's profitability and the fact that cash was used for capital expansion and dividend payments. We recommend that the dividend payout be reduced from its high level and that the funds be reinvested in the business; the reduction of dividends by more than $7 would result in a positive net cash flow for the year, which is needed for immediate liquidity.

EXAMPLE 2-2

Y Company presents the following statement of cash flows.

Y Company

Statement of Cash Flows
for the Year Ended December 31, 20X0

Operating activities:		
Net income		$134,000
Adjustments to reconcile net income to		
cash provided by operating activities:		
Depreciation	$21,000	
Changes in operating assets and liabilities:		
Decrease in accounts receivable	10,000	
Increase in prepaid items	(6,000)	
Increase in accounts payable	35,000	60,000
Cash provided by operating activities		$194,000
Cash flows from investing activities		
Purchase of land	($70,000)	
Purchase of building	(200,000)	
Purchase of equipment	(68,000)	
Cash used by investing activities		(338,000)
Cash flows from financing activities		
Issuance of bonds	150,000	
Payment of cash dividends	(18,000)	
Cash provided by financing activities		132,000
Net decrease in cash		$(12,000)

An analysis of the statement of cash flows reveals that the company is profitable and that cash flow from operating activities exceeds net income, which indicates good internal cash generation. The ratio of cash flow from operating activities to net income is a solid 1.45 ($194,000/$134,000). A high ratio is desirable because it shows that earnings are backed up by cash. The decline in accounts receivable may indicate better collection efforts; the increase in accounts payable shows the company can obtain interest-free financing. The company is definitely in the process of expanding for future growth, as demonstrated by the purchase of land, building, and equipment. The debt position of the company has increased, indicating greater risk for investors. The dividend payout was 13.4 percent ($18,000/$134,000), which is good news for stockholders, who look positively on companies that pay dividends. The decrease of $12,000 in cash flow for the year is a negative sign.

STATEMENT OF CASH FLOWS AND CORPORATE PLANNING

Current profitability is only one important factor in predicting corporate success; current and future cash flows are also essential. In fact, it is possible for a profitable company to have a cash crisis; for example, a company with significant credit sales but a very long collection period may show a profit without actually having the cash from those sales.

Financial managers are responsible for planning how and when cash will be used and obtained. When planned expenditures require more cash than planned activities are likely to produce, financial managers must decide what to do. They may decide to obtain debt or equity funds or to dispose of some fixed assets or a whole business segment. Alternatively, they may decide to cut back on planned activities by modifying operational plans, such as ending a special advertising campaign or delaying new acquisitions, or to revise planned payments to financing sources, such as bondholders or stockholders. Whatever is decided, the financial manager's goal is to balance the cash available and the needs for cash over both the short and the long term.

Evaluating the statement of cash flows is essential if you arc to appraise accurately an entity's cash flows from operating, investing, and financing activities and its liquidity and solvency positions. Inadequacy in cash flow has possible serious implications, including declining profitability, greater financial risk, and even possible bankruptcy.

OTHER SECTIONS OF THE ANNUAL REPORT

Other sections in the annual report in addition to the financial statements are helpful in understanding the company's financial health.

These sections include the highlights, review of operations, footnotes, supplementary schedules, and auditor's report.

Highlights

The highlights section provides comparative financial statement information and covers important points such as profitability, sales, dividends, market price of stock, and asset acquisitions. At a minimum, the company provides sales, net income, and earnings per share figures for the last two years.

Review of Operations

The review of operations section discusses the company's products, services, facilities, and future directions in both numbers and narrative form.

Report of Independent Public Accountants

The independent accountant is a certified public accountant (CPA) in public practice who has no financial or other interest in the client whose financial statements are being examined. In this part of the annual report, he or she expresses an opinion on the fairness of the financial statement numbers.

CPAs render four types of audit opinions: an unqualified opinion, a qualified opinion, a disclaimer of opinion, and an adverse opinion. The auditor's opinion is heavily relied on since he or she is knowledgeable, objective, and independent.

Unqualified Opinion. An unqualified opinion means the CPA is satisfied that the company's financial statements present fairly its financial position and results of operations and gives the financial manager confidence that the financial statements are an accurate reflection of the company's financial health and operating performance.

A typical standard report presenting an unqualified opinion follows.

Independent Auditor's Report

We have audited the accompanying balance sheet of ABC Company as of December 31, 20X2 and the related statements of income, retained earnings, and cash flows for the year then ended. These financial statements are the responsibility of the Company's management. Our responsibility is to express an opinion on these financial statements based on our audit.

We conducted our audit in accordance with generally accepted auditing standards. Those standards require that we plan and perform the audit to obtain reasonable assurance about whether the financial statements are free of material misstatement. An audit includes examining, on a test basis, evidence supporting the amounts and disclosures in the financial statements. An audit also includes assessing the accounting principles used and significant estimates made by management, as well as evaluating the overall financial statement presentation. We believe that our audit provides a reasonable basis for our opinion.

In our opinion, the financial statements referred to above present fairly, in all material respects, the financial position of ABC Company as of December 31, 20X2, and the results of its operations and its cash flows for the year then ended in conformity with generally accepted accounting principles.

If the company is facing a situation with an uncertain outcome that may substantially affect its financial health, such as a lawsuit, the CPA may still give an unqualified opinion. However, there will probably be an explanatory paragraph describing the material uncertainty; this uncertainty will undoubtedly affect readers' opinions of the financial statement information. As a financial manager, you are well advised to note the contingency (potential problem, such as a dispute with the government) and its possible adverse financial effects on the company.

Qualified Opinion. The CPA may issue a qualified opinion if your company has placed a "scope limitation" on his or her work. A scope limitation prevents the independent auditor from doing one or more of the following: (1) gathering enough evidential matter to permit the expression of an unqualified opinion; (2) applying a required auditing procedure; or (3) applying one or more auditing procedures considered necessary under the circumstances.

If the scope limitation is fairly minor, the CPA may issue an "except for" qualified opinion. This may occur, for example, if the auditor is unable to confirm accounts receivable or observe inventory.

Disclaimer of Opinion. When a severe scope limitation exists, the auditor may decide to offer a disclaimer of opinion. A disclaimer indicates that the auditor was unable to form an opinion on the fairness of the financial statements.

Adverse Opinion. The auditor may issue an adverse opinion when the financial statements do *not* present the company's financial position, results of operations, retained earnings, and cash flows fairly and in conformity with generally accepted accounting principles. By issuing an adverse opinion, the CPA is stating that the financial statements may be misleading.

Obviously, the financial manager wants the independent auditor to render an unqualified opinion. Disclaimers and adverse opinions are viewed very negatively by readers such as investors and creditors, who then put little if any faith in the company's financial statements.

Footnotes

Financial statements themselves are concise and condensed, and any explanatory information that cannot readily be abbreviated is added in greater detail in the footnotes. In such cases, the report contains a statement similar to this: "The accompanying footnotes are an integral part of the financial statements."

Footnotes provide detailed information on financial statement figures, accounting policies, explanatory data such as mergers and stock options, and any additional disclosure.

Footnote disclosures usually include accounting methods, estimated figures such as inventory pricing, pension fund, and profit-sharing arrangements, terms and characteristics of long-term debt, particulars of lease agreements, contingencies, and tax matters.

The footnotes appear at the end of the financial statements and explain the figures in those statements both in narrative form and in numbers. It is essential that the financial manager evaluate footnote information to arrive at an informed opinion about the company's financial stature and earning potential.

Supplementary Schedules and Tables

Supplementary schedules and tables enhance the financial manager's comprehension of the company's financial position. Some of the more common schedules are five-year summary of operations, two-year quarterly data, and segmental information. This summary provides income statement information for the past five years, including dividends on preferred stock and common stock. It also reveals operating trends. Some companies provide ten-year comparative data.

Two-Year Quarterly Data. This schedule gives a quarterly breakdown of sales, profit, high and low stock price, and the common stock dividend. Quarterly operating information is particularly useful for a seasonal business, because it helps readers to track the business's highs and lows more accurately. The quarterly market price reveals fluctuations in the market price of stock, while the dividend quarterly information reveals how regularly the company pays dividends.

Segmental Disclosure. This important supplementary schedule presents financial figures for the segments of the business, enabling readers to evaluate each segment's profit potential and risk. Segmental data may be organized by industry, foreign area, major customer, or government contract.

A segment is reportable if any *one* of the following conditions exists:

▬ Revenue is 10 percent or more of total corporate revenue.

▬ Operating profit is 10 percent or more of total corporate operating profit.

▬ Identifiable assets are 10 percent or more of total corporate assets.

The company must also disclose if foreign operations, sales to a major customer, or domestic contract revenue provide 10 percent or more of total sales. The percentage derived and the source of the sales must be stated.

Useful segment information that may be disclosed includes sales, operating profit, total assets, fixed assets, intangible assets, inventory, cost of sales, depreciation, and amortization.

History of Market Price

While this information is optional, many companies provide a brief history of the market price of stock, such as quarterly highs and lows. This information reveals the variability and direction in market price of stock.

HOW TO READ A QUARTERLY REPORT

In addition to the annual report, publicly held companies issue quarterly reports that provide updated information on sales and earnings and describe any material[1] changes that have occurred in the business or its operations. These quarterly reports may provide unaudited financial statements or updates on operating highlights, changes in outstanding shares, compliance with debt restrictions, and pending lawsuits.

At a minimum, quarterly reports must provide data on sales, net income, taxes, nonrecurring revenue and expenses, accounting changes,

---

[1] The Securities and Exchange Commission defines materiality as a change in an account of 10 percent or more relative to the prior year. However, many CPA firms use 5 percent as a materiality guideline.

contingencies (e.g., tax disputes), additions or deletions of business segments, and material changes in financial position.

The company may provide financial figures for the quarter itself (e.g., the third quarter, from July 1 to September 30) or cumulatively from the beginning of the year (cumulative up to the third quarter, or January 1 to September 30). Prior-year data must be provided in a form that allows for comparisons.

The financial manager should read the quarterly report in conjunction with the annual report.

CHAPTER PERSPECTIVE

The financial manager should have a good understanding of the financial statements of the company in order to make an informed judgment on the financial position and operating performance of the entity. The balance sheet reveals the company's financial status as of a given date, while the income statement reports the earnings components for the year. The statement of cash flows allows readers to analyze the company's sources and uses of cash. These financial statements are included in the annual report, along with other vital information including footnote disclosures, the auditor's report, management's discussion of operations, and supplementary schedules.

Analyzing Financial Statements

CHAPTER

3

INTRODUCTION AND MAIN POINTS

In this chapter, we discuss how to analyze a company's financial statements, comprised of the balance sheet and income statement. Financial statement analysis attempts to answer the following basic question:

1. How well is the business doing?
2. What are its strengths?
3. What are its weaknesses?
4. How does it fare in the industry?
5. Is the business improving or deteriorating?

A complete set of financial statements, as explained in Chapter 2, includes the balance sheet, income statement, and statement of cash flows. The first two are vital in financial statement analysis, which is accomplished by the use of various tools, such as horizontal, vertical, and ratio analysis.

In this chapter you will learn:
- What financial statement analysis is and why it is important.
- The basic components of ratio analysis.
- Distinguishing between trend analysis and industry comparison.
- How to calculate and interpret various ratios.
- The limitations of ratio analysis.

WHAT IS FINANCIAL STATEMENT ANALYSIS?

The analysis of financial statements means different things to different people, depending on their particular interests. Creditors, current and prospective investors, and the corporation's own management look at different parts of the analysis to find the answers to the questions that are of greatest concern to them.

Creditors are primarily interested in the company's debt-paying ability. A short-term creditor, such as a vendor or supplier, is ultimately concerned with the business's ability to pay its bills and wants to be assured that the business is liquid. A long-term creditor, such as a bank or bondholder, on the other hand, is interested in the company's ability to repay interest and principal on borrowed funds.

Investors are interested in the current and future level of return (earnings) and risk (liquidity, debt, and activity). Investors evaluate a stock based on an examination of the company's financial statements. This evaluation considers overall financial health, economic and political conditions, industry factors, and future outlook of the company. The analysis attempts to ascertain how the stock is priced in proportion to its market value. A stock is valuable to you only if you can predict the future financial performance of the business; financial statement analysis gives you much of the data to develop predictions.

Management is concerned with all the questions raised by creditors and investors, since both must be satisfied if the company is to obtain the capital it needs.

HORIZONTAL AND VERTICAL ANALYSIS

Comparison of two or more years' financial data is known as *horizontal analysis.* Horizontal analysis concentrates on trends in the accounts in dollar *and* percentage terms. It is typically presented in comparative financial statements (see Figures 3.1a and 3.1b). Annual reports usually present comparative financial data for five years.

Horizontal analysis helps you pinpoint areas of wide divergence that require investigation. For example, in the income statement shown in Figure 3.1b, the significant rise in sales returns, taken with the reduction in sales for 20X1-20X2, should cause concern. Compare these results with those of competitors.

It is essential to present both the dollar amount of change and the percentage of change, since the use of one without the other may result in erroneous conclusions. In our example, the interest expense from 20X0-20X1 went up by 100 percent, but the increase in dollars was only $1,000 and may not need further investigation. Similarly, a large number change may translate into a small percentage change and not be of any great importance.

Key changes and trends can also be highlighted by the use of *common-size statements.* A common-size statement is one that shows each item in percentage terms. Preparation of common-size statements is known as *vertical analysis,* in which a material financial statement item is used as a base value and all other accounts on the financial statement are compared to it. In the balance sheet, for example, total assets equal 100 percent, and each individual asset is stated as a percentage of total assets. Similarly, total liabilities and stockholders' equity are assigned a value of 100 percent and each liability or equity account is then stated as a percentage of total liabilities and stockholders' equity, respectively. Figure 3.2 shows a common-size income statement based on the data provided in Figure 3.1b.

Placing all assets in common-size form shows the relative importance of current assets compared to noncurrent assets. It also shows any significant changes that have taken place in the composition of the current assets over the last year. In Figure 3.2, for example, receivables have increased and cash has declined in relative importance. The deterioration in the cash position may be a result of the company's inability to collect from customers. For the income statement, a value of 100 percent is assigned to net sales, and all other revenue and expense accounts are related to it. It is possible to see at a glance how each dollar of sales is distributed among the various costs, expenses, and profits. For example, notice from Figure 3.2 that 64.8 cents of every dollar of sales was needed to cover cost of goods sold in 20X2, as compared to only 57.3 cents in the prior year; also notice that only 9.9 cents out of every dollar of sales remained for profits in 20X2, down from 13.6 cents in the prior year. You should also compare the vertical percentages of the business to those of the competition and to the industry norms in order to determine how the company is faring within its industry. Further, in making industry comparisons, size of firms within industries should be considered.

WORKING WITH FINANCIAL RATIOS

Horizontal and vertical analysis compares one figure to another within the same category. However, it is also essential to compare figures from different categories. This is accomplished by ratio analysis. In this section, we discuss how to calculate and interpret the various financial ratios. The results of the ratio analysis will allow you to:

1. Appraise the position of a business.
2. Identify trouble spots that need attention.
3. Make projections and forecasts about the course of future operations.

Think of ratios as measures of the relative health or sickness of a business. Just as a doctor takes readings of a patient's temperature, blood pressure, and heart rate, you can take readings of a business's liquidity, profitability, leverage, efficiency in using assets, and market value. Just as the doctor compares the readings to generally accepted guidelines, you compare your results to generally accepted norms.

To obtain useful conclusions from the ratios, you must make two comparisons:

▬ *Industry comparison.* This comparison allows you to answer the question, "How does a business fare in the industry?" You must compare the company's ratios to those of competing companies in the in-

	20X2	20X1	20X0	Incr. or Decr. 20X2–20X1	Incr. or Decr. 20X1–20X0	% Incr. or Decr. 20X2–20X1	% Incr. or Decr. 20X1–20X0
ASSETS							
Current Assets:							
Cash	$28	$36	$36	–8	0	–22.2%	0.0%
Marketable Securities	$22	$15	$7	7	8	46.7%	114.3%
Accounts Receivable	$21	$16	$10	5	6	31.3%	60.0%
Inventory	$53	$46	$49	7	–3	15.2%	–6.1%
Total Current Assets	$124	$113	$102	11	11	9.7%	10.8%
Plant and Equip.	$103	$91	$83	12	8	13.2%	9.6%
Total Assets	$227	$204	$185	23	19	11.3%	10.3%
LIABILITIES							
Current Liabilities	$56	$50	$51	6	–1	12.0%	–2.0%
Long-Term Debt	$83	$74	$69	9	5	12.2%	7.2%
Total Liabilities	$139	$124	$120	15	4	12.1%	3.3%
STOCKHOLDERS' EQUITY							
Common Stock, $10 par, 4,600 shares	$46	$46	$46	0	0	0.0%	0.0%
Retained Earnings	$42	$34	$19	8	15	23.5%	78.9%
Total Stockholders' Equity	$88	$80	$65	8	15	10.0%	23.1%
Total Liab. and Stockholders' Equity	$227	$204	$185	23	19	11.3%	10.3%

Figure 3.1a *TLC, Inc., Comparative Balance Sheet (in thousands of dollars), December 31, 20X2, 20X1, 20X0*

	20X2	20X1	20X0	Incr. or Decr. 20X2–20X1	Decr. 20X1–20X0	% Incr. 20X2–20X1	or Decr. 20X1–20X0
Sales	$98.3	$120.0	$56.6	–$21.7	$63.4	–18.1%	112.0%
Sales Returns & Allowances	$18.0	$10.0	$4.0	$8.0	$6.0	80.0%	150.0%
Net Sales	$80.3	$110.0	$52.6	–$29.7	$57.4	–27.0%	109.1%
Cost of Goods Sold	$52.0	$63.0	$28.0	–$11.0	$35.0	–17.5%	125.0%
Gross Profit	$28.3	$47.0	$24.6	–$18.7	$22.4	–39.8%	91.1%
Operating Expenses							
Selling Expenses	$12.0	$13.0	$11.0	–$1.0	$2.0	–7.7%	18.2%
General Expenses	$5.0	$8.0	$3.0	$3.0	$5.0	–37.5%	166.7%
Total Operating Expenses	$17.0	$21.0	$14.0	$4.0	$7.0	–19.0%	50.0%
Income from Operations	$11.3	$26.0	$10.6	–$14.7	$15.4	–56.5%	145.3%
Nonoperating Income	$4.0	$1.0	$2.0	$3.0	–$1.0	300.0%	–50.0%
Income before Interest & Taxes	$15.3	$27.0	$12.6	–$11.7	$14.4	–43.3%	114.3%
Interest Expense	$2.0	$2.0	$1.0	$0.0	$1.0	0.0%	100.0%
Income before Taxes	$13.3	$25.0	$11.6	–$11.7	$13.4	–46.8%	115.5%
Income Taxes (40%)	$5.3	$10.0	$4.6	$4.7	$5.4	–46.8%	115.5%
Net Income	$8.0	$15.0	$7.0	–$7.0	$8.0	–46.8%	115.5%

Figure 3.1b *TLC, Inc., Comparative Income Statement (in thousands of dollars), December 31, 20X2, 20X1, 20X0*

	20X2 Amount	%	20X1 Amount	%
Sales	$98.3	122.4%	$120.0	109.1%
Sales Returns & Allowances	$18.0	22.4%	$10.0	9.1%
Net Sales	$80.3	100.0%	$110.0	100.0%
Cost of Goods Sold	$52.0	64.8%	$63.0	57.3%
Gross Profit	$28.3	35.2%	$47.0	42.7%
Operating Expenses				
Selling Expenses	$12.0	14.9%	$13.0	11.8%
General Expenses	$5.0	6.2%	$8.0	7.3%
Total Operating Expenses	$17.0	21.2%	$21.0	19.1%
Income from Operations	$11.3	14.1%	$26.0	23.6%
Nonoperating Income	$4.0	5.0%	$1.0	0.9%
Income before Interest & Taxes	$15.3	19.1%	$27.0	24.5%
Interest Expense	$2.0	2.5%	$2.0	1.8%
Income before Taxes	$13.3	16.6%	$25.0	22.7%
Income Taxes (40%)	$5.3	6.6%	$10.0	9.1%
Net Income	$8.0	9.9%	$15.0	13.6%

Figure 3.2 *TLC, Inc., Income Statement and Common Size Analysis (in thousands of dollars) for the Years Ended December 31, 20X2 & 20X1*

dustry or with industry standards (averages). (You can obtain industry norms from financial services such as Value Line, Dun and Bradstreet, and Standard & Poor's.)

■ *Trend analysis.* To see how the business is doing over time, you can track a given ratio for one company over several years to determine any trends and see the direction of the company's financial health or operational performance.

Financial ratios can be grouped into the following types: liquidity, asset utilization (activity), solvency (leverage and debt service), profitability, and market value.

Liquidity Ratios

Liquidity is a company's ability to satisfy maturing short-term debt. It is crucial to carrying out the business, especially during periods of adversity. Poor liquidity may increase a company's cost of financing and can render it unable to pay bills and dividends. However, too much liquidity is not good because excessive cash balances means the company is earning a lower rate of return. The three basic measures of liquidity are (a) net working capital, (b) the current ratio, and (c) the quick (acid-test) ratio.

Throughout the discussion that follows, refer to Figures 3.1a and 3.1b to make sure you understand where the numbers come from.

Net working capital equals current assets minus current liabilities. Net working capital for 20X2 is:

$$
\begin{aligned}
\text{Net working capital} &= \text{Current assets} - \text{Current liabilities} \\
&= \$124 \quad\quad\quad - \$56 \\
&= \$\ 68
\end{aligned}
$$

In 20X1, net working capital was $63. The one-year rise is favorable.

The *current ratio* equals current assets divided by current liabilities. The ratio reflects the company's ability to satisfy current debt from current assets.

$$
\text{Current ratio} = \left(\frac{\text{Current assets}}{\text{Current liabilities}} \right)
$$

For 20X2, the current ratio is:

$$
\left(\frac{\$124}{\$56} \right) = 2.21
$$

In 20X1, the current ratio was 2.26. The ratio's decline over the year points to a slight reduction in liquidity.

A more stringent liquidity test is the *quick (acid-test) ratio*. Inventory and prepaid expenses are excluded from the total of current assets used in this ratio; only the more liquid (or quick) assets are totaled and divided by current liabilities.

$$
\text{Acid-test ratio} = \frac{\text{Cash} + \text{Marketable Securities}}{\text{Current Liabilities}}
$$

The quick ratio for 20X2 is:

$$
\left(\frac{\$28 + \$21 + \$22}{\$56} \right) = 1.27
$$

In 20X1, the ratio was 1.34. A small reduction in the ratio over the period points to a lower level of liquidity.

The overall liquidity trend for TLC shows a slight deterioration, as reflected in the lower current and quick ratios, although it is better than the industry norms (see Figure 3.3 for industry averages). But a mitigating factor is the increase in net working capital.

Asset Utilization Ratios

Asset utilization (activity, turnover) ratios reflect the way in which a company uses its assets to obtain revenue and profit. One example is how well receivables are turned into cash. The higher the ratio, the more efficiently the business manages its assets.

Accounts receivable ratios comprise the accounts receivable turnover and the average collection period.

Accounts receivable turnover is the number of times accounts receivable are collected in the year. It is derived by dividing net credit sales by average accounts receivable. You can calculate average accounts receivable by adding the beginning and ending balances and then dividing by 2.

$$\text{Accounts receivable turnover} = \frac{\text{Net credit sales}}{\text{Average accounts receivable}}$$

For 20X2, the average accounts receivable is:

$$\frac{\$21 + \$16}{2} = \$18.5$$

The accounts receivable turnover for 20X2 is:

$$\frac{\$80.3}{\$18.5} = 4.34$$

In 20X1, the turnover was 8.46. There is a sharp reduction in the turnover rate, suggesting a collection problem.

The *average collection period* is the length of time it takes to collect receivables; it represents the number of days receivables are held.

$$\text{Average collection period} = \frac{365 \text{ days}}{\text{Accounts receivable turnover}}$$

In 20X2, the collection period is:

$$\frac{365}{4.34} = 84.1 \text{ days}$$

It takes this firm about 84 days to convert receivables to cash. In 20X1, the collection period was 43.1 days. The significant lengthening of the collection period may be a cause for some concern; it may result from the presence of many doubtful accounts or from poor credit management.

Inventory ratios are especially useful when a buildup in inventory exists. Inventory ties up cash; holding large amounts of inventory can result in both lost opportunities for profit and increased storage costs.

Before you extend credit or lend money to a company, you should examine its *inventory turnover* and *average age of inventory.*

$$\text{Inventory turnover} = \frac{\text{Cost of goods sold}}{\text{Average inventory}}$$

The inventory turnover for 20X2 is:

$$\frac{\$52}{\$49.5} = 1.05$$

For 20X1, the turnover was 1.33.

$$\text{Average age of inventory} = \frac{365}{\text{Inventory turnover}}$$

In 20X2, the average age is:

$$\frac{365}{1.05} = 347.6 \text{ days}$$

In the previous year, the average age was 274.4 days.

The reduction in the turnover and increase in inventory age suggests that inventory is being held onto for a longer time. You should ask why the inventory is not selling as quickly

The *operating cycle* is the number of days it takes to convert inventory and receivables to cash.

$$\text{Operating cycle} = \text{average collection period} + \text{average age of inventory}$$

In 20X2, the operating cycle is:

$$84.1 \text{ days} + 347.6 \text{ days} = 431.7 \text{ days}$$

In the previous year, the operating cycle was 317.5 days. The increase is unfavorable, because it means that additional funds are tied up in noncash assets and that cash is being collected more slowly.

By calculating the *total asset turnover,* you can find out whether the company is efficiently employing its total assets to obtain sales revenue. A low ratio may indicate that too many assets are being held compared to the sales revenue generated.

$$\text{Total asset turnover} = \frac{\text{Net sales}}{\text{Average total assets}}$$

In 20X2, the ratio is:

$$\frac{\$80.3}{(\$204 + \$227)/2} = \frac{\$80.3}{\$215.5} = .37$$

In 20X1, the ratio was .57 ($110/$194.5). Thus, there has been a sharp reduction in asset utilization.

TLC, Inc., has suffered a sharp deterioration in activity ratios, pointing to a need for improved credit and inventory management, although the 20X2 ratios are not far out of line with the industry averages (see Figure 3.3). It appears that problems are inefficient collection and obsolescence of inventory.

Solvency (Leverage and Debt Service) Ratios

Solvency is the company's ability to satisfy long-term debt as it becomes due. You should be concerned about the long-term financial and operating structure of any company in which you might be interested. Another important consideration is *financial leverage,* the size of debt in the company's capital structure. (Capital structure is the mix of long-term sources of funds used by the company.)

Solvency also depends on earning power; in the long run a company cannot satisfy its debts unless it earns a profit. A leveraged capital structure subjects the company to fixed interest charges, contributing to earnings instability. Excessive debt may also make it difficult for the corporation to borrow funds at reasonable rates during tight money markets.

The *debt ratio* reveals the amount of money a company owes to its creditors. Excessive debt means greater risk to the investor. (Equity holders come after creditors in bankruptcy.)

$$\text{Debt ratio} = \frac{\text{Total liabilities}}{\text{Total assets}}$$

In 20X2, the ratio is:

$$\frac{\$139}{\$227} = .61$$

The *debt-equity ratio* reveals if the company has a great amount of debt in its capital structure. Large debts mean that the borrower has to pay significant periodic interest and principal. Also, a heavily indebted firm takes a greater risk of running out of cash in difficult times. The interpretation of this ratio depends on several variables, including the ratios of other companies in the industry, the degree of access to additional debt financing, and the stability of operations.

$$\text{Debt-equity ratio} = \frac{\text{Total liabilities}}{\text{Stockholders' equity}}$$

In 20X2, the ratio is:

$$\frac{\$139}{\$88} = 1.58$$

In the previous year, the ratio was 1.55. The situation is therefore relatively static.

Times interest earned (interest coverage ratio) tells you how many times the business's before-tax earnings would cover interest. It is a safety margin indicator in that it reflects how large a reduction in earnings a company can tolerate.

$$\text{Times interest earned} = \frac{\text{Income before interest and taxes}}{\text{Interest expense}}$$

For 20X2, the ratio is:

$$\frac{\$15.3}{\$2.0} = 7.65$$

In 20X1, interest was covered 13.5 times. The reduction in coverage during the period is a bad sign; it means that less earnings are available to satisfy interest charges.

You must also note liabilities that have not yet been accounted for in the balance sheet by closely examining footnote disclosures. For example, you should find out about pending lawsuits, noncapitalized leases, and future guarantees.

As revealed in Figure 3.3, the company's overall solvency is poor compared to the industry averages, although it has remained fairly constant. There has been no significant change in its ability to satisfy long-term debt. Note, however, that significantly less profit is available to cover interest payments.

Profitability Ratios

A company's ability to earn good profit and return on investment is an indicator of its financial well-being and the efficiency with which it is managed. Poor earnings have a detrimental effect on both the market price of stock and dividends, and total dollar net income has little meaning unless it is compared to the resources used in getting that profit.

The *gross profit margin* is the percentage of each dollar remaining once the company has paid for goods acquired. A high margin reflects good earning potential.

$$\text{Gross profit margin} = \frac{\text{Gross profit}}{\text{Net sales}}$$

Ratios	Definitions	20X1	20X2	(a) 20X2 Industry Average	20X2 Ind. Comp	Evaluation Trend 20X1–20X2	(b) Overall
LIQUIDITY							
Net working capital	Current assets – current liabilities	63	68	56	good	good	good
Current Ratio	Current assets/current liabilities	2.26	2.21	2.05	OK	OK	OK
Quick (Acid-test) ratio	(Cash + marketable securities + accounts receivable)/current liabilities	1.34	1.27	1.11	OK	OK	OK
ASSET UTILIZATION							
Accounts receivable turnover	Net credit sales/average accounts receivable	8.46	4.34	5.5	OK	poor	poor
Average collection period	365 days/accounts receivable turnover	43.1 days	84.1 days	66.4 days	OK	poor	poor
Inventory turnover	Cost of goods sold/average inventory	1.33	1.05	1.2	OK	poor	poor
Average age of inventory	365 days/inventory turnover	274.4 days	347.6 days	N/A	N/A	poor	poor
Operating cycle	Average collection period + average age of inventory	317.5 days	431.7 days	N/A	N/A	poor	poor
Total asset turnover	Net sales/average total assets	0.57	0.37	0.44	OK	poor	poor
SOLVENCY							
Debt ratio	Total liabilities/total assets	0.61	0.61	N/A	N/A	OK	OK
Debt-equity ratio	Total liabilities/stockholders' equity	1.55	1.58	1.3	poor	poor	poor

		13.5 times	7.65 times	10 times	OK	poor	poor
Times interest earned	Income before interest and taxes/interest expense	13.5 times	7.65 times	10 times	OK	poor	poor
PROFITABILITY							
Gross profit margin	Gross profit/net sales	0.45	0.35	0.48	poor	poor	poor
Profit margin	Net income/net sales	0.14	0.1	0.15	poor	poor	poor
Return on total assets	Net income/average total assets	0.077	0.037	0.1	poor	poor	poor
Return on equity (ROE)	Earnings available to common stockholders/average stockholders' equity	0.207	0.095	0.27	poor	poor	poor
MARKET VALUE							
Earnings per share (EPS)	(Net income – preferred dividend)/common shares outstanding	3.26	1.74	4.51	poor	poor	poor
Price/earnings (P/E) ratio	Market price per share/EPS	7.98	6.9	7.12	OK	poor	poor
Book value per share	(Total stockholders' equity – preferred stock)/common shares outstanding	17.39	19.13	N/A	N/A	good	good
Price/book value ratio	Market price per share/book value per share	1.5	0.63	N/A	N/A	poor	poor
Dividend yield	Dividends per share/market price per share						
Dividend payout	Dividends per share/EPS						

(a) Obtained from sources not included in this chapter

(b) Represent subjective evaluation

Figure 3.3 *Summary of Financial Ratios: Trend and Industry Comparisons; TLC, Inc., 20X2 and 20X1*

In 20X2, the ratio is:

$$\frac{\$28.3}{\$80.3} = .35$$

The ratio was .43 in 20X1. The reduction shows that the company now receives less profit on each dollar of sales, perhaps because it is paying more for the merchandise it sells.

Profit margin shows the earnings generated from revenue and is a key indicator of operating performance. It provides an idea of the firm's pricing, cost structure, and efficiency.

$$\text{Profit margin} = \frac{\text{Net income}}{\text{Net sales}}$$

The ratio in 20X2 is:

$$\frac{\$8}{\$80.3} = .10$$

For the previous year, the profit margin was .14. The decline in the ratio shows a downward trend in earning power. (Note that these percentages are available in the common-size income statement in Figure 3.2).

Return on investment is an important indicator because it allows you to evaluate the profit you will earn if you invest in the business. Two key ratios are the return on total assets and the return on equity.

The *return on total assets* shows whether management is efficient in using available resources to get profit.

$$\text{Return on total assets} = \frac{\text{Net income}}{\text{Average total assets}}$$

In 20X2, the return is:

$$\frac{\$8}{(\$227 + \$204)/2} = .037$$

In 20X1, the return was .077. There has been a deterioration in the productivity of assets in generating earnings.

The *return on equity* (ROE) reflects the rate of return earned on the stockholders' investment.

$$\text{Return on common equity} = \frac{\text{Net income available to stockholders}}{\text{Average stockholders' equity}}$$

The return in 20X2 is:

$$\frac{\$8}{(\$88 + \$80)/2} = 0.095$$

TABLE 3-1

INDUSTRIES WITH HIGH RETURN ON EQUITY (ROE) RATES (IN EXCESS OF 20%) 1998

Industry	ROE (%)
Cars and Trucks	62.4
Personal Care	31.0
Eating Places	22.9
Food Processing	24.8
Beverages	32.0
Business Machines and Services	20.6
Telephone	28.6

Source: *Corporate Scorecard,* by *Business Week,* McGraw-Hill, March 1999, pp. 75–91.

In 20X1, the return was .207. There has been a significant drop in return to the owners.

The overall profitability of the company has decreased considerably, causing a decline in both the return on assets and return on equity. Perhaps the lower earnings resulted from higher costs of short-term financing caused by the decline in liquidity and activity ratios. Moreover, as turnover rates in assets go down, profit declines because of reduced sales and higher costs of carrying higher current asset balances. As indicated in Figure 3.3, industry comparisons reveal that the company is faring very poorly.

Table 3-1 shows industries with high return on equity (in excess of 20 percent).

Market Value Ratios

Market value ratios and dividend-related ratios relate the company's stock price to its dividends, earnings, or book value per share.

Earnings per share (EPS) is the ratio most widely watched by investors. EPS shows the net income per common share owned after reducing net income by the preferred dividends. If preferred stock is not part of the company's capital structure, EPS is determined by dividing net income by common shares outstanding. EPS is a gauge of corporate operating performance and of expected future dividends.

TABLE 3-2

1998 HIGHLY PROFITABLE COMPANIES (IN TERMS OF EPS)

Company	EPS ($)
Ford	17.76
U.S. Home	4.68
Alcoa	4.84
CIGNA	6.05
IBM	6.57
Washington Post	41.10

Source: *Corporate Scorecard,* by *Business Week,* McGraw-Hill, March 1999, pp. 75–91.

$$\text{EPS} = \frac{\text{Net income} - \text{Preferred dividend}}{\text{Common shares outstanding}}$$

EPS in 20X2 is:

$$\frac{\$8,000}{4,600 \text{ shares}} = \$1.74$$

For 20X1, EPS was $3.26. The sharp reduction over the year should cause alarm among investors. As you can see in Figure 3.3, the industry average EPS in 20X2 ($4.51) is much higher than that of TLC, Inc. ($1.74).

Table 3-2 provides a list of highly profitable companies, as measured by EPS.

The *price/earnings (P/E) ratio*, also called the earnings multiple, reflects the company's relationship to its stockholders. The P/E ratio represents the amount investors are willing to pay for each dollar of the company's earnings. A high multiple (cost per dollar of earnings) is favored since it shows that investors view the business positively. On the other hand, investors looking for value prefer a relatively lower multiple (cost per dollar of earnings) as compared with companies of similar risk and return, a lower P/E ratio in such a case suggests that the company's stock may be undervalued.

$$\text{Price/earnings ratio} = \frac{\text{Market price per share}}{\text{Earnings per share}}$$

Assume a market price per share of $12 on December 31, 20X2, and $26 on December 31, 20X1. The P/E ratios are:

TABLE 3-3

P/E RATIOS, 1998

Company	Industry	P/E Ratio
Boeing	Aerospace	32
General Motors	Cars & Trucks	21
Goodyear	Tire & Rubber	13
Gap	Retailing	52
Intel	Semiconductor	37
Pfizer	Drugs & Research	88

Source: *Corporate Scorecard,* by *Business Week,* McGraw-Hill, March 1999, pp. 75–91.

$$20X2 : \frac{\$12}{\$1.74} = 6.9$$

$$20X1 : \frac{\$26}{\$3.26} = 7.98$$

From the lower P/E multiple, you can infer that the stock market now has a lower opinion of the business. However, some investors would argue that the stock is undervalued at $12. Nevertheless, the 54 percent decline in stock price over the year ($14/$26) should cause deep investor concern.

Table 3-3 shows price-earnings ratios of several companies.

Book value per share equals the net assets available to common stockholders divided by shares outstanding. By comparing it to market price per share, you can get another view of how investors feel about the business.

Book value per share

$$= \frac{\text{Total stockholders' equity} - \text{Preferred stock}}{\text{Common shares outstanding}}$$
$$= \frac{\$88,000 - 0}{4,600}$$
$$= \$19.13$$

In 20X1, book value per share was $17.39.

The increased book value per share is a favorable sign.

The *price/book value ratio* shows the market value of the company in comparison to its historical accounting value. A company with old

TABLE 3-4

DIVIDEND YIELD RATIOS 1998

Company	Dividend Payout Ratio
General Electric	1.2%
General Motors	2.3
Intel	0.1
Wal-Mart	0.4
Pfizer	0.5
Hewlett Packard	0.9

Source: MSN Money Central Investor (http://investor.msn.com), April 11, 1999.

assets may have a high ratio, whereas one with new assets may have a low ratio. Hence, you should note the changes in the ratio as part of your effort to appraise the corporate assets.

$$\text{Price/book value} = \frac{\text{Market price per share}}{\text{Book value per share}}$$

In 20X2, the ratio is:

$$\frac{\$12}{\$19.13} = .63$$

In 20X1, the ratio was 1.5. The significant drop in the ratio may indicate that investors now hold a lower opinion of the company than they did formerly. Market price of the stock may have dropped because of a deterioration in liquidity, activity, and profitability ratios. The major indicators of a company's performance are intertwined, and problems in one area may spill over into another. This appears to have happened to the company in our example.

Dividend ratios help you determine the current income from an investment. Two relevant ratios are:

$$\text{Dividend yield} = \frac{\text{Dividends per share}}{\text{Market price per share}}$$

$$\text{Dividend payout} = \frac{\text{Dividends per share}}{\text{Earnings per share}}$$

Table 3-4 shows the dividend payout ratios.

There is no such thing as a "right" payout ratio. Stockholders look unfavorably upon reduced dividends because lower payouts are a sign of a possible deterioration in a company's financial health. However, companies with ample opportunities for growth at high rates of return on assets tend to have low payout ratios.

AN OVERALL EVALUATION—SUMMARY OF FINANCIAL RATIOS

No single ratio or group of ratios is adequate for assessing all aspects of a company's financial condition. Figure 3.3 summarizes the 20X1 and 20X2 ratios calculated in the previous sections, along with the industry average ratios for 20X2, and shows the formula used to calculate each ratio. The last three columns of the figure contain subjective assessments of TLC's financial condition, based on trend analysis and 20X2 comparisons to the industry norms (as a rule, five-year ratios are needed for trend analysis to be meaningful).

Appraising the trend in the company's ratios from 20X1 to 20X2, we see from the drop in the current and quick ratios that there has been a slight detraction in short-term liquidity, although the ratios have been above the industry averages. But working capital has improved. A material deterioration in the activity ratio has occurred, indicating that an improvement in credit management and inventory policies is required. The declines are not terribly alarming, however, because these ratios are not way out of line with industry averages. Also, total utilization of assets, as indicated by the total asset turnover, shows a deteriorating trend.

Leverage (amount of debt) has been constant. However, there is less profit available to satisfy interest charges. TLC's profitability has deteriorated over the year and, in 20X2, is consistently below the industry average in every measure. Consequently, the return on owner's investment and the return on total assets has gone down. The earnings decrease may be partly the result of the company's high cost of short-term financing and partly the result of operating inefficiency. The higher costs may be due to receivable and inventory difficulties that forced a decline in the liquidity and activity ratios. Furthermore, as receivables and inventory turn over less, profit falls off from the reduced sales and the costs of carrying more in current asset balances.

The company's market value, as measured by the price/earnings (P/E) ratio, is respectable compared with other companies in the industry. But it shows a declining trend.

In summary, it appears that the company is doing satisfactorily in the industry in many categories. The 20X1-20X2 period, however, seems to indicate that the company is heading for financial trouble in terms of earnings, activity, and short-term liquidity. The business needs to concentrate on increasing operating efficiency and asset utilization.

LIMITATIONS OF RATIO ANALYSIS

While ratio analysis is an effective tool for assessing a business's financial condition, it's important to recognize its limitations:

1. Accounting policies vary among companies and can inhibit useful comparisons. For example, the use of different depreciation methods (straight-line vs. double declining balance) affects profitability and return ratios. Depreciation methods are discussed in detail in Chapter 10.

2. Management may manipulate the figures in order to make them look more impressive. For example, it can reduce needed research expense just to bolster net income. This practice, however, almost always hurts the company in the long run.

3. A ratio is static and does not reveal future flows. For example, it cannot answer questions such as, "How much cash do you have in your pocket now?" or "Is cash on hand sufficient, considering your expenses and income over the next month?"

4. A ratio does not indicate the quality of its components. For example, a high quick ratio may be based partly on receivables that may not be collected.

5. Reported liabilities, such as a lawsuit in which the company may be found liable, may be undervalued.

6. The company may have multiple lines of business, making it difficult to identify the industry group of which it is a part.

7. Industry averages cited by financial advisory services are only approximations. Hence, you may have to compare a company's ratios to those of competing companies in the industry to assess its standing accurately.

CHAPTER PERSPECTIVE

The analysis of financial statements is of interest to creditors, current and prospective investors, and the company's own management. This chapter has presented various financial statement analysis tools that are useful in evaluating the company's current and future financial condition. These techniques include horizontal, vertical, and ratio analysis, which provide relative measures of the performance and financial health of the company. Two methods—trend analysis and industry comparison—for analyzing financial ratios were demonstrated.

While ratio analysis is an effective tool for assessing a company's financial condition, its limitations must be recognized.

Financial Forecasting and Budgeting

INTRODUCTION AND MAIN POINTS

Financial forecasting, an essential element of planning, is the basis for budgeting and for estimating future financing requirements. Financing may derive from either internal or external sources. Internal financing refers to cash flow generated by the company's normal operating activities; external financing refers to capital provided by parties outside the company, such as investors and banks. Companies are able to estimate their need for external financing by forecasting future sales and related expenses.

After studying the material in this chapter:

■ You will be able to apply the percent-of-sales method to determine the amount of external financing needed.

■ You will have an understanding of the corporation's budgetary system, including the cash budget and the forecasted (pro forma) income statement and balance sheet.

■ You will be able to formulate the master budget, step by step.

■ You will see how a budget can be developed using an electronic spreadsheet.

THE PERCENT-OF-SALES METHOD OF FINANCIAL FORECASTING

The basic steps in projecting a company's financing needs are:

1. Project the company's sales. The sales forecast is the basis for most other forecasts.
2. Project additional variables, such as expenses.
3. Estimate the level of investment in current and fixed assets the company will need to make to support the projected sales.
4. Calculate the company's financing needs.

The most widely used method for projecting the company's financing needs is the *percent-of-sales* method. This method requires financial planners to estimate future expenses, assets, and liabilities as a percent of sales for that period. They then use those percentages together with projected sales, to construct forecasted balance sheets.

The following example illustrates the process.

EXAMPLE 4-1

Assume that sales for 20X1 are $20, projected sales for 20X2 are $24, net income is 5 percent of sales, and the dividend payout ratio is 40 percent. Figure 4.1 is a step-by-step illustration of the method for calculating external financing needs. (All dollar amounts are in millions.)

The steps for the computations are as follows:

Step 1. Express those balance sheet items that vary directly with sales as a percentage of sales. Any item such as long-term debt that does not vary directly with sales is designated "n.a.," or "not applicable."

Step 2. Multiply these percentages by the 20X2 projected sales ($24) to obtain the projected amounts (shown in the last column).

Step 3. Insert figures for long-term debt, common stock, and paid-in capital from the 20X1 balance sheet.

Step 4. Compute 20X2 retained earnings as shown in footnote (b).

Step 5. Sum the asset accounts, obtaining total projected assets of $7.2. Add to that total the projected liabilities and equity to obtain $7.12, the total internal financing provided. Since liabilities and equity must total $7.2, but only $7.12 is projected, there is a shortfall of $0.08. This is the external financing needed.

Although you can forecast the additional funds required by setting up a pro forma balance sheet as described above, it is often easier to use the following formula:

External funds needed (EFN)	=	Required increase in assets	−	Spontaneous increase in liabilities	−	Increase in retained earnings

$$\text{EFN} = (A/S)\, \Delta S - (L/S)\, \Delta S - (PM)(PS)(1-d)$$

where

A/S = Assets that increase spontaneously with sales as a percentage of sales

L/S = Liabilities that increase spontaneously with sales as a percentage of sales

ΔS = Change in sales

PM = Profit margin on sales

PS = Projected sales

d = Dividend payout ratio

EXAMPLE 4-2
In Example 4-1,

$$A/S = \$6/\$20 = 30\%$$
$$L/S = \$2/\$20 = 10\%$$
$$\Delta S = (\$24 - \$20) = \$4$$
$$PM = 5\% \text{ on sales}$$
$$PS = \$24$$
$$d = 40\%$$

Plugging these figures into the formula yields:

$$EFN = 0.3(\$4) - 0.1(\$4) - (0.05)(\$24)(1 - 0.4)$$
$$= \$1.2 - \$0.4 - \$0.72$$
$$= \$0.08$$

The amount of external financing needed is $80,000, which can be raised by issuing any combination of notes payable, bonds, and stocks.

The major advantage of the percent-of-sales method of financial forecasting is that it is simple and inexpensive to use. It assumes that the company is operating at full capacity and therefore does not have sufficient productive capacity to absorb a projected increase in sales; thus an additional investment in assets will be necessary. The method must be used with extreme caution if excess capacity exists in certain asset accounts.

To obtain a more precise projection of the company's future financing needs, a cash budget (discussed in the next section) is required.

TYPES OF BUDGETS

A budget represents a company's annual financial plan. A comprehensive (master) budget is a formal statement of management's expectation for sales, expenses, volume, and other financial transactions for the coming period. It consists basically of a pro forma (projected or planned) income statement, pro forma balance sheet, and cash budget.

A budget is a tool for both planning and control. At the beginning of the period, the budget is a plan or standard; at the end of the period it serves as a control device by which management can measure its success in achieving the goals outlined in the budget and plan to improve future performance.

With the aid of computer technology, budgeting can be used to evaluate a variety of "what-if" scenarios. Such analyses makes it easier for management to find the best course of action among various

	Present (20X1)	% of Sales (20X1 Sales = $20)	Projected (20X2 Sales = $24)	
Assets				
Current assets	2	10	2.4	
Fixed assets	4	20	4.8	
Total assets	6		7.2	

LIABILITIES AND STOCKHOLDERS' EQUITY

	Present	% of Sales	Projected	
Current liabilities	2	10	2.4	
Long-term debt	2.5	n.a.	2.5	
Total liabilities	4.5		4.9	
Common stock	0.1	n.a.	0.1	
Capital surplus	0.2	n.a.	0.2	
Retained earnings	1.2		1.92[a]	
Total equity	1.5		2.22	
Total liabilities and stockholders' equity	6		7.12	Total financing provided
			0.08[b]	External financing needed
			7.2	Total

---

[a] 20X2 retained earnings = 20X1 retained earnings + projected net income
                  − cash dividends paid
           = $1.2 + 5%($24) − 40%[5%($24)]
           = $1.2 + $1.2 − $0.48 = $2.4 − $0.48 = $1.92

[b] External financing needed = projected total assets − (projected total liabilities
                                + projected equity)
           = $7.2 − ($4.9 + 2.22) = $7.2 − $7.12 = $0.08

Figure 4.1 *Pro Forma Balance Sheet (in Millions of Dollars)*

alternatives. If management does not like what it sees on the budgeted financial statements, it can alter its contemplated planning decisions.

The budget is classified into two broad categories:
1. Operating budget.
2. Financial budget.

The *operating budget* consists of:
- Sales budget
- Production budget
- Direct material budget
- Direct labor budget
- Factory overhead budget
- Selling and administrative expense budget
- Pro forma income statement

The *financial budget* consists of:
- Cash budget
- Pro forma balance sheet

PREPARING THE BUDGET

The major steps in preparing the budget are:
1. Prepare a sales forecast.
2. Determine expected production volume.
3. Estimate manufacturing costs and operating expenses.
4. Determine cash flow and other financial effects.
5. Formulate projected financial statements.

Figure 4.2 shows a simplified diagram of the various parts of the comprehensive (master) budget.

To illustrate how these budgets are put together, we will prepare a sample financial plan for a manufacturing company called the Johnson Company, which produces and markets a single product. We assume that the company develops its master budget on a quarterly basis and distinguishes between variable costs and fixed costs in its planning. (Variable costs are those costs that vary in proportion to sales or production volume; fixed costs do not vary but remain constant regardless of volume.)

Sales Forecasts

The sales forecast gives the expected level of sales for the company's goods or services throughout some future period and is instrumental in the company's planning and budgeting functions. It is the key to other forecasts and plans. There is a wide range of techniques of sales forecasting which the company may choose from; however, there are basically two approaches to forecasting: qualitative and quantitative.

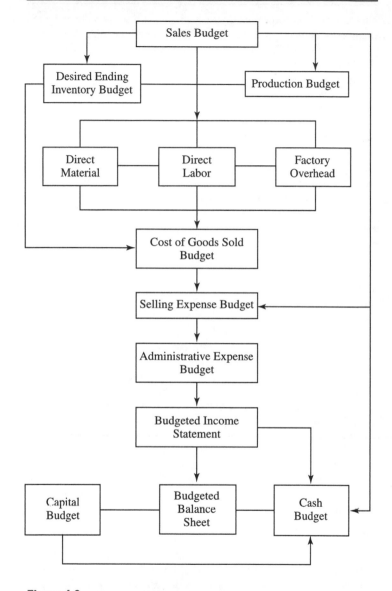

Figure 4.2 *Comprehensive (Master) Budget*

The *qualitative approach,* which includes forecasts based on judgment and opinion, includes such methods as executive opinions, the Delphi technique, sales force polling, and consumer surveys. The *quantitative approach* is as follows:

- Forecasts based on historical data
  - Naive methods
  - Moving averages
  - Exponential smoothing
  - Trend analysis
- Associative (causal) forecasts
  - Simple regression
  - Multiple regression
  - Econometric modeling

The discussion on forecasting methodology is reserved for business forecasting texts.

The Sales Budget

The sales budget is the starting point in preparing the master budget, since estimated sales volume influences nearly all other items in the master budget. The sales budget ordinarily indicates the quantity in units of each product the company expects to sell. That number is multiplied by the expected unit selling price to construct the sales budget. The sales budget also includes a computation of expected cash collections from credit sales, which will be used later for cash budgeting.

The Production Budget

After sales are budgeted, the production budget is developed by determining the number of units expected to be manufactured in order to meet budgeted sales and inventory requirements. The expected volume of production is determined by subtracting the estimated inventory at the beginning of the period from the sum of the units expected to be sold and the desired inventory at the end of the period.

$$\begin{array}{l}\text{Expected}\\\text{production}\\\text{volume}\end{array} = \text{Planned sales} + \begin{array}{l}\text{Desired}\\\text{ending}\\\text{inventory}\end{array} - \text{Beginning inventory}$$

EXAMPLE 4-3

THE JOHNSON COMPANY

Sales Budget
for the Year Ending December 31, 20X2

	Quarter				Total
	1	2	3	4	
Expected sales in units	800	700	900	800	3,200
Unit sales price	×$80	×$80	×$80	×$80	×$80
Total sales	$64,000	$56,000	$72,000	$64,000	$256,000

SCHEDULE OF EXPECTED CASH COLLECTIONS

	1	2	3	4	Total
Accounts receivable, 12/31/20X1	9,500[*]				$9,500
1st quarter sales ($64,000)	44,800[†]	$17,920[‡]			62,720
2d quarter sales ($56,000)		39,200	$15,680		54,880
3d quarter sales ($72,000)			50,400	$20,160	70,560
4th quarter sales ($64,000)				44,800	44,800
Total cash collections	$54,300	$57,120	$66,080	$64,960	$242,460

[*] The entire $9,500 accounts receivable balance is assumed to be collectible in the first quarter.
[†] 70% of a quarter's sales are collected in the quarter of sale.

[‡] 28% of a quarter's sales are collected in the quarter following; the remaining 2 are uncollectible.

Monthly Cash Collections from Customers

Frequently, there are time lags between monthly sales made *on account* and their related monthly cash collections. For example, in any month, credit sales are collected as follows: 15 percent in month of sale, 60 percent in the following month, and 25 percent in the month after. The following are given for a hypothetical company (in thousands):

	April— Actual	May— Actual	June— Budgeted	July— Budgeted
Credit sales	$320	$200	$300	$280

The budgeted cash receipts for June and July are computed as follows:

For June:

From April sales	$320 × 0.25	$ 80
From May sales	200 × 0.6	120
From June sales	300 × 0.15	45
Total budgeted collections in June		$245

For July:

From May sales	$200 × 0.25	$ 50
From June sales	300 × 0.6	180
From July sales	280 × 0.15	42
Total budgeted collections in July		$272

EXAMPLE 4-4

THE JOHNSON COMPANY

Production Budget
for the Year Ending December 31, 20X2

	Quarter				Total
	1	2	3	4	
Planned sales (Example 4-3)	800	700	900	800	3,200
Desired ending inventory*	70	90	80	100[†]	100
Total Needs	870	790	980	900	3,300
Less: Beginning inventory[‡]	80	70	90	80	80
Units to be produced	790	720	890	820	3,220

---

* 10% of the next quarter's sales

[†] Estimated

[‡] The same as the previous quarter's ending inventory

The Direct Material Budget

After the level of production has been computed, a direct material budget should be constructed to show how much material will be required and how much must be purchased to meet production requirements. The amount to be purchased depends on the expected usage of materials and existing inventory levels. The formula for computing the purchase is:

Purchase in units = Usage

+ Desired ending material inventory units

− Beginning inventory units

The direct material budget is usually accompanied by a computation of expected cash payments for materials.

EXAMPLE 4-5

THE JOHNSON COMPANY
Direct Material Budget
for the Year Ending December 31, 20X2

	Quarter				Total
	1	2	3	4	
Units to be produced (Ex. 4-4)	790	720	890	820	3,220
Material needs per unit (lbs)	× 3	× 3	× 3	× 3	× 3
Material needs for production	2,370	2,160	2,670	2,460	9,660
Desired ending inventory of materials*	216	267	246	250†	250
Total needs	2,586	2,427	2,916	2,710	9,910
Less: Beginning inventory of materials‡	237	216	267	246	237
Materials to be purchased	2,349	2,211	2,649	2,464	9,673
Unit price	× $2	× $2	× $2	× $2	× $2
Purchase cost	$4,698	$4,422	$5,298	$4,928	$19,346

SCHEDULE OF EXPECTED CASH DISBURSEMENTS

Accounts payable, 12/31/20X1	$2,200				$2,200
1st quarter purchases ($4,698)	2,349	2,349§			4,698
2d quarter purchases ($4,422)		2,211	2,211		4,422
3d quarter purchases ($5,298)			2,649	2,649	5,298
4th quarter purchases ($4,928)				2,464	2,464
Total disbursements	$4,549	$4,560	$4,860	$5,113	$19,082

---

* 10% of the next quarter's units needed for production

† Estimated

‡ The same as the prior quarter's ending inventory

§ 50% of a quarter's purchases are paid for in the quarter of purchase; the remainder are paid for in the following quarter.

The Direct Labor Budget

The production requirements in the production budget provide the starting point for the preparation of the direct labor budget. To compute direct labor requirements, multiply expected production volume for each period by the number of direct labor hours required to produce a single unit. The result is then multiplied by the direct labor cost per hour to obtain budgeted total direct labor costs.

EXAMPLE 4-6

THE JOHNSON COMPANY

Direct Labor Budget
for the Year Ending December 31, 20X2

	Quarter				Total
	1	2	3	4	
Units to be produced (Ex. 4-4)	790	720	890	820	3,220
Direct labor hours per unit	× 5	× 5	× 5	× 5	× 5
Total hours	3,950	3,600	4,450	4,100	16,100
Direct labor cost per hour	× $5	× $5	× $5	× $5	× $5
Total direct labor cost	$19,750	$18,000	$22,250	$20,500	$80,500

The Factory Overhead Budget

The factory overhead budget provides a schedule of all manufacturing costs other than direct materials and direct labor, such as depreciation, property taxes and factory rent. In developing the cash budget, it is important to remember that depreciation does not entail a cash outlay and therefore must be deducted from the total factory overhead when you compute cash disbursement for factory overhead.

EXAMPLE 4-7

In the following illustration of a factory overhead budget, we assume that

▬ Total factory overhead budgeted = $6,000 fixed (per quarter), plus $2 per hour of direct labor.

▬ Depreciation expenses are $3,250 each quarter.

▬ All overhead costs involving cash outlays are paid for in the quarter incurred.

EXAMPLE 4-7, continued

THE JOHNSON COMPANY

Factory Overhead Budget
for the Year Ending December 31, 20X2

	Quarter				Total
	1	2	3	4	
Budgeted direct labor hours (Example 4-6)	3,950	3,600	4,450	4,100	16,100
Variable overhead rate	× $2	× $2	× $2	× $2	× $2
Variable overhead budgeted	7,900	7,200	8,900	8,200	32,200
Fixed overhead budgeted	6,000	6,000	6,000	6,000	24,000
Total budgeted overhead	13,900	13,200	14,900	14,200	56,200
Less: Depreciation	3,250	3,250	3,250	3,250	13,000
Cash disbursement for overhead	10,650	9,950	11,650	10,950	43,200

The Ending Inventory Budget

The ending inventory budget provides the information required for the construction of budgeted financial statements. Specifically, it helps compute the cost of goods sold on the budgeted income statement and the dollar value of the ending materials and finished goods inventory that appears on the budgeted balance sheet.

EXAMPLE 4-8

THE JOHNSON COMPANY

Ending Inventory Budget
for the Year Ending December 31, 20X2
Ending Inventory

	Units	Unit Cost	Total
Direct materials	250 pounds (Example 4-5)	$ 2	$500
Finished goods	100 units (Example 4-4)	$41[*]	$4,100

---

[*] The unit variable cost of $41 is computed as follows:

	Units	Unit Cost	Total
Direct materials (Example 4-5)	$2	3 pounds	$6
Direct labor (Example 4-6)	5	5 hours	25
Variable overhead (Example 4-7)	2	5 hours	10
Total variable manufacturing cost			$41

The Selling and Administrative Expense Budget

The selling and administrative expense budget lists the operating expenses incurred in selling the products and in managing the business. To complete the budgeted income statement (sales less variable costs less fixed costs), you must compute variable selling and administrative expense per unit.

EXAMPLE 4-9

THE JOHNSON COMPANY

Selling and Administrative Expense Budget
for the Year Ending December 31, 20X2

	Quarter				Total
	1	2	3	4	
Expected sales in units	800	700	900	800	3,200
Variable selling and administrative expense per unit[*]	× $4	× $4	× $4	× $4	× $4
Budgeted variable expense	$3,200	$2,800	$3,600	$3,200	$12,800
Fixed selling and administrative expenses:					
Advertising	1,100	1,100	1,100	1,100	4,400
Insurance	2,800				2,800
Office salaries	8,500	8,500	8,500	8,500	34,000
Rent	350	350	350	350	1,400
Taxes			1,200		1,200
Total budgeted selling and administrative expenses[†]	$15,950	$12,750	$14,750	$13,150	$56,600

[*] Assumed; includes sales agents' commissions, shipping, and supplies

[†] Paid for in the quarter incurred

The Cash Budget

The cash budget helps managers anticipate the expected cash inflow and outflow for a designated time period, keep cash balances in reasonable relationship to needs, and avoid both unnecessarily idle cash and possible cash shortages. The cash budget usually consists of four major sections:

1. The *receipts* section, including the beginning cash balance, cash in from customers, and other receipts.
2. The *disbursements* section, comprising all cash payments that are planned during the budget period.
3. The *cash surplus* or *deficit* section, which shows the difference between the cash receipts section and the cash disbursements section.

EXAMPLE 4-10

THE JOHNSON COMPANY

Cash Budget
for the Year Ending December 31, 20X2

	From Example	Quarter 1	Quarter 2	Quarter 3	Quarter 4	Total
Cash balance, beginning		10,000*	9,401	5,461	9,106	10,000
Add: Receipts:						
Collections from customers	4-3	54,300	57,120	66,080	64,960	242,460
Total cash available		64,300	66,521	71,541	74,066	252,460
Less: Disbursements:						
Direct materials	4-5	4,549	4,560	4,860	5,113	19,082
Direct labor	4-6	19,750	18,000	22,250	20,500	80,500
Factory overhead	4-7	10,650	9,950	11,650	10,950	43,200
Selling and Admin.	4-9	15,950	12,750	14,750	13,150	56,600
Machinery purchase	Given	—	24,300	—	—	24,300
Income tax	Given	4,000	—	—	—	4,000
Total disbursements		54,899	69,560	53,510	49,713	227,682
Cash surplus (deficit)		9,401	(3,039)	18,031	24,353	24,778
Financing:						
Borrowing		—	8,500	—	—	8,500
Repayment		—	—	(8,500)	—	(8,500)
Interest		—	—	(425)	†	(425)
Total financing		—	8,500	(8,925)	—	(425)
Cash balance, ending		9,401	5,461	9,106	24,353	24,353

---

* From balance sheet 20X1, page 76.

† $8,500 \times \frac{1}{2} \times 10\% = \$425$

4. The *financing* section, which provides a detailed account of the borrowings and repayments expected during the budgeting period. In this illustration, we assume that:

▬ The company desires to maintain a $5,000 minimum cash balance at the end of each quarter.

▬ All borrowing and repayment must be in multiples of $500 at an interest rate of 10 percent per annum. Interest is computed and paid as the principal is repaid. Borrowing takes place at the beginning of each quarter, and repayment is at the end of each quarter.

The Budgeted Income Statement

The budgeted income statement summarizes projections for the various components of revenue and expenses for the budgeting period. The budget can be divided into quarters or even months if the company wishes to keep tight control over its operations.

EXAMPLE 4-11

THE JOHNSON COMPANY

Budgeted Income Statement
for the Year Ending December 31, 20X2

	Example		
Sales (3,200 units @ $80)	4-3		$256,000
Less: Variable expenses			
Variable cost of goods sold			
(3,200 units @ $41)	4-4	$131,200	
Variable selling &			
administrative	4-9	12,800	144,000
Contribution margin			112,000
Less: Fixed expenses			
Factory overhead	4-7	24,000	
Selling and administrative	4-9	43,800	67,800
Net operating income			44,200
Less: Interest expense	4-10		425
Income before taxes			43,775
Less: Income taxes	20%*		8,755
Net income			35,020

---

* Assumed.

The budgeted balance sheet is developed by adjusting the balance sheet for the year just ended, using all the activities that are expected to take place during the budgeting period. The budgeted balance sheet must be prepared because:

■ It might disclose some unfavorable financial conditions that management will want to avoid.

■ It serves as a final check on the mathematical accuracy of all the other schedules.

■ It helps management perform a variety of ratio calculations.

■ It highlights future resources and obligations.

EXAMPLE 4-12
In this illustration, we use the balance sheet for the year 20X1.

THE JOHNSON COMPANY

Balance Sheet
as of December 31, 20X1

ASSETS		LIABILITIES AND STOCKHOLDERS' EQUITY	
Current Assets:		Current Liabilities:	
Cash	10,000	Accounts Payable	2,200
Accounts Receivable	9,500	Income Tax Payable	4,000
Material Inventory	474	Total Current Liabilities	6,200
Finished Goods Inventory	3,280		
Total Current Assets	23,254		
Fixed Assets:		Stockholders' Equity:	
Land	50,000	Common Stock, No-Par	70,000
Building and Equipment	100,000	Retained Earnings	37,054
Accumulated Depreciation	(60,000)		
	90,000		
		Total Liabilities and	
Total Assets	113,254	Stockholders' Equity	113,254

THE JOHNSON COMPANY

Budgeted Balance Sheet
as of December 31, 20X2

ASSETS		LIABILITIES AND STOCKHOLDERS' EQUITY	
Current Assets:		Current Liabilities:	
Cash	24,353[a]	Accounts Payable	2,464[i]
Accounts Receivable	23,040[b]	Income Tax Payable	8,755[j]
Material Inventory	500[c]	Total Current	
Finished Goods		Liabilities	11,219
Inventory	4,100[d]		
Total Current Assets	$51,993		
Fixed Assets:		Stockholders' Equity:	
Land	50,000[e]	Common Stock,	
Building and		No-Par	70,000[k]
Equipment	124,300[f]	Retained Earnings	72,074[l]
Accumulated			
Depreciation	(73,000)[g]		
	101,300[h]	Total Liabilities and	
Total Assets	153,293	Stockholders' Equity	153,293

Computations:

[a] From Example 4-10 (cash budget).

[b] $9,500 (from balance sheet 20X1) + $256,000 sales (from Example 4-3) − $242,460 receipts (from Example 4-3) = $23,040.

[c] and [d] From Example 4-8 (ending inventory budget).

[e] No change.

[f] $100,000 (from balance sheet 20X1) + $24,300 (from Example 4-10) = $124,300.

[g] $60,000 (from balance sheet 20X1) + $13,000 (from Example 4-7) = $73,000.

[h] $50,000 + $124,300 − $73,000 = $101,300.

[i] $2,200 (from balance sheet 20X1) + $19,346 (from Example 4-5) − $19,082 (Example 4-5) = $2,464 (all accounts payable relate to material purchases), or 50% of 4th quarter purchase = 50% ($4,928) = 2,464.

[j] From Example 4-11 (budgeted income statement).

[k] No change.

[l] $37,054 (from balance sheet 20X1) + $35,020 net income (from Example 4-11) = $72,074.

Some Financial Ratio Calculations

To predict the Johnson Company's financial condition for the budgeting year, you can calculate a sample of financial ratios. (Assume 20X1 after-tax net income was $15,000.)

	20X1	20X2
Current ratio		
(Current assets/	= $23,254/$6,200	= $51,993/$11,219
current liabilities)	= 3.75	= 4.63
Return on total assets		
(Net income after		
taxes/	= $15,000/$113,254	= $35,020/$153,293
total assets)	= 13.24%	= 22.85%

Sample calculations indicate that the Johnson Company may well improve its liquidity in 20X2, as measured by the current ratio, and its overall performance as measured by return on total assets will likely improve. This could be an indication that the company's contemplated plan may work out well.

COMPUTER-BASED MODELS AND SPREADSHEET PROGRAM MODELS FOR BUDGETING

Examples 4-3 to 4-12 showed a detailed procedure for developing a master budget. However, in practice computer and software technology allows financial planners and budget analysts to take a short-cut, computerized approach to budgeting. More and more companies are developing computer-based models for financial planning and budgeting, using powerful, yet easy-to-use, financial modeling languages such as Comshare's Interactive Financial Planning System (IFPS) and Up Your Cash Flow. The models help not only to build a budget for profit planning but also to answer a variety of "what-if" scenarios. The resultant calculations provide a basis for choice among alternatives under conditions of uncertainty. Furthermore, budget modeling can be accomplished using spreadsheet programs such as Microsoft's Excel.

In this section we will illustrate the use of Excel to develop a financial model. For illustrative purposes, we will present two examples of projecting an income statement.

EXAMPLE 4-13

JKS Furniture Company, Inc., expects the following for the coming 12 months, 20X2:
- Sales for first month = $60,000.
- Cost of sales = 42 percent of sales, all variable.
- Operating expenses = $10,000 fixed plus 5 percent of sales.
- Taxes = 30 percent of net income.
- Sales increase by 5 percent each month.

Based on this information, Figure 4.3 presents a spreadsheet for the contribution income statement for the next 12 months and in total.

Figure 4.4 shows a spreadsheet for the contribution income statement for the next 12 months and in total, assuming that sales increase by 10 percent and operating expenses = $10,000 plus 10 percent of sales. This is an example of "what-if" scenarios.

EXAMPLE 4-14

Delta Gamma Company wishes to prepare a 3-year projection of net income using the following 1998 base year information:

Sales revenues	$4,500,000
Cost of sales	2,900,000
Selling and administrative expenses	800,000
Net income before taxes	800,000

The projection uses following assumptions:
▬ Sales revenues increase by 6 percent in 1999, 7 percent in 2000, and 8 percent in 2001.
▬ Cost of sales increase by 5 percent each year.
▬ Selling and administrative expenses increase only 1 percent in 1999 and will remain at the 1999 level thereafter.
▬ The income tax rate = 46 percent.

Figure 4.5 presents a spreadsheet for the income statement for the next 3 years.

CHAPTER PERSPECTIVE

Financial forecasting, an essential element of planning, is a vital function of financial managers. Forecasts of future sales and their related expenses provide the business with the information needed to project financing requirements. The chapter discussed two major methods: (1) a short-cut technique of financial forecasting, referred to as the percent-of-sales method, and (2) the budgetary system, including the cash budget. Financial forecasting and budgeting are simplified by the use of electronic spreadsheet software, such as Excel.

	1	2	3	4	5	6	7	8	9	10	11	12	TOTAL	PER-CENT
Sales	$60,000	$63,000	$66,150	$69,458	$72,930	$76,577	$80,406	$84,426	$88,647	$93,080	$97,734	$102,620	$955,028	100
Less: VC Cost of sales	$25,200	$26,460	$27,783	$29,172	$30,631	$32,162	$33,770	$35,459	$37,232	$39,093	$41,048	$43,101	$401,112	42
Operating exp.	$3,000	$3,150	$3,308	$3,473	$3,647	$3,829	$4,020	$4,221	$4,432	$4,654	$4,887	$5,131	$47,751	5
CM	$31,800	$33,390	$35,060	$36,812	$38,653	$40,586	$42,615	$44,746	$46,983	$49,332	$51,799	$54,389	$506,165	53
Less: FC Operating exp.	$10,000	$10,000	$10,000	$10,000	$10,000	$10,000	$10,000	$10,000	$10,000	$10,000	$10,000	$10,000	$120,000	13
Net income	$21,800	$23,390	$25,060	$26,812	$28,653	$30,586	$32,615	$34,746	$36,983	$39,332	$41,799	$44,389	$386,165	40
Less: Tax	$6,540	$7,017	$7,518	$8,044	$8,596	$9,176	$9,785	$10,424	$11,095	$11,800	$12,540	$13,317	$115,849	12
NI after tax	$15,260	$16,373	$17,542	$18,769	$20,057	$21,410	$22,831	$24,322	$25,888	$27,533	$29,259	$31,072	$270,315	28

Figure 4.3 *Projected Income Statement*

	1	2	3	4	5	6	7	8	9	10	11	12	TOTAL	PER-CENT
Sales	$60,000	$66,000	$72,600	$79,860	$87,846	$96,631	$106,294	$116,923	$128,615	$141,477	$155,625	$171,187	$1,283,057	134
Less: VC Cost of sales	$25,200	$27,720	$30,492	$33,541	$36,895	$40,585	$44,643	$49,108	$54,018	$59,420	$65,362	$71,899	$538,884	56
Operating exp.	$6,000	$6,600	$7,260	$7,986	$8,785	$9,663	$10,629	$11,692	$12,862	$14,148	$15,562	$17,119	$64,153	7
CM	$28,800	$31,680	$34,848	$38,333	$42,166	$46,383	$51,021	$56,123	$61,735	$67,909	$74,700	$82,170	$615,867	64
Less: FC Operating exp.	$10,000	$10,000	$10,000	$10,000	$10,000	$10,000	$10,000	$10,000	$10,000	$10,000	$10,000	$10,000	$120,000	13
Net income	$18,800	$21,680	$24,848	$28,333	$32,166	$36,383	$41,021	$46,123	$51,735	$57,909	$64,700	$72,170	$495,867	52
Less: Tax	$5,640	$6,504	$7,454	$8,500	$9,650	$10,915	$12,306	$13,837	$15,521	$17,373	$19,410	$21,651	$148,760	16
NI after tax	$13,160	$15,176	$17,394	$19,833	$22,516	$25,468	$28,715	$32,286	$36,215	$40,536	$45,290	$50,519	$347,107	36

Figure 4.4 *Projected Income Statement*

	1998	1999	2000	2001
Sales	$4,500,000	$4,770,000	$5,103,900	$5,512,212
Cost of sales	2,900,000	3,045,000	3,197,250	3,357,113
Gross margin	1,600,000	1,725,000	1,906,650	2,155,100
Selling & administrative exp.	800,000	808,000	808,000	808,000
Net income before tax	800,000	917,000	1,098,650	1,347,100
Tax	368,000	421,820	505,379	619,666
Net income after tax	$ 432,000	$ 495,180	$ 593,271	$ 727,434

Figure 4.5   *3-Year Income Projections (1998–2001)*

Analyzing and Improving Management Performance

INTRODUCTION AND MAIN POINTS

Companies must be able to measure managerial performance if they are to control operations and achieve organizational goals. As companies grow or their activities become more complex, they often attempt to decentralize decision making as much as possible by restructuring into several divisions and treating each as an independent business. The managers of these subunits or segments are evaluated on the basis of the effectiveness with which they use the assets entrusted to them.

Perhaps the most widely used single measure of success of an organization and its subunits is the rate of return on investment (ROI). A related measure is the return to stockholders, known as the return on equity (ROE). After studying the material in this chapter:

■ You will be able to explain ROI.

■ You will be able to identify the components of the Du Pont formula and explain how it can be used for profit improvement.

■ You will see how financial leverage affects the stockholder's return.

■ You will have an understanding of the relationship between ROI and ROE.

RETURN ON INVESTMENT

ROI, which relates net income to invested capital (total assets), provides a standard for evaluating how efficiently management employs the average dollar invested in a business's assets. An increase in ROI can translate directly into a higher return on the stockholders' equity. ROI is calculated as:

$$\text{ROI} = \frac{\text{Net profit after taxes}}{\text{Total assets}}$$

EXAMPLE 5-1

Consider the following financial data:

If Total assets = $100,000, and Net profit after taxes = $18,000

$$\text{Then, ROI} = \frac{\text{Net profit after taxes}}{\text{Total assets}} = \frac{\$18,000}{\$100,000} = 18\%$$

The problem with this formula is that it tells you only how well a company utilized its assets and how it fared compared to others in its industry. It has very little value from the standpoint of profit planning, meaning determining ways to increase profits.

DU PONT FORMULA

ROI can be broken down into two factors—profit margin and asset turnover. In the past, managers have tended to focus only on profit margin and have ignored the turnover of assets. However, having excessive funds tied up in assets can be just as much a drag on profitability as can excessive expenses. The Du Pont Corporation was the first major company to recognize the importance of looking at both net profit margin and total asset turnover in assessing the performance of an organization. The ROI breakdown, known as the *Du Pont formula,* is expressed as a product of these two factors, as shown below.

$$\text{ROI} = \frac{\text{Net profit after taxes}}{\text{Total assets}}$$

$$= \frac{\text{Net profit after taxes}}{\text{Sales}} \times \frac{\text{Sales}}{\text{Total assets}}$$

$$= \text{Net profit margin} \times \text{Total asset turnover}$$

The breakdown of ROI is based on the thesis that company profitability is directly related to management's ability to manage assets efficiently and to control expenses effectively. Net profit margin (the percentage of profit earned on sales) is a measure of profitability or operating efficiency. On the other hand, total asset turnover (the number of times the investment in assets turns over each year to generate sales) measures how well a company manages its assets.

EXAMPLE 5-2

Assume the same data as in Example 5-1. Also assume sales of $200,000.

$$\text{Then, ROI} = \frac{\text{Net profit after taxes}}{\text{Total assets}} = \frac{\$18,000}{\$100,000} = 18\%$$

Alternatively,

$$\text{Net profit margin} = \frac{\text{Net profit after taxes}}{\text{Sales}} = \frac{\$18,000}{\$200,000} = 9\%$$

$$\text{Total asset turnover} = \frac{\text{Sales}}{\text{Total assets}} = \frac{\$200,000}{\$100,000} = 2 \text{ times}$$

Therefore,

$$\text{ROI} = \text{net profit margin} \times \text{total asset turnover}$$
$$= 9\% \times 2 \text{ times} = 18\%$$

Financial managers can gain a great deal of insight into how to improve profitability and improve investment strategy from this breakdown. (Net profit margin and total asset turnover are hereafter called margin and turnover, respectively.) This breakdown has several advantages for profit planning over the original formula:

1. It recognizes the importance of turnover as a key to overall return on investment. In fact, turnover is just as important as profit margin in enhancing overall return.
2. It recognizes the importance of sales.
3. It stresses the possibility of trading margin for turnover in an attempt to improve the overall performance of a company. In other words, a low turnover can be made up by a high margin, and vice versa.

EXAMPLE 5-3
The breakdown of ROI into its two components shows that a number of combinations of margin and turnover can yield the same rate of return, as shown below:

	Margin	×	Turnover	=	ROI
(1)	9%	×	2 times	–	18%
(2)	6	×	3	–	18
(3)	3	×	6	=	18
(4)	2	×	9	=	18

The turnover-margin relationship and its resulting ROI are illustrated in Figure 5.1.

IS THERE AN OPTIMAL ROI?
No one ROI is satisfactory for all companies. Sound and successful operation results in an optimum combination of profits, sales, and capital employed, but the precise combination necessarily varies with the nature of the business and the characteristics of the product. An industry

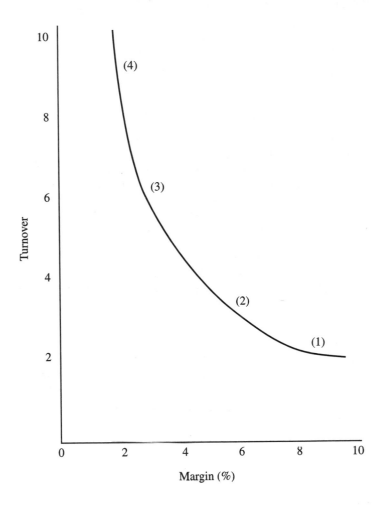

Figure 5.1 *The Margin-Turnover Relationship*

whose products are tailored to customers' specifications will have different margins and turnover ratios than an industry that mass-produces highly competitive consumer goods. For example, a supermarket operation inherently works with low margin and high turnover, while a jewelry store typically has a low turnover and high margin.

USING THE DU PONT FORMULA FOR PROFIT IMPROVEMENT

The breakdown of ROI into margin and turnover gives management insight into planning for profit improvement by revealing where weaknesses exist—margin or turnover, or both. Management can then take various actions to enhance ROI:

- Improve margin
- Improve turnover
- Improve both

Improving margin, a popular way of improving performance, may be accomplished by reducing expenses, raising selling prices, or increasing sales faster than expenses. Expenses may be reduced by:

(a) Using less costly materials (although this can be dangerous in today's quality-oriented environment).

(b) Automating processes as much as possible to increase labor productivity. (This will probably increase assets, thereby reducing turnover.)

(c) Bringing discretionary fixed costs under scrutiny and curtailing or eliminating various programs. Discretionary fixed costs include advertising, research and development, and management development programs.

Companies that can raise selling prices and retain profitability without losing business even in poor economic times are said to have pricing power. Pricing power is also the ability to pass on cost increases to consumers without attracting domestic and import competition, political opposition, regulation, or threats of product substitution. As a rule, companies that offer unique, high-quality goods and services (where the service is more important than the cost) are most likely to have pricing power.

Improved turnover may be achieved by increasing sales while holding the investment in assets relatively constant or by reducing assets. Some of the strategies to reduce assets are:

(a) Disposing of obsolete and redundant inventory. Computers have made it easy to monitor inventory continuously, allowing for better control.

(b) Devising methods to speed up the collection of receivables and to evaluate credit terms and policies.

(c) Identifying unused fixed assets.
(d) Using the cash obtained by implementing the previous methods to repay outstanding debts, repurchase outstanding issues of stock, or invest in other profit-producing activities.

Figure 5.2 shows the relationship of ROI to the underlying ratios—margin and turnover—and their components.

EXAMPLE 5-4

Assume that management sets a 20 percent ROI as a profit target. It is currently making an 18 percent return on its investment.

$$\text{ROI} = \frac{\text{Net profit after taxes}}{\text{Total assets}} = \frac{\text{Net profit after taxes}}{\text{Sales}} \times \frac{\text{Sales}}{\text{Total assets}}$$

Present situation:

$$18\% = \frac{18,000}{200,000} \times \frac{200,000}{100,000}$$

There are several strategies the company can use to achieve its goals.

Alternative 1: Increase the margin while holding turnover constant. Pursuing this strategy requires maintaining current selling prices and working to increase efficiency in order to reduce expenses. This strategy can reduce expenses by $2,000 without affecting sales and investment and thus yield a 20 percent target ROI, as follows:

$$20\% = \frac{20,000}{200,000} \times \frac{200,000}{100,000}$$

Alternative 2: Increase turnover by reducing investment in assets while holding net profit and sales constant. The company might reduce working capital or sell some land, reducing investment in assets by $10,000 without affecting sales and net income and yielding the 20 percent target ROI as follows:

$$20\% = \frac{18,000}{200,000} \times \frac{200,000}{90,000}$$

Alternative 3: Increase both margin and turnover by disposing of obsolete and redundant inventories or by initiating an active advertising campaign. For example, the company could trim $5,000 worth of inventory, thereby reducing the inventory holding charge by $1,000. This strategy would increase ROI to 20 percent.

$$20\% = \frac{19,000}{200,000} \times \frac{200,000}{95,000}$$

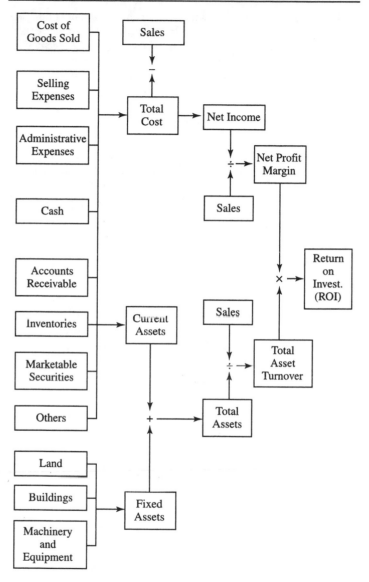

Figure 5.2 *Relationship of Factors Influencing ROI*

Excessive investment in assets is just as much of a drag on profitability as are excessive expenses. In this case, cutting unnecessary inventories also helps reduce the costs of carrying those inventories, thus improving both margin and turnover at the same time. In practice, alternative 3 is much more common than alternatives 1 or 2.

IMPROVING RETURN TO STOCKHOLDERS THROUGH FINANCIAL LEVERAGE

Generally, a high level of management performance, defined as a high or above-average ROI, produces a high return to equity holders. However, even a poorly managed company that suffers from a below-average performance can generate an above-average return on the stockholders' equity, or return on equity (ROE). It can do this through the use of borrowed funds that can magnify the returns paid out to stockholders.

A variant on the Du Pont formula, called the modified Du Pont formula, reflects this effect. The formula ties together the company's ROI and its degree of financial leverage, that is, its use of borrowed funds. Financial leverage is measured by the equity multiplier (the ratio of a company's total asset base to its equity investment or, stated another way, dollars of assets held per dollar of stockholders' equity). This ratio, which is calculated by dividing total assets by stockholders' equity, gives an indication of the extent to which a company's assets are financed by stockholders' equity and borrowed funds.

The return on equity (ROE) is calculated as:

$$\text{ROE} = \frac{\text{Net profit after taxes}}{\text{Stockholders' equity}}$$

$$= \frac{\text{Net profit after taxes}}{\text{Total assets}} \times \frac{\text{Total assets}}{\text{Stockholders' equity}}$$

$$= \text{ROI} \times \text{Equity multiplier}$$

ROE measures the returns earned on both preferred and common stockholders' investments. The use of the equity multiplier to convert the ROI to the ROE reflects the impact of the leverage (use of debt) on the stockholders' return (see Figure 5.3).

EXAMPLE 5-5

In Example 5-1, assume stockholders' equity of $45,000. Then,

$$\text{Equity multiplier} = \frac{\text{Total assets}}{\text{Stockholders' equity}}$$

$$= \frac{\$100,000}{\$45,000} = 2.22$$

$$= \frac{1}{(1 - \text{ debt ratio})}$$

$$= \frac{1}{(1 - .55)} = \frac{1}{.45} = 2.22$$

$$\text{ROE} = \frac{\text{Net profit after taxes}}{\text{Stockholders' equity}} = \frac{\$18,000}{\$45,000} = 40\%$$

$$\text{ROE} = \text{ROI} \times \text{Equity multiplier} = 18\% \times 2.22 = 40\%$$

If the company used only equity to fund its operations, ROI and ROE would both be 18 percent. However 55 percent of the company's capital was supplied by creditors ($45,000/$100,000 = 45 percent is the equity-to-asset ratio; $55,000/$100,000 = 55 percent is the debt ratio). Since the entire 18 percent ROI goes to stockholders, who put up only 45 percent of the capital, the ROE is higher than 18 percent. This example illustrates a successful use of leverage.

EXAMPLE 5-6

To further demonstrate the interrelationship between a company's financial structure and the return it generates on its stockholders' investments, we compare two companies that generate $300,000 in operating income. Both businesses have $800,000 in total assets, but they have different capital structures. One employs no debt; the other uses $400,000 in borrowed funds. The comparative capital structures are:

	A	B
Total assets	$800,000	$800,000
Total liabilities	—	400,000
Stockholders' equity (a)	800,000	400,000
Total liabilities and stockholders' equity	$800,000	$800,000

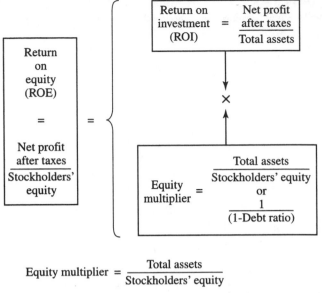

$$\text{Equity multiplier} = \frac{\text{Total assets}}{\text{Stockholders' equity}}$$

$$= \frac{\text{Total assets}}{\text{Total assets} - \text{Total liabilities}}$$

$$= \frac{1}{1 - \dfrac{\text{Total liabilities}}{\text{Total assets}}}$$

$$= \frac{1}{(1 - \text{Debt ratio})}$$

Figure 5.3 *ROI, ROE, and Financial Leverage*

Firm B pays 10 percent interest for borrowed funds. The comparative income statements and ROEs for A and B are as follows:

Operating income	$300,000	$300,000
Interest expense	—	(40,000)
Profit before taxes	$300,000	$260,000
Taxes (30% assumed)	(90,000)	(78,000)
Net profit after taxes (b)	$210,000	$182,000
ROE [(b)/(a)]	26.25%	45.5%

Although the absence of debt allows company A to register higher profits after taxes, the owners of company B enjoy a significantly higher return on their investments. This contrast demonstrates the benefits that can accrue from using debt—up to a limit. Too much debt can increase a company's financial risk and thus its cost of financing.

If the assets in which the borrowed funds are invested earn a return greater than the interest rate required by the creditors, the leverage is positive and the common stockholders benefit. The advantage of the modified Du Pont formula is that the company can break its ROE into a profit margin portion (net profit margin), an efficiency-of-asset-utilization portion (total asset turnover), and a use-of-leverage portion (equity multiplier).

Since the added interest costs created by financial leverage affect net profit margin, management must analyze the parts of the ROE equation to determine how to earn the highest return for stockholders and to identify the combination of asset return and leverage that will work best in its competitive environment. Most companies try to keep a level equal to the average for their industry.

A Word of Caution

Unfortunately, leverage is a two-edged sword. If assets do not earn a rate of return high enough to cover fixed finance charges, then stockholders suffer, since part of the profits generated by the assets they have provided to the company must go to make up the shortfall to the long-term creditors.

CHAPTER PERSPECTIVE

This chapter covered in detail various strategies for increasing the return on investment (ROI). The breakdown of ROI into margin and turnover, popularly known as the Du Pont formula, provides insight into: (a) the strengths and weaknesses of a business and its segments, and (b) what needs to be done in order to improve performance. Another version of the Du Pont formula—the modified Du Pont formula—relates ROI to ROE (stockholders' return) through financial leverage and shows how leverage can benefit company shareholders.

Understanding the Concept of Time Value of Money

6

INTRODUCTION AND MAIN POINTS

Money has a time value; a dollar received now is worth more than a dollar to be received later. The reasoning behind this principle does not reflect concern that inflation might reduce the buying power of the dollar received later; it is based on the fact that you can invest the dollar now and have more than a dollar at a specified later date.

Time value of money is a critical consideration in financial and investment decisions. It is an element of compound interest calculations used to determine future results of investments and of discounting, which is inversely related to compounding and is used to evaluate the future cash flow associated with capital budgeting projects.

After studying the material in this chapter:

■ You will understand the concept of future value, with both annual and intrayear compounding.

■ You will be able to distinguish between future value and present value concepts.

■ You will be able to calculate the future value of a single payment and an annuity.

■ You will be able to calculate the present value of a single payment and an annuity.

■ You will see how to utilize future value and present value tables.

■ You will be able to determine some important financial variables such as a sinking fund amount, the monthly payment of an amortized loan, and annual percentage rate (APR).

CALCULATING FUTURE VALUES

A dollar in hand today is worth more than a dollar to be received tomorrow because of the interest you can earn by putting it in a savings account or other investment account. Further, over time that interest will earn interest, a practice known as *compounding*. For our discussion of the concepts of compounding and time value, we define the following terms:

$$F_n = \text{future value} = \text{the amount of money at the end of year}$$
$$P = \text{principal}$$
$$i = \text{annual interest rate}$$
$$n = \text{number of years}$$

Then,

$$F_1 = \text{the amount of money at the end of year 1}$$
$$= \text{principal and interest} = P + iP = P(1 + i)$$
$$F_2 = \text{the amount of money at the end of year 2}$$
$$= F_1(1 + i) = P(1 + i)(1 + i) = P(1 + i)^2$$

The future value of an investment compounded annually at rate i for n years is

$$F_n = P(1 + i)^n = P \cdot T_1(i, n)$$

where $T_1(i, n)$ is the compound amount of $1 (see Table 6-1).

EXAMPLE 6-1
You place $1,000 in a savings account earning 8 percent interest compounded annually. How much money will you have in the account at the end of 4 years?

$$F_n = P(1 + i)^n$$
$$F_4 = \$1,000(1 + 0.08)^4 = \$1,000T_1 \ (8\%, \ 4 \ \text{years})$$

From Table 6-1, the T_1 for 4 years at 8 percent is 1.361. Therefore,

$$F_4 = \$1,000(1.361) = \$1,361$$

EXAMPLE 6-2
You invested a large sum of money in the stock of TLC Corporation. The company paid a $3 dividend per share. The dividend is expected to increase by 20 percent per year for the next 3 years. You wish to project the dividends for years 1 through 3.

$$F_n = P(1 + i)^n$$
$$F_1 = \$3(1 + 0.2)^1 = \$3T_1(20\%, 1) = \$3(1.200) = \$3.60$$
$$F_2 = \$3(1 + 0.2)^2 = \$3T_1(20\%, 2) = \$3(1.440) = \$4.32$$
$$F_3 = \$3(1 + 0.2)^3 = \$3T_1(20\%, 3) = \$3(1.728) = \$5.18$$

Intrayear Compounding

Interest is often compounded more frequently than once a year. Banks, for example, compound interest quarterly, daily, and even continuously. If interest is compounded m times a year, then the general formula for solving the future value becomes

$$F_n = P \left(1 + \frac{i}{m}\right)^{n \cdot m} = P \cdot T_1(i/m, n \cdot m)$$

The formula reflects more frequent compounding $(n \cdot m)$ at a smaller interest rate per period (i/m). For example, in the case of semiannual compounding $(m = 2)$, the above formula becomes

$$F_n = P \left(1 + \frac{i}{2}\right)^{n \cdot 2} = P \cdot T_1(i/2, n \cdot 2)$$

EXAMPLE 6-3

You deposit $10,000 in an account offering an annual interest rate of 20 percent. You will keep the money on deposit for five years. The interest rate is compounded quarterly. The accumulated amount at the end of the fifth year is calculated as follows:

$$F_n = P \left(1 + \frac{i}{m}\right)^{n \cdot m} = P \cdot T_1(i/m, n \cdot m)$$

where

$$
\begin{aligned}
P &= \$10,000 \\
i/m &= 20\%/4 = 5\% \\
n \cdot m &= 5 \cdot 4 = 20
\end{aligned}
$$

Therefore,

$$
\begin{aligned}
F_5 = \$10,000(1 + .05)^{20} &= \$10,000 \; T_1(5\%, 20) \\
&= \$10,000(2.653) \\
&= \$26,530
\end{aligned}
$$

EXAMPLE 6-4

Assume that $P = \$1,000$, $i = 8\%$, and $n = 2$ years. Then for annual compounding $(m = 1)$:

$$
\begin{aligned}
F_2 = \$1,000(1 + 0.08)^2 &= \$1,000 \; T_1(8\%, 2) \\
&= \$1,000(1.166) \\
&= \$1,166.00
\end{aligned}
$$

Semiannual compounding (m = 2):

$$F_2 = \$1,000 \left(1 + \frac{0.08}{2}\right)^{2 \cdot 2}$$
$$= \$1,000(1 + .04)^4$$
$$= \$1,000 \, T_1(4\%, 4)$$
$$= \$1,000(1.170)$$
$$= \$1,170.00$$

Quarterly compounding (m = 4):

$$F_2 = \$1,000 \left(1 + \frac{0.08}{4}\right)^{2 \cdot 4}$$
$$= \$1,000(1 + .02)^8$$
$$= \$1,000 \, T_1(2\%, 8)$$
$$= \$1,000(1.172)$$
$$= \$1,172.00$$

As the example shows, the more frequently interest is compounded, the greater the amount that accumulates. This is true for any rate of interest over any period of time.

Future Value of an Annuity

An annuity is defined as a series of payments (or receipts) of a fixed amount of money for a specified number of periods. Each payment is assumed to occur at the end of the period. The future value of an annuity involves depositing or investing an equal sum of money at the end of each year for a certain number of years and allowing it to grow.

$$\text{Let } S_n = \text{ the future value of an n-year annuity}$$
$$A = \text{ the amount of an annuity}$$

Then we can write

$$S_n = A(1 + i)^{n-1} + A(1 + i)^{n-2} + \ldots + A(1 + i)^0$$
$$= A[(1 + i)^{n-1} + (1 + i)^{n-2} + \ldots(1 + i)^0]$$
$$= A \cdot \sum_{t=0}^{n-1}(1 + i)^t$$
$$= A \left[\frac{(1 + i)^n - 1}{i}\right]$$
$$= A \cdot T_2(i, n)$$

where $T_2(i, n)$ represents the future value of an annuity of $1 for n years compounded at i percent (see Table 6-2).

EXAMPLE 6-5
You wish to determine the sum of money you will have in a savings account at the end of 6 years after depositing $1,000 at the end of each year for the next 6 years. The annual interest rate is 8 percent. The T_2 (8%, 6 years) is given in Table 6-2 as 7.336. Therefore,

$$S_6 = \$1,000 \, T_2(8\%, 6) = \$1,000(7.336) = \$7,336$$

EXAMPLE 6-6
You deposit $30,000 semiannually into a fund for 10 years. The annual interest rate is 8 percent. The amount accumulated at the end of the tenth year is calculated as follows:

$$S_n = A \cdot T_2(i, n)$$

where

$$
\begin{aligned}
A &= \$30,000 \\
i &= 8\%/2 = 4\% \\
n &= 10 \times 2 = 20
\end{aligned}
$$

Therefore,

$$
\begin{aligned}
S_n &= \$30,000 \, T_2(4\%, \ 20) \\
&= \$30,000(29.778) \\
&= \$893,340
\end{aligned}
$$

CALCULATING PRESENT VALUES OF MONEY

Present value, defined as the present worth of future sums of money, is calculated by a process that is actually the opposite of that for finding the compounded future value. In connection with present value calculations known as discounting, the interest rate, i, is called the *discount rate,* more commonly called the *cost of capital,* the minimum rate of return required by the investor. (Determining the cost of capital is discussed in detail in Chapter 9.)

Recall that

$$F_n = P(1 + i)^n$$

Therefore,

$$P = \frac{F}{(1 + i)^n} = F_n \left[\frac{1}{(1 + i)^n} \right] = F_n \cdot T_3(i, n)$$

where $T_3(i, n)$ represents the present value of $1 (see Table 6-3).

EXAMPLE 6-7
You have been given an opportunity to receive $20,000 six years from now. If you can earn 10 percent on your investments, what is the most you should pay for this opportunity? To answer this question, you must compute the present value of $20,000 to be received six years from now at a 10 percent rate of discount. F_6 is $20,000, i is 10 percent, and n is six years. $T_3(10\%, 6)$ from Table 6-3 is 0.565.

$$
\begin{aligned}
P &= \$2,000 \left[\frac{1}{(1 + 0.1)^6} \right] \\
&= \$20,000\ T_3(10\%, 6) \\
&= \$20,000(0.565) \\
&= \$11,300
\end{aligned}
$$

Since you can earn 10 percent on your investment, paying $11,300 for the opportunity discussed is pointless. In either case, you will wind up with $20,000 in six years.

Present Value of Mixed Streams of Cash Flows
The present value of a series of mixed payments (or receipts) is the sum of the present value of each individual payment. We know that the present value of each individual payment is the payment times the appropriate T_3 value.

You are thinking of starting a new product line that will cost $32,000 up front. Your annual projected cash inflows are:

year 1 $10,000
year 2 $20,000
year 3 $5,000

If you must earn a minimum of 10 percent on your investment, should you undertake this new product line?

The present value of this series of mixed streams of cash inflows is calculated as follows:

Year	Cash Inflows	$\times T_3(10\%, n)$	Present Value
1	$10,000	0.909	$9,090
2	$20,000	0.826	$16,520
3	$5,000	0.751	$3,755
			$29,365

Since the present value of your projected cash inflows is less than the initial investment required, you should not undertake this project.

Present Value of an Annuity

Interest received from bonds, pension funds, and insurance obligations all involve annuities. To compare these financial instruments, we need to know the present value of each. The present value of an annuity (P_n) can be found by using the following equation:

$$P_n = A \cdot \left[\frac{1}{(1+i)^1} \right] + A \cdot \left[\frac{1}{(1+i)^2} \right] + \cdots + A \cdot \left[\frac{1}{(1+i)^n} \right]$$

$$= A \left[\frac{1}{(1+i)^1} + \frac{1}{(1+i)^2} + \cdots + \frac{1}{(1+i)^n} \right]$$

$$= A \cdot \sum_{t=1}^{n} \frac{1}{(1+i)^t} = \frac{1}{i} \left[1 - \frac{1}{(1+i)} \right]$$

$$= A \cdot T_4(i, n)$$

where $T_4(i, n)$ represents the present value of an annuity of \$1 discounted at i percent for n years (see Table 6-4).

EXAMPLE 6-8

Assume that the cash inflows in Example 6-7 form an annuity of \$10,000 for 3 years. Then the present value is

$$P_n = A \cdot T_4(i, n)$$
$$P_3 = \$10,000 T_4(10\%, 3 \text{ years})$$
$$= \$10,000(2.487)$$
$$= \$24,870$$

Perpetuities

Some annuities, called perpetuities, go on forever. An example of a perpetuity is preferred stock, which yields a constant dollar dividend indefinitely. The present value of a perpetuity is found as follows:

$$\text{Present value of a perpetuity} = \frac{\text{receipt}}{\text{discount rate}} = \frac{A}{i}$$

EXAMPLE 6-9

Assume that a perpetual bond has an \$80-per-year interest payment and that the discount rate is 10 percent. The present value of this perpetuity is:

$$P = \frac{A}{i} = \frac{\$80}{0.10} = \$800$$

APPLICATIONS OF FUTURE VALUES AND PRESENT VALUES

Future and present values have numerous applications in financial and investment decisions. Six of the most common applications are presented below.

Calculating Deposits to Accumulate a Future Sum (or Sinking Fund)

To determine the annual deposit (or payment) that is necessary to accumulate a future sum (or sinking fund), we can use the formula for finding the future value of an annuity.

$$S_n = A \cdot T_2(i, n)$$

Solving for A, we obtain:

$$\text{Annual deposit amount } = A = \frac{S_n}{T_2(i, n)}$$

EXAMPLE 6-10

You wish to determine the equal annual end-of-year deposits required to accumulate $5,000 at the end of 5 years. The interest rate is 10 percent. The annual deposit is:

$$S_5 = \$5,000$$
$$T_2(10\%, 5 \text{ years}) = 6.105 \text{ (from Table 6-2)}$$
$$A = \frac{\$5,000}{6.105}$$
$$= \$819$$

In other words, if you deposit $819 at the end of each year for 5 years at 10 percent interest, you will have accumulated $5,000 at the end of the fifth year.

EXAMPLE 6-11

You need a sinking fund for the retirement of a bond 30 years from now. The interest rate is 10 percent. The annual year-end contribution needed to accumulate $1,000,000 is

$$S_{30} = \$1,000,000$$
$$T_2(10\%, 30 \text{ years}) = 164.49$$
$$A = \frac{\$1,000,000}{164.49}$$
$$= \$6,079.40$$

Amortized Loans

An amortized loan is a loan that is repaid in equal periodic payments. Examples include auto loans, mortgage loans, and most commercial loans. The periodic payment can be computed as follows:

$$P_n = A \cdot T_4(i, n)$$

Solving for A, we obtain

$$\text{Amount of loan } = A = \frac{P_n}{T_4(i, n)}$$

EXAMPLE 6-12

You borrow $200,000 for 5 years at an interest rate of 14 percent. The annual year-end payment on the loan is calculated as follows:

$$P_5 = \$200,000$$
$$T_4(14\%, 5 \text{ years}) = 3.433 \text{ (from Table 6-4)}$$
$$\text{Amount of loan } = A = \frac{P_5}{T_4(14\%, 5 \text{ years})}$$
$$= \frac{\$200,000}{3.433}$$
$$= \$58,258.08$$

EXAMPLE 6-13

You take out a 40-month bank loan of $5,000 at a 12 percent annual interest rate. You want to find out the monthly loan payment.

$$i = 12\%/12 \text{ months} = 1\%$$
$$P_{40} = \$5,000$$
$$T_4(1\%, 40 \text{ months}) = 32.835 \text{ (from Table 6-4)}$$

Therefore,

$$A = \frac{\$5,000}{32.835} = \$152.28$$

So, to repay the principal and interest on a $5,000, 12 percent, 40-month loan, you have to pay $152.28 a month for the next 40 months.

EXAMPLE 6-14

Assume that a company borrows $2,000 to be repaid in three equal installments at the end of each of the next 3 years. The bank charges 12 percent interest. The amount of each payment is

$$P_3 = \$2,000$$
$$T_4(12\%, 3 \text{ years}) = 2.402$$

Therefore,

$$A = \frac{\$2,000}{2.402} = \$832.64$$

Developing Loan Amortization Schedules

The breakdown of each loan payment into interest and principal is often displayed in a loan amortization schedule. The interest component of the payment is largest in the first period (because the principal balance is the highest) and subsequently declines, whereas the principal portion is smallest in the first period and increases thereafter, as shown in the following example.

EXAMPLE 6-15
Using the same data as in Example 6-14, we set up the following amortization schedule:

Year	Payment	Interest	Repayment of Principal	Remaining Balance
0				$2,000.00
1	$832.64	$240.00[a]	$592.64[b]	$1,407.36
2	$832.64	$168.88	$663.76	$ 743.60
3	$832.64	$ 89.23	$743.41[c]	

(a) Interest is computed by multiplying the loan balance at the beginning of the year by the interest rate. Therefore, interest in year 1 is $2,000(0.12) = $240; in year 2, interest is $1,407.36(0.12) = $168.88; and in year 3, interest is $743.60(0.12) = $89.23. All figures are rounded.

(b) The reduction in principal equals the payment less the interest portion ($832.64 − $240.00 = $592.64)

(c) Not exact because of accumulated rounding errors.

Calculating Annual Percentage Rates

Different types of investments use different compounding periods. For example, most bonds pay interest semiannually, whereas banks generally pay interest quarterly. If a financial manager wishes to compare investments with different compounding periods, he or she needs to put them on a common basis. The annual percentage rate or effective annual rate, which is used for this purpose, is computed as follows:

$$APR = \left[1 + \frac{i}{m}\right]^m - 1.0$$

where i = the stated, nominal, or quoted rate and m = the number of compounding periods per year.

EXAMPLE 6-16

If the nominal rate is 6 percent, compounded quarterly, the APR is

$$APR = \left[1 + \frac{i}{m}\right]^m - 1.0$$

$$= \left[1 + \frac{0.06}{4}\right]^4 - 1.0$$

$$= (1.015)^4 - 1.0$$

$$= 1.0614 - 1.0$$

$$= 0.0614$$

$$= 6.14\%$$

This means that if one bank offers 6 percent with quarterly compounding, while another offers 6.14 percent with annual compounding, they are both paying the same effective rate of interest.

The annual percentage rate also is a measure of the cost of credit, expressed as a yearly rate. It includes interest as well as other financial charges, such as loan origination and certain closing fees. Lenders are required to disclose the APR, which provides a good basis for comparing the cost of loans, including mortgages.

Calculating Rates of Growth

In finance, it is often necessary to calculate the compound annual rate of growth associated with a stream of earnings. The compound annual growth rate in earnings per share is computed as follows:

$$F_n = P \cdot T_1(i, n)$$

Solving this for T_1, we obtain

$$T_1(i, n) = \frac{F_n}{P}$$

EXAMPLE 6-17

Assume that your company has earnings per share of $2.50 in 20X1 and that 10 years later the earnings per share has increased to $3.70. The compound annual rate of growth in earnings per share is computed as follows:

$$F_{10} = \$3.70 \text{ and } P = \$2.50$$

Therefore,

$$T_1(i, 10) = \frac{\$3.70}{\$2.50} = 1.48$$

From Table 6-1, T_1 of 1.48 at 10 years is at $i = 4\%$. The compound annual rate of growth is therefore 4 percent.

Calculating Bond Values

Bonds call for the payment of a specific amount of interest, usually semiannually, for a stated number of years and the repayment of the face value at the maturity date. Thus, a bond represents an annuity plus a final lump sum payment. Its value is found as the present value of the payment stream.

$$V = \sum_{t=1}^{n} \frac{I}{(1+i)^t} + \frac{M}{(1+i)^n}$$
$$= I \cdot T_4(i, n) + M \cdot T_3(i, n)$$

where I = interest payment per period
M = par value, or maturity value, usually \$1,000
i = investor's required rate of return
n = number of periods

This topic is covered in more detail in Chapter 8.

EXAMPLE 6-18

Assume a 10-year bond with a 10 percent coupon pays interest semi-annually and has a face value of \$1,000. Since interest is paid semi-annually, the number of periods involved is twenty and the semiannual cash inflow is \$100/2 = \$50.

Assume that you have a required rate of return of 12 percent for this type of bond. The present value (V) of this bond is:

$$V = \$50 \cdot T_4(6\%, 20) + \$1,000 \cdot T_3(6\%, 20)$$
$$= \$50(11.470) + \$1,000(0.312)$$
$$= \$573.50 + \$312.00$$
$$= \$885.50$$

Note that the required rate of return (12 percent) is higher than the coupon rate of interest (10 percent). Therefore, the bond value (the price investors are willing to pay for this particular bond) is less than its \$1,000 face value.

USE OF FINANCIAL CALCULATORS AND SPREADSHEET PROGRAMS

Many financial calculators contain pre-programmed formulas for performing present-value and future-value applications. Furthermore, spreadsheet software has built-in financial functions for performing many such applications.

TABLE 6-1
THE FUTURE VALUE OF $1.00
(COMPOUNDED AMOUNT OF $1.00)

$$(1 + i)^n = T_1(i, n)$$

PERIODS	4%	6%	8%	10%	12%	14%	20%
1	1.040	1.060	1.080	1.100	1.120	1.140	1.200
2	1.082	1.124	1.166	1.210	1.254	1.300	1.440
3	1.125	1.191	1.260	1.331	1.405	1.482	1.728
4	1.170	1.263	1.361	1.464	1.574	1.689	2.074
5	1.217	1.338	1.469	1.611	1.762	1.925	2.488
6	1.265	1.419	1.587	1.772	1.974	2.195	2.986
7	1.316	1.504	1.714	1.949	2.211	2.502	3.583
8	1.369	1.594	1.851	2.144	2.476	2.853	4.300
9	1.423	1.690	1.999	2.359	2.773	3.252	5.160
10	1.480	1.791	2.159	2.594	3.106	3.707	6.192
11	1.540	1.898	2.332	2.853	3.479	4.226	7.430
12	1.601	2.012	2.518	3.139	3.896	4.818	8.916
13	1.665	2.133	2.720	3.452	4.364	5.492	10.699
14	1.732	2.261	2.937	3.798	4.887	6.261	12.839
15	1.801	2.397	3.172	4.177	5.474	7.138	15.407
16	1.873	2.540	3.426	4.595	6.130	8.137	18.488
17	1.948	2.693	3.700	5.055	6.866	9.277	22.186
18	2.026	2.854	3.996	5.560	7.690	10.575	26.623
19	2.107	3.026	4.316	6.116	8.613	12.056	31.948
20	2.191	3.207	4.661	6.728	9.646	13.743	38.338
30	3.243	5.744	10.063	17.450	29.960	50.950	237.380
40	4.801	10.286	21.725	45.260	93.051	188.880	1469.800

TABLE 6-2
THE FUTURE VALUE
OF AN ANNUITY OF $1.00*
(COMPOUNDED AMOUNT
OF AN ANNUITY OF $1.00)

$$\frac{(1 + i)^n - 1}{i} = T_2(i, n)$$

PERIODS	4%	6%	8%	10%	12%	14%	20%
1	1.000	1.000	1.000	1.000	1.000	1.000	1.000
2	2.040	2.060	2.080	2.100	2.120	2.140	2.200
3	3.122	3.184	3.246	3.310	3.374	3.440	3.640
4	4.247	4.375	4.506	4.641	4.779	4.921	5.368
5	5.416	5.637	5.867	6.105	6.353	6.610	7.442
6	6.633	6.975	7.336	7.716	8.115	8.536	9.930
7	7.898	8.394	8.923	9.487	10.089	10.730	12.916
8	9.214	9.898	10.637	11.436	12.300	13.233	16.499
9	10.583	11.491	12.488	13.580	14.776	16.085	20.799
10	12.006	13.181	14.487	15.938	17.549	19.337	25.959
11	13.486	14.972	16.646	18.531	20.655	23.045	32.150
12	15.026	16.870	18.977	21.385	24.133	27.271	39.580
13	16.627	18.882	21.495	24.523	28.029	32.089	48.497
14	18.292	21.015	24.215	27.976	32.393	37.581	59.196
15	20.024	23.276	27.152	31.773	37.280	43.842	72.035
16	21.825	25.673	30.324	35.950	42.753	50.980	87.442
17	23.698	28.213	33.750	40.546	48.884	59.118	105.930
18	25.645	30.906	37.450	45.600	55.750	68.394	128.120
19	27.671	33.760	41.446	51.160	63.440	78.969	154.740
20	29.778	36.778	45.762	57.276	75.052	91.025	186.690
30	56.085	79.058	113.283	164.496	241.330	356.790	1181.900
40	95.026	154.762	259.057	442.597	767.090	1342.000	7343.900

*Payments (or receipts) at the *end* of each period.

TABLE 6-3
PRESENT VALUE OF $1.00

$$\frac{1}{(1 + i)^n} = T_3(i, n)$$

PERIODS	4%	6%	8%	10%	12%	14%	16%	18%	20%	22%	24%	26%	28%	30%
1	.962	.943	.926	.909	.893	.877	.862	.847	.833	.820	.806	.794	.781	.769
2	.925	.890	.857	.826	.797	.769	.743	.718	.694	.672	.650	.630	.610	.592
3	.889	.840	.794	.751	.712	.675	.641	.609	.579	.551	.524	.500	.477	.455
4	.855	.792	.735	.683	.636	.592	.552	.516	.482	.451	.423	.397	.373	.350
5	.822	.747	.681	.621	.567	.519	.476	.437	.402	.370	.341	.315	.291	.269
6	.790	.705	.630	.564	.507	.456	.410	.370	.335	.303	.275	.250	.227	.207
7	.760	.665	.583	.513	.452	.400	.354	.314	.279	.249	.222	.198	.178	.159
8	.731	.627	.540	.467	.404	.351	.305	.266	.233	.204	.179	.157	.139	.123
9	.703	.592	.500	.424	.361	.308	.263	.225	.194	.167	.144	.125	.108	.094
10	.676	.558	.463	.386	.322	.270	.227	.191	.162	.137	.116	.099	.085	.073
11	.650	.527	.429	.350	.287	.237	.195	.162	.135	.112	.094	.079	.066	.056
12	.625	.497	.397	.319	.257	.208	.168	.137	.112	.092	.076	.062	.052	.043
13	.601	.469	.368	.290	.229	.182	.145	.116	.093	.075	.061	.050	.040	.033
14	.577	.442	.340	.263	.205	.160	.125	.099	.078	.062	.049	.039	.032	.025
15	.555	.417	.315	.239	.183	.140	.108	.084	.065	.051	.040	.031	.025	.020
16	.534	.394	.292	.218	.163	.123	.093	.071	.054	.042	.032	.025	.019	.015
17	.513	.371	.270	.198	.146	.108	.080	.060	.045	.034	.026	.020	.015	.012
18	.494	.350	.250	.180	.130	.095	.069	.051	.038	.028	.021	.016	.012	.009
19	.475	.331	.232	.164	.116	.083	.060	.043	.031	.023	.017	.012	.009	.007
20	.456	.312	.215	.149	.104	.073	.051	.037	.026	.019	.014	.010	.007	.005
21	.439	.294	.199	.135	.093	.064	.044	.031	.022	.015	.011	.008	.006	.004
22	.422	.278	.184	.123	.083	.056	.038	.026	.018	.013	.009	.006	.004	.003
23	.406	.262	.170	.112	.074	.049	.033	.022	.015	.010	.007	.005	.003	.002
24	.390	.247	.158	.102	.066	.043	.028	.019	.013	.008	.006	.004	.003	.002
25	.375	.233	.146	.092	.059	.038	.024	.016	.010	.007	.005	.003	.002	.001
26	.361	.220	.135	.084	.053	.033	.021	.014	.009	.006	.004	.002	.002	.001
27	.347	.207	.125	.076	.047	.029	.018	.011	.007	.005	.003	.002	.001	.001
28	.333	.196	.116	.069	.042	.026	.016	.010	.006	.004	.002	.002	.001	.001
29	.321	.185	.107	.063	.037	.022	.014	.008	.005	.003	.002	.001	.001	.001
30	.308	.174	.099	.057	.033	.020	.012	.007	.004	.003	.002	.001	.001	
40	.208	.097	.046	.022	.011	.005	.003	.001	.001					

TABLE 6-4

PRESENT VALUE OF AN ANNUITY OF $1 FOR N PERIODS

$$\frac{1}{i} = \left[1 - \frac{1}{(1 + i)^n} \right] = T_4(i, n)$$

n	1%	2%	3%	4%	5%	6%	7%	8%	9%	10%
1	.990	.980	.971	.962	.952	.943	.935	.926	.917	.909
2	1.970	1.942	1.913	1.886	1.859	1.833	1.808	1.783	1.759	1.736
3	2.941	2.884	2.829	2.775	2.723	2.673	2.624	2.577	2.531	2.487
4	3.902	3.808	3.717	3.630	3.546	3.465	3.387	3.312	3.240	3.170
5	4.853	4.713	4.580	4.452	4.329	4.212	4.100	3.993	3.890	3.791
6	5.795	5.601	5.417	5.242	5.076	4.917	4.767	4.623	4.486	4.355
7	6.728	6.472	6.230	6.002	5.786	5.582	5.389	5.206	5.033	4.868
8	7.652	7.326	7.020	6.733	6.463	6.210	5.971	5.747	5.535	5.335
9	8.566	8.162	7.786	7.435	7.108	6.802	6.515	6.247	5.995	5.759
10	9.471	8.983	8.530	8.111	7.722	7.360	7.024	6.710	6.418	6.145
11	10.368	9.787	9.253	8.760	8.306	7.887	7.499	7.139	6.805	6.495
12	11.255	10.575	9.954	9.385	8.863	8.384	7.943	7.536	7.161	6.814
13	12.134	11.348	10.635	9.986	9.394	8.853	8.358	7.904	7.487	7.103
14	13.004	12.106	11.296	10.563	9.899	2.295	8.746	8.244	7.786	7.367
15	13.865	12.849	11.938	11.118	10.380	9.712	9.108	8.560	8.061	7.606
16	14.718	13.578	12.561	11.652	10.838	10.106	9.447	8.851	8.313	7.824
17	15.562	14.292	13.166	12.166	11.274	10.477	9.763	9.122	8.544	8.022
18	16.398	14.992	13.754	12.659	11.690	10.828	10.059	9.372	8.756	8.201
19	17.226	15.679	14.324	13.134	12.085	11.158	10.336	9.604	8.950	8.365
20	18.046	16.352	14.878	13.590	12.462	11.470	10.594	9.818	9.129	8.514
21	18.857	17.011	15.415	14.029	12.821	11.764	10.836	10.017	9.292	8.649
22	19.661	17.658	15.937	14.451	13.163	12.042	11.061	10.201	9.442	8.772
23	20.456	18.292	16.444	14.857	13.489	12.303	11.272	10.371	9.580	8.883
24	21.244	18.914	16.936	15.247	13.799	12.550	11.469	10.529	9.707	8.985
25	22.023	19.524	17.413	15.622	14.094	12.783	11.654	10.675	9.823	9.077
30	25.808	22.397	19.601	17.292	15.373	13.765	12.409	11.258	10.274	9.427
40	32.835	27.356	23.115	19.793	17.159	15.046	13.332	11.925	10.757	9.779
50	39.197	31.424	25.730	21.482	18.256	15.762	13.801	12.234	10.962	9.915

n	11%	12%	13%	14%	15%	16%	17%	18%	19%	20%
1	.901	.893	.885	.877	.870	.862	.855	.847	.840	.833
2	1.713	1.690	1.668	1.647	1.626	1.605	1.585	1.566	1.547	1.528
3	2.444	2.402	2.361	2.322	2.283	2.246	2.210	2.174	2.140	2.106
4	3.102	3.037	2.974	2.914	2.855	2.798	2.743	2.690	2.639	2.589
5	3.696	3.605	3.517	3.433	3.352	3.274	3.199	3.127	3.058	2.991
6	4.231	4.111	3.998	3.889	3.784	3.685	3.589	3.498	3.410	3.326
7	4.712	4.564	4.423	4.288	4.160	4.039	3.922	3.812	3.706	3.605
8	5.146	4.968	4.799	4.639	4.487	4.344	4.207	4.078	3.954	3.837
9	5.537	5.328	5.132	4.946	4.772	4.607	4.451	4.303	4.163	4.031
10	5.889	5.650	5.426	5.216	5.019	4.833	4.659	4.494	4.339	4.192
11	6.207	5.938	5.687	5.453	5.234	5.029	4.836	4.656	4.487	4.327
12	6.492	6.194	5.918	5.660	5.421	5.197	4.988	4.793	4.611	4.439
13	6.750	6.424	6.122	5.842	5.583	5.342	5.118	4.910	4.715	4.533
14	6.982	6.628	6.303	6.002	5.724	5.468	5.229	5.008	4.802	4.611
15	7.191	6.811	6.462	6.142	5.847	5.575	5.324	5.092	4.876	4.675
16	7.379	6.974	6.604	6.265	5.954	5.669	5.405	5.162	4.938	4.730
17	7.549	7.120	6.729	6.373	6.047	5.749	5.475	5.222	4.990	4.775
18	7.702	7.250	6.840	6.467	6.128	5.818	5.534	5.273	5.033	4.812
19	7.839	7.366	6.938	6.550	6.198	5.877	5.585	5.316	5.070	4.843
20	7.963	7.469	7.025	6.623	6.259	5.929	5.628	5.353	5.101	4.870
21	8.075	7.562	7.102	6.687	6.312	5.973	5.665	5.384	5.127	4.891
22	8.176	7.645	7.170	6.743	6.359	6.011	5.696	5.410	5.149	4.909
23	8.266	7.718	7.230	6.792	6.399	6.044	5.723	5.432	5.167	4.925
24	8.348	7.784	7.283	6.835	6.434	6.073	5.747	5.451	5.182	4.937
25	8.442	7.843	7.330	6.873	6.464	6.097	5.766	5.467	5.195	4.948
30	8.694	8.055	7.496	7.003	6.566	6.177	5.829	5.517	5.235	4.979
40	8.951	8.244	7.634	7.105	6.642	6.233	5.871	5.548	5.258	4.997
50	9.042	8.305	7.675	7.133	6.661	6.246	5.880	5.554	5.262	4.999

n	31%	32%	33%	34%	35%	36%	37%	38%	39%	40%
1	.763	.758	.752	.746	.741	.735	.730	.725	.719	.714
2	1.346	1.331	1.317	1.303	1.289	1.276	1.263	1.250	1.237	1.224
3	1.791	1.766	1.742	1.719	1.696	1.673	1.652	1.630	1.609	1.589
4	2.130	2.096	2.062	2.029	1.997	1.966	1.935	1.906	1.877	1.849
5	2.390	2.345	2.302	2.260	2.220	2.181	2.143	2.106	2.070	2.035
6	2.588	2.534	2.483	2.433	2.385	2.339	2.294	2.251	2.209	2.168
7	2.739	2.677	2.619	2.562	2.508	2.455	2.404	2.355	2.308	2.263
8	2.854	2.786	2.721	2.658	2.598	2.540	2.485	2.432	2.380	2.331
9	2.942	2.868	2.798	2.730	2.665	2.603	2.544	2.487	2.432	2.379
10	3.009	2.930	2.855	2.784	2.715	2.649	2.587	2.527	2.469	2.414
11	3.060	2.978	2.899	2.824	2.752	2.683	2.618	2.555	2.496	2.438
12	3.100	3.013	2.931	2.853	2.779	2.708	2.641	2.576	2.515	2.456
13	3.129	3.040	2.956	2.876	2.799	2.727	2.658	2.592	2.529	2.469
14	3.152	3.061	2.974	2.892	2.814	2.740	2.670	2.603	2.539	2.477
15	3.170	3.076	2.988	2.905	2.825	2.750	2.679	2.611	2.546	2.484
16	3.183	3.088	2.999	2.914	2.834	2.757	2.685	2.616	2.551	2.489
17	3.193	3.097	3.007	2.921	2.840	2.763	2.690	2.621	2.555	2.492
18	3.201	3.104	3.012	2.926	2.844	2.767	2.693	2.624	2.557	2.494
19	3.207	3.109	3.017	2.930	2.848	2.770	2.696	2.626	2.559	2.496
20	3.211	3.113	3.020	2.933	2.850	2.772	2.698	2.627	2.561	2.497
21	3.215	3.116	3.023	2.935	2.852	2.773	2.699	2.629	2.562	2.498
22	3.217	3.118	3.025	2.936	2.853	2.775	2.700	2.629	2.562	2.498
23	3.219	3.120	3.026	2.938	2.854	2.775	2.701	2.630	2.563	2.499
24	3.221	3.121	3.027	2.939	2.855	2.776	2.701	2.630	2.563	2.499
25	3.222	3.122	3.028	2.939	2.856	2.776	2.702	2.631	2.563	2.499
30	3.225	3.124	3.030	2.941	2.857	2.777	2.702	2.631	2.564	2.500
40	3.226	3.125	3.030	2.941	2.857	2.778	2.703	2.632	2.564	2.500
50	3.226	3.125	3.030	2.941	2.857	2.778	2.703	2.632	2.564	2.500

CHAPTER PERSPECTIVE

Money received in the future is not as valuable as money received today. The time value of money is a critical factor in many financial and investment applications, such as determining the size of deposits necessary to accumulate a future sum and the periodic payment of an amortized loan. The time value of money concept permits comparison of sums of money that are available at different times. In this chapter, we developed the two basic concepts of future value and present value and showed how these values are calculated. We also discussed their application to various financial and investment situations.

Understanding Return and Risk

INTRODUCTION AND MAIN POINTS

You can never predict with certainty the outcome of any financial or investment decision. Each decision presents certain risks and return characteristics.

Because of this reality, all major decisions must be viewed in terms of expected return and expected risk and their combined impact on the market value of your company. You must also take into account the trade-off between the return you expect to receive from the decision and the risk you must assume to earn.

After studying the material in this chapter:

— You will be able to define return and how it is measured.

— You will be able to distinguish between arithmetic return and geometric return.

— You will be able to calculate and understand risk statistics: the variance, standard deviation, and coefficient of variation.

— You will be able to identify the types of risk.

— You will understand the nature of diversification and how it reduces risk.

— You will be able to calculate a beta value and understand its use in designing a portfolio.

WHAT IS RETURN?

Return, a key consideration in financial and investment decisions, is simply the reward for investing. The return on an investment consists of the following sources of income:

(a) Periodic cash payments, called *current income.*

(b) Appreciation (or depreciation) in market value, called *capital gains* (or *losses*).

Current income, which is received on a periodic basis, may take the form of interest, dividends, or rent. Capital gains or losses represent changes in market value; a capital gain is the amount by which the proceeds from the sale of an investment exceeds its original purchase price, while a capital loss represents the amount by which the sale price of investment falls short of its original purchase price.

Measuring Return

How you measure the return on a given investment depends primarily on how you define the relevant period over which you hold the investment (the *holding period*). The term *holding period return* (HPR) refers to the total return earned from holding an investment for that period of time. It is computed as follows:

$$\text{HPR} = \frac{\text{Current income} + \text{Capital gain (or loss)}}{\text{Purchase price}}$$

EXAMPLE 7-1

Consider the investment in stocks A and B over a one-year period of ownership:

	Stock	
	A	B
Purchase price (beginning of year)	$100	$100
Cash dividend received (during the year)	$ 13	$ 18
Sales price (end of year)	$107	$ 97

The current income from the investment in stocks A and B over the one-year period is $13 and $18, respectively. For stock A, a capital gain of $7 ($107 sales price − $100 purchase price) is realized over the period. For stock B, a $3 capital loss ($97 sales price − $100 purchase price) results.

Combining the capital gain return (or loss) with the current income, the total return on each investment is summarized as follows:

	Stock	
Return	A	B
Cash dividend	$13	$18
Capital gain (loss)	7	(3)
Total return	$20	$15

Thus, the return on investments A and B are:

$$\text{HPR (stock A)} = \frac{\$13 + (\$107 - \$100)}{\$100}$$

$$= \frac{\$13 + \$7}{\$100}$$

$$= \frac{\$20}{\$100}$$

$$= 20\%$$

$$\text{HPR (stock B)} = \frac{\$18 + (\$97 - \$100)}{\$100}$$

$$= \frac{\$18 - \$3}{\$100}$$

$$= \frac{\$15}{\$100}$$

$$= 15\%$$

ARITHMETIC AND GEOMETRIC AVERAGE RETURNS

It is one thing to measure the return over a single holding period and quite another to describe a series of returns over time. When a financial manager holds an investment for more than one period, it is important to understand how to compute the average of the successive rates of return. Two types of multi-period average (mean) returns—the arithmetic average return and geometric average return—are commonly used.

The *arithmetic return* is simply the arithmetic average of successive one-period rates of return. It is defined as:

$$\text{Arithmetic return} = 1/n \sum r_t$$

where n = the number of time periods and r_t = the single holding period return in time t. The arithmetic average return, however, can be quite misleading when it is used for multi-period return calculations.

A more accurate measure of the actual return generated by an investment over multiple periods is the *geometric average return,* commonly called the *compounded annual rate of return.* The geometric return over n periods is computed as follows:

$$\text{Geometric return} = \sqrt[n]{(1 + r)(1 + r)\ldots(1 + r)} - 1$$

The following example illustrates the accuracy of the geometric return as a measure of return for multiple-period situations.

EXAMPLE 7-2

Consider the following data, in which the price of a stock doubles in one period and then depreciates back to the original price. Dividend income (current income) is zero.

	Time Periods		
	t = 0	t = 1	t = 2
Price (end of period)	$80	$160	$80
HPR	—	100%	−50%

The arithmetic average return is the average of 100 percent and −50 percent, which is 25 percent, as shown below:

$$\frac{100\% + (-50\%)}{2} = 25\%$$

In reality, though, the stock purchased for $80 and sold for the same price two periods later did not earn a 25 percent return; it clearly earned zero return. This can be shown by computing the geometric average return.

Note that n = 2, $r_1 = 100\% = 1$, and $r_2 = -50\% = -0.5$

Then,

$$
\begin{aligned}
\text{Geometric return} &= \sqrt[2]{(1+1)(1-0.5)} - 1 \\
&= \sqrt[2]{(2)(0.5)} - 1 \\
&= \sqrt{1} - 1 \\
&= 1 - 1 \\
&= 0\%
\end{aligned}
$$

EXPECTED RATE OF RETURN

A financial manager is primarily concerned with predicting future returns from an investment in a security. This outcome is the expected rate of return. Historical (actual) rates of return can provide a useful basis for formulating these future expectations.

Probabilities may be used to evaluate the expected return. The expected rate of return ($\bar{r}$) is the weighted average of possible returns from a given investment, weights being probabilities. Mathematically,

$$\bar{r} = \sum r_i p_i$$

where r_i is the ith possible return, p_i is the probability of the ith return, and n_4 is the number of possible returns.

EXAMPLE 7-3

Consider the possible rates of return, depending upon the states of the economy, recession, normal, and prosperity, that you might earn next year on a $50,000 investment in either stock A or stock B:

Stock A

State of economy	Return (r_i)	Probability (p_i)
Recession	−5%	.2
Normal	20	.6
Prosperity	40	.2

Stock B

State of economy	Return (r_i)	Probability (p_i)
Recession	10%	.2
Normal	15	.6
Prosperity	20	.2

The expected rates of return can be calculated as follows:
For stock A,

$$\bar{r} = (-5\%)(.2) + (20\%)(.6) + (40\%)(.2) = 19\%$$

For stock B,

$$\bar{r} = (10\%)(.2) + (15\%)(.6) + (20\%)(.2) = 15\%$$

RISK AND THE RISK-RETURN TRADE-OFF

The concept of a risk-return trade-off is integral to the subject of finance. All financial decisions involve some sort of risk-return trade-off; the greater the risk, the greater the return expected. Proper assessment and balance of the various risk-return trade-offs available is part of creating a sound financial and investment plan. Figure 7.1 depicts the risk-return trade-off (the risk-free rate is the rate of return commonly required on a risk-free security such as a U.S. Treasury bill).

In the case of investment in stock, you, as an investor, demand higher return from a speculative stock to compensate for the higher level of risk. In the case of working capital management, the less inventory you keep, the higher the expected return (since less of your current assets are tied up); however, there is increased risk of running out of stock and thus losing potential revenue.

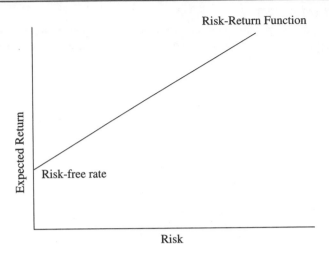

Figure 7.1 *Return vs. Risk*

REDUCING RISK BY DIVERSIFYING

Diversification—spreading your investments over a range of investment instruments to minimize the risk of losing all your assets should one investment go bad—is one way to minimize risk. In a diversified portfolio containing stocks, bonds, real estate, and savings accounts, the values of the investments do not all increase or decrease at the same time or in the same magnitude, and you can therefore protect yourself against fluctuations. Similarly, your company may diversify into different lines of businesses that are not subject to the same economic and political influences and thus protect itself against fluctuations in earnings.

MEASURING RISK

Risk refers to variations in earnings and includes the chance you may lose money on an investment. The standard deviation, a statistical measure of dispersion of the probability distribution of possible returns, is one measure of risk. The smaller the deviation, the tighter the distribution and thus the lower the riskiness of the investment. Mathematically,

$$\sigma = \sqrt{\sum (r_i - \bar{r})^2 \, p_i}$$

To calculate σ, proceed as follows:

Step 1. First compute the expected rate of return ($\bar{r}$).

Step 2. Subtract each possible return from $\bar{r}$ to obtain a set of deviations ($r_i - \bar{r}$).

Step 3. Square each deviation, multiply the squared deviation by the probability of occurrence for its respective return, and sum these products to obtain the variance $(\sigma)^2$:

$$\sigma^2 = \sum (r_i - \bar{r})^2 \, p_i$$

Step 4. Finally, take the square root of the variance to obtain the standard deviation (σ).

EXAMPLE 7-4

To follow this step-by-step approach, it is convenient to set up a table, as follows:

Stock A

Return (r_i)	Probability (p_i)	(step 1) $r_i p_i$	(step 2) $(r_i - \bar{r})$	$(r_i - \bar{r})^2$	(step 3) $(r_i - \bar{r})^2 p_i$
−5%	.2	−1%	−24%	576	115.2
20	.6	12	1	1	.6
40	.2	8	21	441	88.2
		$\bar{r} = 19\%$		$\sigma^2 =$	204
				(step 4) $\sigma = \sqrt{204}$	
				$\sigma = 14.18\%$	

Stock B

Return (r_i)	Probability (p_i)	(step 1) $r_i p_i$	(step 2) $(r_i - \bar{r})$	$(r_i - \bar{r})^2$	(step 3) $(r_i - \bar{r})^2 p_i$
10%	.2	2%	−5%	25	5
15	.6	9	0	0	0
20	.2	4	5	25	5
		$\bar{r} = 15\%$		$\sigma^2 = 10$	
				(step 4) $\sigma = \sqrt{10}$	
				$\sigma = 3.16\%$	

The financial manager must be careful in using the standard deviation to compare risk, since it is only an absolute measure of dispersion (risk) and does not consider the risk in relationship to an expected return. To compare securities with differing expected returns, managers commonly use the *coefficient of variation,* computed by dividing the standard deviation for a security by its expected value:

$$\sigma/\bar{r}$$

The higher the coefficient, the more risky the security.

EXAMPLE 7-5
Using the following data, we can compute the coefficient of variation for each stock as follows:

	Stock A	Stock B
$\bar{r}$	19%	15%
σ	14.28%	3.16%

The coefficient of variation is computed as follows:
For stock A,
$$\sigma/\bar{r} = 14.18/19 = .75$$

For stock B,
$$\sigma/\bar{r} = 3.16/15 = .21$$

Although stock A produces a considerably higher return than stock B, stock A is overall more risky than stock B, based on the computed coefficient of variation.

TYPES OF RISK

While all investments are subject to risk, different types of risk affect various investment alternatives differently. Among the kinds of risk that financial managers must consider are:

■ *Business risk*—the risk that the company will have general business problems. This kind of risk depends on changes in demand, input prices, and technological obsolescence.

■ *Liquidity risk*—the possibility that an asset may not be sold on short notice for its market value. If an investment must be sold at a high discount, it is said to have a substantial amount of liquidity risk.

■ *Default risk*—the risk that the issuing company is unable to make interest payments or principal repayments on debt. For example, there is a great amount of default risk inherent in the bonds of a company experiencing financial difficulty.

■ *Market risk*—risk associated with changes in stock price resulting from broad swings in the stock market as a whole. The prices of many stocks are affected by trends such as bull or bear markets.

■ *Interest rate risk*—fluctuations in the value of an asset as the interest rates and conditions of the money and capital markets change.

Interest rate risk applies to fixed income securities, such as bonds and real estate. As a rule, for example, if interest rates rise (fall), bond prices fall (rise).

■ *Purchasing power risk*—the possibility that you will receive a lesser amount of purchasing power than was originally invested. Bonds are most affected by this risk since the issuer repays them in cheaper dollars during an inflationary period.

BETA

That portion of a security's risk (called *unsystematic risk*) that is unique to that security can be controlled through diversification. Business, liquidity, and default risks fall into this category. Nondiversifiable risk, more commonly referred to as *systematic risk,* results from forces outside the company's control and is therefore not unique to the given security. Purchasing power, interest rate, and market risks fall into this category. Systematic risk is measured by *beta.*

Beta (b) measures a security's volatility relative to an average security. A particular stock's beta can help you predict how much the security will go up or down, provided that you know which way the market will go, and therefore figure out risk and expected return.

Most of the unsystematic risk affecting a security can be diversified away in an efficiently constructed portfolio; therefore, this type of risk does not need to be compensated with a higher level of return. The only relevant risk for which the investor can expect to receive compensation is systematic risk or beta risk.

Under the *capital asset pricing model* (CAPM), there is a relationship between a stock's expected (or required return) and its beta. The following formula is very helpful in determining a stock's expected return.

$$r_j = r_f + b(r_m - r_f)$$

In words,

Expected return $=$ Risk-free rate $+$ Beta $\times$ (Market risk premium)

where r_j $=$ the expected (or required) return on security j; r_f $=$ the risk-free rate on a security such as a T-bill; r_m $=$ the expected return on the market portfolio (such as Standard & Poor's 500 Stock Composite Index or Dow Jones 30 Industrials); and b $=$ beta, an index of systematic (nondiversifiable, noncontrollable) risk.

The market risk premium ($r_m - r_f$), which equals the expected market return (r_m) minus the risk-free rate (r_f), is the additional return above that which you could earn on, say, a T-bill, to compensate for your assuming a given level of risk (as measured by beta). Thus, the formula shows that the required (expected) return on a given security is equal to the return required for securities that have no risk plus a risk premium.

The idea behind the formula is that the relevant measure of risk is the risk of the individual security, or its beta. The higher the beta for a security, the greater the return expected (or demanded) by the investor.

EXAMPLE 7-6

Assume that $r_f = 6$ percent and $r_m = 10$ percent. If a stock has a beta of 2.0, its risk premium should be 14 percent:

$$r_j = r_f + b(r_m - r_f)$$
$$6\% + 2.0(10\% - 6\%) = 6\% + 8\% = 14\%$$

This means that you would expect (or demand) an extra 8 percent (risk premium) on this stock on top of the risk-free return of 6 percent. Therefore, the total expected (required) return on the stock should be 14 percent:

$$6\% + 8\% = 14\%$$

HOW TO READ BETA

Beta (b) measures a security's volatility relative to an average security; it is a measure of a security's return over time compared to that of the overall market. For example, if your company's beta is 2.0 and the stock market goes up 10 percent, your company's common stock goes up 20 percent; if the market goes down 10 percent, your company's stock price goes down 20 percent. There are general standards for interpreting betas:

Beta	What It Means
0	The security's return is independent of the market. An example is a risk-free security such as a T-bill.
0.5	The security is only half as responsive as the market.
1.0	The security has the same responsive or risk as the market (i.e., average risk). This is the beta value of the market portfolio such as Standard & Poor's 500 or Dow Jones 30 Industrials.
2.0	The security is twice as responsive, or risky, as the market.

An investment portfolio with high beta stocks will do poorly in a bear market but offer better returns in a bull market; Table 7-1 shows betas for selected stocks.

TABLE 7-1

BETA VALUES FOR SELECTED STOCKS
(APRIL 1999)

Company	Beta Value
Microsoft	1.4
Pfizer	0.9
Intel	1.4
Wal-Mart	0.9
GTE	0.6
General Motors	1.1
IBM	1.3
AOL	2.5

Source: AOL Personal Finance Channel and MSN Money Central Investor
(http://investor.msn.com), April 12, 1999.

CHAPTER PERSPECTIVE

Risk and return are two of the major factors you should consider in making financial and investment decisions. Always remember that the higher the return, the higher the risk. Beta can help you estimate the expected return and risk of a security. In order to reduce the risk, you might want to diversify your investment holdings.

The chapter covered a wide range of tools and measures associated with return and risk. The need to understand the different types of risk was emphasized.

Valuing Stocks and Bonds

INTRODUCTION AND MAIN POINTS

Valuation is the process of determining the worth (or value) of an asset. Just like a company's investors, the company's financial managers must have a good understanding of how to value its stocks, bonds, and other securities to judge whether or not they are a good buy. Failure to understand the concepts and computational procedures used in valuing a security may preclude the managers' making sound financial decisions that maximize the value of the company's common stock.

In this chapter, we use the concept of the time value of money to analyze the values of bonds and stocks and discuss basic bond and stock valuation models under varying assumptions. In all cases, bond and stock values are the present value of the future cash flows expected from the security.

In this chapter, you will learn:
■ The key inputs and concepts underlying the security valuation process.
■ How to value bonds.
■ How to identify and calculate various yields on a bond.
■ How to distinguish between preferred stock and common stock.
■ The various methods of common stock valuation.
■ How to determine the investor's expected rate of return on preferred stock and common stock.

VALUING A SECURITY

The process of determining the value of a security involves finding the present value of the asset's expected future cash flows using the investor's required rate of return. The basic security valuation model can be defined mathematically as follows:

$$V = \sum_{t=1}^{n} \frac{C_t}{(1 + r)^t}$$

where V = intrinsic value or present value of a security
C_t = expected future cash flows in period $t = 1, ..., n$
r = the investor's required rate of return

BONDS

A bond is a certificate or security certifying that its holder loaned funds to a company in return for fixed future interest and repayment of principal.

Certain terms and features are commonly used to describe bonds, including:

■ *Par value*—the face value (maturity value), usually $1,000.

■ *Coupon rate*—the nominal interest rate that determines the actual interest to be received on a bond. It is an annual interest based on par value. For example, if you own a $1,000 bond having a coupon rate of 6 percent, you will receive an annual interest payment of $60.

■ *Maturity date*—the final date on which repayment of the bond principal is due.

■ *Yield*—the effective interest rate you are earning on the bond investment. The yield is different than the coupon interest rate. If a bond is bought below its face value (i.e., purchased at a discount), the yield is higher than the coupon rate; if it is acquired above face value (i.e., bought at a premium), the yield is below the coupon rate.

VALUING BONDS

To value a bond, you need to know three basic elements: (1) the amount of the cash flows to be received by the investor, equal to the periodic interest to be received and the par value to be paid at maturity; (2) the maturity date of the loan; and (3) the investor's required rate of return.

The periodic interest can be received annually or semiannually. The value of a bond is simply the present value of these cash flows. Two versions of the bond valuation model are presented below.

If the interest payments are made annually, then

$$V = \sum_{t=1}^{n} \frac{I}{(1 + r)^t} + \frac{M}{(1 + r)^n} = I \cdot T_4(r, n) + M \cdot T_3(r, n)$$

where I = interest payment each year
          = coupon interest rate $\times$ par value
    M = par value, or maturity value, typically $1,000
    r = the investor's required rate of return
    n = number of years to maturity
    T_4 = present value interest factor of an annuity of $1
          (which can be found in Table 6-4 in Chapter 6)
    T_3 = present value interest factor of $1 (which can be
          found in Table 6-3 in Chapter 6)

Both T_4 and T_3 were discussed in detail in Chapter 6 on the time value of money.

EXAMPLE 8-1

Consider a bond, maturing in 10 years and having a coupon rate of 8 percent. The par value is $1,000. Investors consider 10 percent to be an appropriate required rate of return in view of the risk level associated with this bond. The annual interest payment is $80 (8% $\times$ $1,000). The present value is:

$$
\begin{aligned}
V &= \sum_{t-1}^{n} \frac{I}{(1+r)^t} + \frac{M}{(1+r)^n} \\
&= I \cdot T_4(r, n) + M \cdot T_3(r, n) \\
&= \sum_{t=1}^{10} \frac{\$80}{(1+0.1)^t} + \frac{\$1,000}{(1+0.1)^{10}} \\
&= \$80 \cdot T_4(10\%, 10) + \$1,000 \cdot T_3(10\%, 10) \\
&= \$80(6.145) + \$1,000(0.386) \\
&= \$491.60 + 386.00 \\
&= \$877.60
\end{aligned}
$$

If the interest is paid semiannually, then

$$
\begin{aligned}
V &= \sum_{t=1}^{2n} \frac{I/2}{(1+2/r)^t} + \frac{M}{(1+2/r)^{2n}} \\
&= \frac{I}{2} \cdot T_4(r/2, 2n) + M \cdot T_3(r/2, 2n)
\end{aligned}
$$

EXAMPLE 8-2

Assume the same data as in Example 8-1, except the interest is paid semiannually.

$$
\begin{aligned}
V &= \sum_{t=1}^{2n} \frac{I/2}{(1+r/2)^t} + \frac{M}{(1+2/r)^{2n}} \\
&= \frac{I}{2} \cdot T_4(r/2, 2n) + M \cdot T_3(r/2, 2n) \\
&= \sum_{t=1}^{20} \frac{\$40}{(1+0.05)^t} + \frac{\$1000}{(1+0.05)^{20}} \\
&= \$40 \cdot T_4(5\%, 20) + \$1,000 \cdot T_3(5\%, 20) \\
&= \$40(12.462) + \$1,000(0.377) \\
&= \$498.48 + \$377.00 \\
&= \$875.48
\end{aligned}
$$

CALCULATING YIELD (EFFECTIVE RATE OF RETURN) ON A BOND

Bonds are evaluated on many different types of returns, including current yield and yield to maturity.

Current yield. The current yield is the annual interest payment divided by the current price of the bond. This figure is reported in *The Wall Street Journal,* among other newspapers.

EXAMPLE 8-3

Assume a 12 percent coupon rate $1,000 par value bond selling for $960. The current yield is:

$$\$120/\$960 = 12.5\%$$

The problem with this measure of return is that it does not take into account the maturity date of the bond. A bond with 1 year to run and another with 15 years to run would have the same current yield quote if interest payments were $120 and the price were $960. Clearly, the 1-year bond would be preferable under this circumstance because you would get not only $120 in interest but also a gain of $40 ($1000 − $960).

Yield to maturity. The expected rate of return on a bond, better known as the bond's yield to maturity, is computed by solving the following equation (the bond valuation model) for r:

$$V = \sum_{t=1}^{2n} \frac{I}{(1+r)^t} + \frac{M}{(1+r)^n} = I \cdot T_4(r, n) + M \cdot T_3(r, n)$$

Because the yield to maturity takes into account the maturity date of the bond, it is the real return you would receive from interest income plus capital gain, assuming you hold the bond to maturity.

Finding the bond's yield r involves trial and error. It is best explained by an example.

EXAMPLE 8-4

Suppose you are offered a 10-year, 8 percent coupon, $1,000 par value bond at a price of $877.60. What rate of return could you earn if you bought the bond and held it to maturity? Recall that in Example 8-1 the value of the bond ($877.60) was obtained using the required rate of return of 10 percent. Compute this bond's yield to see if it is 10 percent.

First, set up the bond valuation model:

$$V = \$877.60 = \sum_{t=1}^{10} \frac{\$80}{(1+r)^t} + \frac{\$1,000}{(1+r)^{10}}$$

$$= \$80 \cdot T_4(r, 10) + \$1,000 \cdot T_3(r, 10)$$

Since the bond is selling at a discount under the par value ($877.60 versus $1,000), the bond's yield is above the going coupon rate of 8 percent. Therefore, try a rate of 9 percent. Substituting factors for 9 percent in the equation, we obtain:

$$V = \$80(6.418) + \$1,000(0.422)$$
$$= \$513.44 + \$422.00$$
$$= \$935.44$$

The calculated bond value, $935.44, is above the actual market price of $877.60, so the yield is not 9 percent. To lower the calculated value, the rate must be raised. Trying 10 percent, we obtain:

$$V = \$80(6.145) + \$1,000(0.386)$$
$$= \$491.60 + \$386.00$$
$$= \$877.60$$

This calculated value is exactly equal to the market price of the bond; thus, 10 percent is the bond's yield to maturity.

The formula that can be used to find the approximate yield to maturity on a bond is:

$$\text{Yield} = \frac{I + (M - V)/n}{(M + V)/2}$$

where I = dollars of interest paid per year

M = the par value, typically $1,000 per bond

V = a bond's current value (price)

n = number of years to maturity

This formula can also be used to obtain a starting point for the trial-and-error method discussed in Example 8-4.

EXAMPLE 8-5

Using the same data as in Example 8-4 and the short-cut method, the rate of return on the bond is:

$$\begin{aligned}
\text{Yield} &= \frac{\$80 + (\$1,000 - \$877.60)/10}{(\$1,000 + \$877.60)/2} \\
&= \frac{\$80 + \$12.24}{\$938.80} \\
&= \frac{\$92.24}{\$938.80} \\
&= 9.8\%
\end{aligned}$$

Since the bond was bought at a discount, the yield (9.8 percent) is actually greater than the coupon rate of 8 percent.

PREFERRED STOCK

Preferred stock carries a fixed dividend that is paid quarterly and that is stated in dollar terms per share or as a percentage of par (stated) value of the stock. It is considered a hybrid security because it possesses features of both common stock and corporate bonds. It resembles common stock in that:

■ It represents equity ownership and is issued without stated maturity dates.

■ It pays dividends.

However, it is like a corporate bond in that:

■ It provides for prior claims on earnings and assets.

■ Its dividend is fixed for the life of the issue.

■ It can carry call and convertible features and sinking fund provisions.

Since preferred stocks are traded on the basis of the yield offered to investors, they are viewed as fixed income securities and, as a result, compete with bonds in the marketplace. Convertible preferred stock (which can be exchanged for common stock), however, trades more like common stock, depending on conversion prices.

VALUING PREFERRED STOCK

The value of preferred stock is the present worth of a series of equal cash flow streams (dividends), continuing indefinitely. Since the dividends in each period are equal for preferred stock, the valuation model is:

$$V = D/r$$

where V = present value of a preferred stock
       D = annual dividend
       r = the investor's required rate of return

EXAMPLE 8-6

ABC preferred stock pays an annual dividend of $4.00. You, as an investor, require a 16% return on your investment. Then the value of the ABC preferred stock can be determined as follows:

$$V = D/r = \$4.00/.16 = \$25$$

CALCULATING EXPECTED RETURN ON PREFERRED STOCK

To compute the preferred stockholder's expected rate of return, we use the valuation equation for preferred stock presented in Example 8-6. Solving it for r,

$$r = D/V$$

which indicates that the expected rate of return of a preferred stock equals the dividend yield (annual dividend/market price).

EXAMPLE 8-7

A preferred stock paying $5.00 a year in dividends and having a market price of $25 would have a current yield of 20%, computed as follows:

$$r = D/V = \$5/\$25 = 20\%$$

COMMON STOCK

Common stock is an equity investment that represents the ownership of a corporation. It is the equivalent of the capital account for a sole proprietorship or capital contributed by each partner for a partnership.

The corporation's stockholders have certain rights and privileges including:

▬ *Control of the firm.* The stockholders elect the company's directors, who in turn select officers to manage the business.

■ *Preemptive rights.* This is the right to purchase new stock. A preemptive right entitles a common stockholder to maintain his or her proportional ownership through the opportunity to purchase, on a pro rata basis, any new stock being offered or any securities convertible into common stock.

A distinction should be made between growth and value stocks. A *growth stock* shows better market price and profit potential. However, it pays little or no dividends. A *value stock* is underpriced and/or has high dividends.

VALUING COMMON STOCK

The value of a common stock is the present value of all future cash inflows expected to be received by the investor, including dividends and the future price of the stock at the time it is sold.

Single Holding Period

For an investor holding a common stock for only one year, the value of the stock is the present value of both the expected cash dividend to be received in one year (D_1) and the expected market price per share of the stock at year-end (P_1). If r represents an investor's required rate of return, the value of common stock (P_0) is:

$$P_0 = \frac{D_1}{(1+r)^1} + \frac{P_1}{(1+r)^1}$$

EXAMPLE 8-8

Assume an investor is considering the purchase of stock A at the beginning of the year. The dividend at year-end is expected to be $1.50, and the market price by the end of the year is expected to be $40. If the investor's required rate of return is 15%, the value of the stock is:

$$
\begin{aligned}
P_0 &= \frac{D_1}{(1+r)^1} + \frac{P_1}{(1+r)^1} = \frac{\$1.50}{(1+0.15)} + \frac{\$40}{(1+0.15)} \\
&= \$1.50T_3(15\%, 1) + \$40T_3(15\%, 1) \\
&= \$1.50(0.870) + \$40(0.870) \\
&= \$1.31 + \$34.80 \\
&= \$36.11
\end{aligned}
$$

MULTIPLE HOLDING PERIOD

Since common stock has no maturity date and can be held for many years, a more general, multi-period model is needed to project its value.

The common stock valuation model is:

$$P_0 = \sum_{t=1} \frac{D_t}{(1+r)^t}$$

where D_t = dividend in period t.

Dividends may be classified as zero growth or constant growth. In the case of zero growth (i.e., $D_0 = D_1 = \ldots = D$), then the valuation model is:

$$P_0 = \frac{D}{r}$$

This model is most applicable to the valuation of preferred stocks or to the common stocks of very mature companies, such as large utilities.

EXAMPLE 8-9

Assuming dividend (D) equals $2.50 and r equals 10 percent, then the value of the stock is:

$$P_0 = \frac{\$2.50}{0.1} = \$25$$

In the case of constant growth, if we assume that dividends grow at a constant rate of g every year [i.e., $D_t = D_0(1+g)^t$], then the general model is:

$$P_0 = \frac{D_1}{r-g}$$

In words,

$$\text{Common stock value} = \frac{\text{dividend in year 1}}{\text{(required rate of return)} - \text{(growth rate)}}$$

This formula, known as the Gordon's valuation model, is most applicable to the valuation of the common stock of very large or broadly diversified firms.

EXAMPLE 8-10

Consider a common stock that paid a $3 dividend per share at the end of the last year and is expected to pay a cash dividend every year at a growth rate of 10 percent. Assume the investor's required rate of return is 12 percent. The value of the stock is:

$$D_1 = D_0(1+g) = \$3(1+0.10) = \$3.30$$
$$P_0 = \frac{D_1}{r-g} = \frac{\$3.30}{0.12 - 0.10} = \$165$$

CALCULATING THE EXPECTED RETURN ON COMMON STOCK

The formula for computing the expected rate of return on common stock can be derived easily from the valuation models.

The single-holding period return formula is derived from:

$$P_o = \frac{D_1}{(1+r)} + \frac{P_1}{(1+r)}$$

Solving for r gives:

$$r = \frac{D_1 + (P_1 - P_o)}{P_o}$$

In words,

$$\text{Rate of return} = \frac{\text{annual dividend} + \text{capital gain}}{\text{beginning price}}$$

$$= \frac{\text{annual dividend}}{\text{beginning price}} + \frac{\text{capital gain}}{\text{beginning price}}$$

$$= \text{dividend yield} + \text{capital gain yield}$$

This formula is the same as the holding period return (HPR), introduced in Chapter 7.

EXAMPLE 8-11

Consider a stock that sells for $50. The company is expected to pay a $3 cash dividend at the end of the year, and the stock market price at the end of the year is expected to be $55 a share. Thus the expected return is:

$$
\begin{aligned}
r &= \frac{D_1 + (P_1 - P_o)}{P_o} \\
&= \frac{\$3.00 + (\$55 - \$50)}{\$50} \\
&= \frac{\$3.00 + \$5.00}{\$50} \\
&= 16\%
\end{aligned}
$$

or:

$$\text{Dividend yield} = \frac{\$3.00}{\$50} = 6\%$$

$$\text{Capital gain yield} = \frac{\$5.00}{\$50} = 10\%$$

$$
\begin{aligned}
r &= \text{Dividend yield} + \text{Capital gain yield} \\
&= 6\% + 10\% \\
&= 16\%
\end{aligned}
$$

Assuming a constant growth in dividends, the formula for the expected rate of return on an investment in stock is:

$$P_0 = \frac{D_1}{r - g}$$

Solving for r gives:

$$r = \frac{D_1}{P_0} + g$$
$$= \text{Dividend yield} + \text{Annual growth rate}$$

EXAMPLE 8-12
Suppose that your company's dividend per share is $4.50 and that it is expected to grow at a constant rate of 6 percent. The current market price of the stock is $30. Then the expected rate of return is:

$$r = \frac{D_1}{P_0} + g$$
$$= \frac{\$4.50}{\$30} + 6\%$$
$$= 15\% + 6\%$$
$$= 21\%$$

CHAPTER PERSPECTIVE

In this chapter we have discussed the valuation of bonds, preferred stock, and common stock. Valuation is a present value concept that involves estimating future cash flows and discounting them at a required rate of return. The value of a bond is essentially the present value of all future interest and principal payments; the value of a stock is a function of the expected future dividends and the rate of return required by investors (the Gordon's market valuation model). The chapter also discussed how to calculate the expected return from a stock investment and the yield on a bond.

Cost of Capital

INTRODUCTION AND MAIN POINTS

The cost of capital is defined as the rate of return that a company must offer on its securities in order to maintain its market value. Financial managers must know the cost of capital in order to (1) make capital budgeting decisions, (2) help to establish the optimal capital structure, and (3) make decisions concerning leasing, bond refunding, and working capital management. The cost of capital is computed as a weighted average of the various capital components, items on the right-hand side of the balance sheet such as debt, preferred stock, common stock, and retained earnings.

After studying the material in this chapter:

▬ You will be able to compute individual costs of financing including long-term debt, bonds, preferred stock, common stock, and retained earnings.

▬ You will be able to determine the overall cost of capital.

▬ You will be able to discuss the various weighting schemes.

▬ You will be able to explain how the weighted marginal cost of capital can be used with the investment opportunity schedule to find the optimal capital budget.

COMPUTING INDIVIDUAL COSTS OF CAPITAL

Each element of capital has a component cost that is identified by the following:

k_i = before-tax cost of debt
$k_d = K_i(1 - t)$ = after-tax cost of debt, where t = tax rate
k_p = cost of preferred stock
k_s = cost of retained earnings (or internal equity)
k_e = cost of external equity capital, or cost of issuing new common stock
k_o = company's overall cost of capital, or a weighted average cost of capital

Cost of Debt

You can compute before-tax cost of debt by determining the internal rate of return (or yield to maturity) on the bond cash flows. However, there is a short-cut formula that may be used for approximating the yield to maturity on a bond:

$$k_i = \frac{I + (M - V)/n}{(M + V)/2}$$

where I = annual interest payments in dollars
  M = par or face value, usually $1,000 per bond
  V = market value or net proceeds from the sale of a bond
  n = term of the bond n years

Since the interest payments are tax deductible, you must state the cost of debt on an after-tax basis, which is:

$$k_d = k_i(1 - t)$$

where t is the tax rate.

EXAMPLE 9-1

Assume that the Carter Company issues a $1,000, 8 percent, 20-year bond whose net proceeds are $940. The tax rate is 40 percent. Then, the before-tax cost of debt, k_i, is:

$$
\begin{aligned}
k_i &= \frac{I + (M - V)/n}{(M + V)/2} \\
&= \frac{\$80 + (\$1,000 - \$940)/20}{(\$1,000 + \$940)/2} \\
&= \frac{\$83}{\$970} \\
&= 8.56\%
\end{aligned}
$$

Therefore, the after-tax cost of debt is:

$$
\begin{aligned}
k_d &= k_i(1 - t) \\
&= 8.56\%(1 - 0.4) \\
&= 5.14\%
\end{aligned}
$$

Cost of Preferred Stock

The cost of preferred stock, k_p, is found by dividing the annual preferred stock dividend, d_p, by the net proceeds from the sale of the preferred stock, p, as follows:

$$k_p = \frac{d_p}{p}$$

Since preferred stock dividends are not tax deductible, no tax adjustment is required.

EXAMPLE 9-2

Suppose that the Carter Company has preferred stock that pays a $13 dividend per share and sells for $100 per share in the market. The flotation (or underwriting) cost is 3 percent, or $3 per share. Then the cost of preferred stock is:

$$k_p = \frac{d_p}{p}$$
$$= \frac{\$13}{\$97}$$
$$= 13.4\%$$

Cost of Equity Capital

The cost of common stock, k_e, is generally viewed as the rate of return investors require on a company's common stock. There are two widely used techniques for measuring the cost of common stock equity capital: the Gordon's growth model and the capital asset pricing model (CAPM) approach.

The Gordon's Growth Model.

The Gordon model is:

$$P_o = \frac{D_1}{r - g}$$

where P_o = value (or market price) of common stock
D_1 = dividend to be received in one year
r = investor's required rate of return
g = rate of growth (assumed to be constant over time)

Solving the model for r yields the formula for the cost of common stock:

$$r = \frac{D_1}{P_o} + g \quad \text{or} \quad k_c = \frac{D_1}{P_o} + g$$

The symbol r is changed to k_e to show that it is used for the computation of cost of capital.

EXAMPLE 9-3

Assume that the market price of the Carter Company's stock is $40. The dividend to be paid at the end of the coming year is $4 per share; it is expected to grow at a constant annual rate of 6 percent. Then the cost of this common stock is:

$$k_e = \frac{D_1}{P_o} + g$$
$$= \frac{\$4}{\$40} + 6\%$$
$$= 16\%$$

The cost of new common stock, or external equity capital, is higher than the cost of existing common stock because of the flotation costs involved in selling the new stock. Flotation costs, sometimes called issuance costs, are the total costs of issuing and selling a security, including printing and engraving, legal fees, and accounting fees.

If f is flotation cost in percent, the formula for the cost of new common stock is:

$$k_e = \frac{D_1}{P_0(1-f)} + g$$

EXAMPLE 9-4

Assume the same data as in Example 9-3, except that the corporation is trying to sell new issues of stock A and its flotation cost is 10 percent. Then:

$$k_e = \frac{D_1}{P_0(1-f)} + g$$
$$= \frac{\$4}{\$40(1-0.1)} + 6\%$$
$$= \frac{\$4}{\$36} + 6\%$$
$$= 11.11\% + 6\%$$
$$= 17.11\%$$

The Capital Asset Pricing Model Approach. To use this alternative approach to measuring the cost of common stock, you must:
1. Estimate the risk-free rate, r_f, generally taken to be the U.S. Treasury bill rate.
2. Estimate the stock's beta coefficient, b, which is an index of systematic (or nondiversifiable market) risk.
3. Estimate the rate of return on the market portfolio, r_m, such as the Standard & Poor's 500 Stock Composite Index or Dow Jones 30 Industrials.
4. Estimate the required rate of return on the company's stock using the CAPM equation:

$$k_e = r_f + b(r_m - r_f)$$

Again, note that the symbol r_j is changed to k_e.

EXAMPLE 9-5

Assuming that r_f is 7%, b is 1.5, and r_m is 13%, then:

$$k_e = r_f + b(r_m - r_f)$$
$$= 7\% + 1.5(13\% - 7\%)$$
$$= 16\%$$

This 16 percent cost of common stock consists of a 7 percent risk-free rate plus a 9 percent risk premium, reflecting the fact that the stock price is 1.5 times more vulnerable than the market portfolio to the factors affecting nondiversifiable, or systematic, risk.

The Arbitrage Pricing Model. The CAPM assumes that required rates of return depend only on one risk factor, the stock's *beta*. The Arbitrage Pricing Model (APM) disputes this and includes any number of risk factors:

$$r = r_f + b_1RP_1 + b_2RP_2 + \cdots + b_nRP_n$$

where r = the expected return for a given stock or portfolio

r_f = the risk-free rate

b_i = the sensitivity (or reaction) of the returns of the stock to unexpected changes in economic forces $i(i = 1, \cdots, n)$

RP_i = the market risk premium associated with an unexpected change in the ith economic force

n = the number of relevant economic forces

The following five economic forces are suggested:
- Changes in expected inflation.
- Unanticipated changes in inflation.
- Unanticipated changes in industrial production.
- Unanticipated changes in the yield differential between low- and high-grade bonds (the default-risk premium).
- Unanticipated changes in the yield differential between long- and short-term bonds (the term structure of interest rates).

EXAMPLE 9-6

Suppose returns required in the market by investors are a function of two economic factors according the following equation, where the risk-free rate is 7 percent:

$$r = 0.07 + b_1(0.04) + b_2(0.01)$$

ABC stock has the reaction coefficients to the factors, such that $b_1 = 1.3$ and $b_2 = 0.90$. Then the required rate of return for the ABC stock is

$$r = 0.07 + (1.3)(0.04) + (0.90)(0.01) = 0.113 = 11.3\%$$

Cost of Retained Earnings

The cost of retained earnings, k_s, is closely related to the cost of existing common stock, since the cost of equity obtained by retained earnings is the same as the rate of return investors require on the company's common stock. Therefore,

$$k_e = k_s$$

Measuring the Overall Cost of Capital

The firm's overall cost of capital is the average of the individual capital costs, weighted by the proportion of each type of capital used. If k_o is the overall cost of capital:

$$k_o = \sum \text{Percentage of the total capital structure supplied}$$
$$\text{by each source of capital}$$
$$\times \text{Cost of capital for each source}$$
$$= w_d k_d + w_p k_p + w_e k_e + w_s k_s$$

where w_d = % of total capital supplied by debts

w_p = % of total capital supplied by preferred stock

w_e = % of total capital supplied by external equity

w_s = % of total capital supplied by retained earnings

(or internal equity)

The weights can be *historical*, *target*, or *marginal*.

Historical Weights

Historical weights are based on a company's existing capital structure and are used if management believes that the existing capital structure is optimal and therefore should be maintained in the future. There are two types of historical weights—book value weights and market value weights.

Book Value Weights. The use of book value weights to calculate a company's weighted cost of capital assumes that new financing will be raised using the same method the company used for its present capital structure. The weights are determined by dividing the book value of each capital component by the sum of the book values of all the long-term capital sources. A sample computation follows:

EXAMPLE 9-7

Assume the following capital structure and cost of each source of financing for the Carter Company:

		Cost
Mortgage bonds ($1,000 par)	$20,000,000	5.14% (from Example 9-1)
Preferred stock ($100 par)	5,000,000	13.40% (from Example 9-2)
Common stock ($40 par)	20,000,000	17.11% (from Example 9-4)
Retained earnings	5,000,000	16.00% (from Example 9-3)
Total	50,000,000	

The book value weights and the overall cost of capital are computed as follows:

Source	Book Value	Weights	Cost	Weighted Cost
Debt	$20,000,000	40%[a]	5.14%	2.06%[b]
Preferred stock	5,000,000	10	13.40%	1.34
Common stock	20,000,000	40	17.11%	6.84
Retained earnings	5,000,000	10	16.00%	1.60
Total	$50,000,000	100%		11.84%

Overall cost of capital $= k_o = 11.84\%$

(a) $20,000,000/$50,000,000 = .40 = 40\%$
(b) $5.14\% \times 40\% = 2.06\%$

Market Value Weights.
Market value weights are determined by dividing the market value of each source by the sum of the market values of all sources. This approach for computing a company's weighted average cost of capital is considered more accurate than the use of book value weights because the market values of the securities closely approximate the actual dollars to be received from their sale.

EXAMPLE 9-8

In addition to the data from Example 9-7, assume that the security market prices are as follows:

$$\text{Mortgage bonds} = \$1,100 \text{ per bond}$$
$$\text{Preferred stock} = \$90 \text{ per share}$$
$$\text{Common stock} = \$80 \text{ per share}$$

The number of securities in each category is:

$$\text{Mortgage bonds} = \frac{\$20,000,000}{\$1,000} = 20,000$$

$$\text{Preferred stock} = \frac{\$5,000,000}{\$100} = 50,000$$

$$\text{Common stock} = \frac{\$20,000,000}{\$40} = 500,000$$

Therefore, the market value weights are:

Source	Number of Securities	Price	Market Value
Debt	20,000	$1,100	$22,000,000
Preferred stock	50,000	$ 90	4,500,000
Common stock	500,000	$ 80	40,000,000
			$66,500,000

The $40 million common stock value must be split in the ratio of 4 to 1 ($20 million common stock and $5 million retained earnings in the original capital structure), since the market value of the retained earnings has been impounded into the common stock.

The company's cost of capital is as follows:

Source	Market Value	Weights	Cost	Weighted Average
Debt	$22,000,000	33.08%	5.14%	1.70%
Preferred stock	4,500,000	6.77	13.40%	0.91
Common stock	32,000,000	48.12	17.11%	8.23
Retained earnings	8,000,000	12.03	16.00%	1.92
	$66,500,000	100.00%		12.76%

Overall cost of capital = k_o = 12.76%

Target Weights

If the company has a target capital structure (that is, a desired debt-equity mix) that it maintains over the long term, then the use of that capital structure and associated weights can be used in calculating the weighted cost of capital.

Marginal Weights

Marginal weights using the *actual* financial mix proposed for financing investments can also be used for calculating the weighted cost of capital. This approach, while attractive, presents a problem. The cost of capital for the individual sources depend on the company's financial risk, which is affected by its financial mix. If the company alters its present capital structure, the individual costs will change, making it more difficult to compute the weighted cost of capital. For this method to work, financial managers must be able to assume that the company's financial mix is relatively stable and that current weights will closely approximate future financing practice.

EXAMPLE 9-9

The Carter Company is considering raising $8 million for plant expansion. Management estimates using the following mix for financing this project:

Debt	$4,000,000	50%
Common stock	2,000,000	25%
Retained earnings	2,000,000	25%
	$8,000,000	100%

The company's cost of capital is computed as follows:

Source	Marginal Weights	Cost	Weighted Cost
Debt	50%	5.14%	2.57%
Common stock	25	17.11%	4.28
Retained earnings	25	16.00%	4.00
	100%		10.85%

Overall cost of capital = k_o = 10.85%

LEVEL OF FINANCING AND THE MARGINAL COST OF CAPITAL

In Example 9-9, the weighted cost of capital was determined with the assumption that no new common stock was to be issued. If new common stock is in fact to be issued, the weighted cost of capital will increase for each dollar of new financing, in order to allow for the flotation costs associated with external equity capital. Therefore, companies generally prefer to use the lower-cost capital sources first.

A schedule or graph relating the company's cost of capital to the level of new financing is called the *weighted marginal cost of capital* (MCC). This schedule determines the discount rate to be used in the capital budgeting process. The steps to be followed in calculating the marginal cost of capital are summarized below.

1. Determine the cost and the percentage of financing for each source of capital (debt, preferred stock, common stock equity).
2. Compute the break points on the MCC curve where the weighted cost will increase. The formula for computing the break points is:

$$\text{Break point} = \frac{\text{maximum amount of the lower-cost source of capital}}{\text{percentage financing provided by the source}}$$

3. Calculate the weighted cost of capital over the range of total financing between break points.
4. Construct a MCC schedule or graph that shows the weighted cost of capital for each level of total new financing. This schedule will be used in conjunction with the company's available *investment opportunities schedule* (IOS) in order to select the investments. As long as a project's *internal rate of return* (IRR) is greater than the marginal cost of new financing, the project should be accepted. The point at which the IRR intersects the MCC gives the optimal capital budget.

EXAMPLE 9-10

A company is contemplating three investment projects, A, B, and C, whose initial cash outlays and expected IRR are shown below. IOS for these projects is:

Project	Cash Outlay	IRR
A	$2,000,000	13%
B	$2,000,000	15%
C	$1,000,000	10%

If these projects are accepted, the financing will consist of 50 percent debt and 50 percent common stock. The company expects to have $1.8 million in earnings available for reinvestment (internally generated funds). The company will consider only the effects of increases in the cost of common stock on its marginal cost of capital.

1. The costs of capital for each source of financing have been computed and are given below:

Source	Cost
Debt	5%
Common stock ($1.8 million)	15%
New common stock	19%

If the firm uses only internally generated common stock, the weighted cost of capital is:

$$k_o = \sum (\text{percentage of the total capital structure supplied by}$$

$$\text{each source of capital} \times \text{cost of capital for each source})$$

In this case, the capital structure is composed of 50 percent debt and 50 percent internally generated common stock. Thus,

$$k_o = (0.5)5\% + (0.5)15\% = 10\%$$

If the company uses only new common stock, the weighted cost of capital is:

$$k_o = (0.5)5\% + (0.5)19\% = 12\%$$

Range of Total New Financing (in millions of dollars)	Type of Capital	Proportion	Cost	Weighted Cost
$0–$3.6	Debt	0.5	5%	2.5%
	Internal common	0.5	15%	7.5
				10.0%
$3.6 and up	Debt	0.5	5%	2.5%
	New common	0.5	19%	9.5
				12.0%

2. Next compute the break point, the level of financing at which the weighted cost of capital increases.

$$\text{Break point} = \frac{\text{maximum amount of the lower-cost source of capital}}{\text{percentage financing provided by the source}}$$

$$= \frac{\$1,800,000}{0.5}$$

$$= \$3,600,000$$

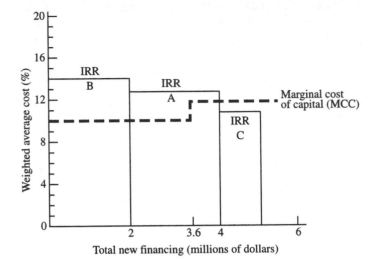

Figure 9.1 *MCC Schedule and IOS Graph*

3. The company may be able to finance $3.6 million in new investments with internal common stock and debt without changing the current mix of 50 percent debt and 50 percent common stock. Therefore, if the total financing is $3.6 million or less, the cost of capital is 10 percent.
4. Construct the MCC schedule on the IOS graph to obtain the discount rate in order to determine which project to accept and to show the optimal capital budget (see Figure 9.1).

The company should continue to invest up to the point where the IRR equals the MCC. The graph in Figure 9.1 shows that the company should invest in projects B and A, since each IRR exceeds the marginal cost of capital. It should reject project C since its cost of capital is greater than the IRR. The optimal capital budget is $4 million, the sum of the cash outlay required for projects A and B.

CHAPTER PERSPECTIVE

Cost of capital is the rate of return that must be achieved in order for the price of a company's stock to remain unchanged and is therefore the minimum acceptable rate of return for the company's new investments. The chapter discussed how to calculate the individual costs of financing sources, various ways to calculate the overall cost of capital, and how to construct the optimal budget for capital spending. Financial officers should be thoroughly familiar with the ways to compute the costs of various sources of financing for financial, capital budgeting, and capital structure decisions.

How to Make Capital Budgeting Decisions

INTRODUCTION AND MAIN POINTS

Capital budgeting is the process of making long-term investment decisions that further the company's goals. The stockholders have entrusted the company with their money, and they expect the company to invest their money wisely. Investments in fixed assets should be consistent with the goal of maximizing the market value of the firm.

Companies must make many financial decisions in order to grow, including selecting product lines, disposing of business segments, choosing to lease or buy equipment, and selecting investments. To make long-term investment decisions in accordance with the company's goals, you must perform three tasks when evaluating capital budgeting projects: (1) estimate cash flows, (2) estimate the cost of capital (or required rate of return), and (3) apply a decision rule to determine whether a project will be good for the company.

After studying the material in this chapter:

■ You will know the types and special features of capital budgeting decisions.

■ You will be able to calculate, interpret, and evaluate five capital budgeting techniques.

■ You will be able to select the best mix of projects to implement with a limited capital spending budget.

■ You will understand how income tax factors affect decisions.

■ You will understand different methods of calculating depreciation.

■ You will be familiar with the effect of Accelerated Cost Recovery System (ACRS) on capital budgeting decisions.

TYPES OF INVESTMENT PROJECTS

Your company must make two types of long-term investment decisions:

1. *Selection decisions*—determining whether to obtain new facilities or expand existing facilities. Typically, such decisions involve:
   (a) Investments in property, plant, and equipment and other types of assets.

(b) Resource commitments in the form of new product development, market research, introduction of a computer, refunding of long-term debt, etc.

(c) Mergers and acquisitions, that is, buying another company to acquire a new product line.

2. *Replacement decisions*—deciding to replace existing facilities with new facilities, such as opting to replace an old machine with a high-tech machine.

FEATURES OF INVESTMENT PROJECTS

Long-term investments have three important characteristics:

1. They typically involve a large initial cash outlay, which usually has a long-term impact on the company's profitability. Therefore, this initial cash outlay must be justified on a cost-benefit basis.

2. They generate recurring cash inflows (for example, increased revenues or savings in cash operating expenses). Because much of this income or savings occurs years into the future, managers must consider the time value of money.

3. Income tax factors may be critical in whether a project is cost-effective. Therefore, they must be taken into account in every capital budgeting decision.

MEASURING INVESTMENT WORTH

Several methods of evaluating investment projects are used by financial managers. They include:

1. Payback period
2. Accounting rate of return (ARR)
3. Net present value (NPV)
4. Internal rate of return (IRR)
5. Profitability index (or cost/benefit ratio)

Payback Period

The payback period is the length of time it will take the company to recover its initial investment. It is computed by dividing the initial investment by the cash inflows generated by either increased revenues or cost savings.

EXAMPLE 10-1

Assume:

Cost of investment	$18,000
Annual after-tax cash savings	$3,000

Then, the payback period is:

$$\text{Payback period} = \frac{\text{initial investment}}{\text{cost savings}} = \frac{\$18,000}{\$3,000} = 6 \text{ years}$$

As a rule, it is wiser to choose the project with the shorter payback period. Such projects are less risky and have greater liquidity.

EXAMPLE 10-2

Consider two projects with uneven after-tax cash inflows. Assume each project costs $1,000.

	Cash Inflow	
Year	A($)	B($)
1	100	500
2	200	400
3	300	300
4	400	100
5	500	
6	600	

When cash inflows are not even, you must find the payback period by trial and error. The payback period of project A is ($1,000 = $100 + $200 + $300 + $400), or 4 years. The payback period of project B is ($1,000 = $500 + $400 + $100) :

$$2 \text{ years} + \frac{\$100}{\$300} = 2\frac{1}{3} \text{ years}$$

Project B is the project of choice in this case, since it has the shorter payback period.

The advantages of using the payback period method of evaluating an investment project are that (1) it is simple to compute and easy to understand, and (2) it handles investment risk effectively. The shortcomings of this method are that (1) it does not recognize the time value of money, and (2) it ignores the impact of cash inflows received after the payback period, which determine the project's profitability.

Accounting Rate of Return

Accounting rate of return (ARR) measures profitability by relating either the required investment or the average investment to future annual net income.

As a decision, you should select the project with the higher rate of return.

EXAMPLE 10-3

Consider the following investment:

Initial investment	$6,500
Estimated life	20 years
Cash inflows per year	$1,000
Depreciation per year (using straight-line method)	$325

The accounting rate of return for this project is:

$$\text{ARR} = \frac{\text{net income}}{\text{investment}} = \frac{\$1,000 - \$325}{\$6,500} = 10.4\%$$

If average investment (usually assumed to be one-half the original investment) is used, then:

$$\text{ARR} = \frac{\$1,000 - \$325}{\$3,250} = 20.8\%$$

The advantages of this method are that it is easily understandable and simple to compute and it recognizes the importance of profitability. Its shortcomings are that it fails to recognize the time value of money and that it uses accounting data instead of cash flow data.

Net Present Value

Net present value (NPV) is the excess of the present value (PV) of future cash inflows to be generated by the project over the amount of the initial investment (I):

$$\text{NPV} = \text{PV} - \text{I}$$

The present value of future cash flows is computed using the so-called cost of capital (or minimum required rate of return) as the discount rate. With an annuity, the present value is

$$\text{PV} = \text{A} \cdot \text{T}_4(\text{i}, \text{n})$$

where A is the amount of the annuity. The value of T_4 is found in Table 6-4 in Chapter 6.

If NPV is positive, you should accept the project. If it is not, you should reject it.

EXAMPLE 10-4

Consider the following investment:

Initial investment	$12,950
Estimated life	10 years
Annual cash inflows	$3,000
Cost of capital (minimum required rate of return)	12%

Present value of the cash inflows is:

$$PV = A \cdot T_4(i, n)$$
$$= \$3,000 \cdot T_4(12\%, 10 \text{ years})$$
$$= \$3,000(5.650) \qquad \$16,950$$

Initial investment (I) $\qquad \underline{12,950}$

Net present value (NPV = PV − I) $\quad \$\ 4,000$

Since the NPV of the investment is positive, the investment should be accepted.

The advantages of the NPV method are that it recognizes the time value of money and it is easy to compute, whether the cash flows form an annuity or vary from period to period.

Internal Rate of Return

Internal rate of return (IRR) is defined as that rate of interest that equates the initial investment I with the present value (PV) of future cash inflows. In other words, at IRR,

$$I = PV$$

or

$$NPV = 0$$

Generally, you should accept the project if the IRR exceeds the cost of capital.

EXAMPLE 10-5

Assume the same data given in Example 10-4, and set the following equality (I = PV):

$$\$12,950 = \$3,000 \cdot T_4(i, 10 \text{ years})$$

$$T_4(i, 10 \text{ years}) = \frac{\$12,950}{\$3,000} = 4.317$$

which stands somewhere between 18 percent and 20 percent in the 10-year line of Table 6-4. The interpolation follows:

	PV of an Annuity of $1 Factor T_4 (i,10 years)	
18%	4.494	4.494
IRR	4.317	
20%		4.192
Difference	0.177	0.302

Therefore,

$$\begin{aligned}
\text{IRR} &= 18\% + \frac{0.177}{0.302}(20\% - 18\%) \\
&= 18\% + 0.586(2\%) \\
&= 18\% + 1.17\% \\
&= 19.17\%
\end{aligned}$$

Since the IRR of the investment is greater than the cost of capital (12 percent), you should accept the project.

The advantage of using the IRR method is that it considers the time value of money and therefore is more exact and realistic than the ARR method. However, it is time-consuming to compute, especially when the cash inflows are not even (most business calculators have a program to calculate IRR), and it fails to recognize the different sizes of investment required for competing projects.

When cash inflows are not even, IRR is computed by the trial and error method, which is not discussed here. Many financial calculators have a key for IRR calculations.

CAN A COMPUTER HELP?

Spreadsheet programs can be used in making IRR calculations. For example, Excel has a function IRR(*values, guess*). Excel considers negative numbers as cash outflows such as the initial investment and positive numbers as cash inflows. Many financial calculators have similar features. As in Example 10-5, suppose that you want to calculate the IRR of a $12,950 investment (the value −12950 entered in year 0 that is followed by 10 monthly cash inflows of $3,000. Using a guess of 12 percent (the value of 0.12), which is in effect the cost of capital), your formula would be @IRR(*values,* 0.12) and Excel would return 19.15 percent, as shown here.

Year 0	1	2	3	4	5	6	7	8	9	10
$ (12,950)	3,000	3,000	3,000	3,000	3,000	3,000	3,000	3,000	3,000	3,000

IRR = 19.15%
NPV = $4,000.67

Note: The Excel formula for NPV is NPV (discount rate, cash inflow values) + I, where I is given as a negative number.

Profitability Index

The profitability index is the ratio of the total present value of future cash inflows to the initial investment, that is, PV/I. This index is used as a means of ranking projects in descending order of attractiveness. If the profitability index is greater than 1, then you should accept the project.

EXAMPLE 10-6

Using the data in Example 10-4, the profitability index is

$$\frac{PV}{I} = \frac{\$16,950}{\$12,950} = 1.31$$

Since the project generates $1.31 for each dollar invested (i.e., its profitability index is greater than 1), you should accept the project.

The profitability index has the advantage of putting all projects on the same relative basis regardless of size.

SELECTING THE BEST MIX OF PROJECTS FOR A LIMITED BUDGET

Many companies limit their overall budgets for capital spending. *Capital rationing* is the process of selecting that mix of acceptable projects that provides the highest overall net present value (NPV). The profitability index is widely used in ranking projects competing for limited funds.

EXAMPLE 10-7

A company with a fixed capital spending budget of $250,000 needs to select a mix of acceptable projects from the following:

Projects	I($)	PV($)	NPV($)	Profitability Index	Ranking
A	70,000	112,000	42,000	1.6	1
B	100,000	145,000	45,000	1.45	2
C	110,000	126,500	16,500	1.15	5
D	60,000	79,000	19,000	1.32	3
E	40,000	38,000	−2,000	0.95	6
F	80,000	95,000	15,000	1.19	4

The ranking derived from the profitability index shows that the company should select projects A, B, and D.

	I	PV
A	$70,000	$112,000
B	100,000	145,000
D	60,000	79,000
	$230,000	$336,000

Therefore,

$$NPV = \$336,000 - \$230,000 = \$106,000$$

Zero-one programming, a special case of *linear programming,* is a more general approach to solving capital rationing problems. Here the objective is to select that mix of projects that maximizes the net present value (NPV) subject to a budget constraint. Using the data given in Example 10-7, we can set up the problem as a zero-one programming problem such that

$$x_j = \begin{cases} 1 \text{ if project}_j \text{ is selected} \\ 0 \text{ if project}_j \text{ is not selected} \end{cases}$$

$$(j = 1, 2, 3, 4, 5, 6)$$

The problem then can be formulated as follows:
Maximize

$$\begin{aligned} NPV = \; & \$42,000x_1 + \$45,000x_2 + \$16,500x_3 + \$19,000x_4 \\ & -\$2,000x_5 + \$15,000x_6 \end{aligned}$$

subject to

$$\begin{aligned} \$70,000x_1 + \$100,000x_2 + \$110,000x_3 + \$60,000x_4 \\ +\$40,000x_5 + \$80,000x_6 \leq \$250,000x_j \\ = x_j(j = 1, 2, ..., 6) \end{aligned}$$

Using the zero-one programming solution routine, the solution to the problem is:

$$x_1 = A = 1, \quad x_2 = B = 1, \quad x_4 = D = 1$$

and the NPV is $106,000. Thus, projects A, B, and D should be selected.

The strength of the use of zero-one programming is its ability to handle mutually exclusive and interdependent projects. For further information on this subject, consult an advanced finance textbook.

HANDLING MUTUALLY EXCLUSIVE INVESTMENTS

A mutually exclusive project is one whose acceptance automatically precludes the acceptance of one or more other projects (for example, choosing between two alternative uses of a single plot of land). If you must choose between mutually exclusive investments, you may find that the NPV and IRR methods may result in contradictory indications under certain conditions:

1. If the projects have different life expectancies.
2. If the projects call for different amounts of investment capital.
3. If the projects are expected to yield different cash flows over time-if, for example, the cash flows of one project will increase over time while those of the other will decrease.

The contradictions between the NPV and the IRR methods result from different assumptions concerning the reinvestment rate on cash flows from the projects. The NPV method discounts all cash flows at the cost of capital, thus implicitly assuming that these cash flows can be reinvested at this rate; on the other hand, the IRR method assumes that cash flows are reinvested at the often unrealistic rate specified by the project's internal rate of return. Thus, the implied investment rate differs from project to project.

The relative desirability of mutually exclusive projects depends on the rate of return the subsequent cash flows can earn. The NPV method generally gives correct ranking, since the cost of capital is the more realistic reinvestment rate; the cost of capital usually closely approximates the market rate of return.

EXAMPLE 10-8

Assume the following:

		Cash Flows				
	0	1	2	3	4	5
A	(100)	120				
B	(100)				201.14	

Computing IRR and NPV at 10 percent gives the following different rankings:

	IRR	NPV at 10%
A	20%	9.01
B	15%	24.90

The difference in ranking between the two methods is caused by the methods' reinvestment rate assumptions. The IRR method assumes

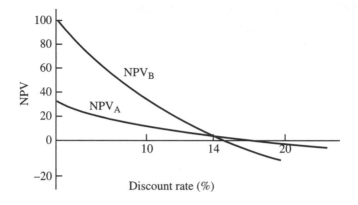

Figure 10.1 *NPV Profiles for Projects A and B*

project A's cash inflow of $120 is reinvested at 20 percent for the subsequent four years; the NPV method assumes $120 is reinvested at 10 percent. The correct decision is to select the project with the higher NPV (that is, Project B), since the NPV method assumes a more realistic reinvestment rate (the cost of capital, 10 percent in this example).

The net present value plotted against various discount rates (costs of capital) results in the NPV profiles for projects A and B (Figure 10.1). An analysis of Figure 10.1 indicates that at a discount rate larger than 14%, A has a higher NPV than B, and should therefore be selected. At a discount rate less than 14%, B has a higher NPV than A and thus should be selected.

THE EFFECT OF INCOME TAXES ON INVESTMENT DECISIONS

Income taxes make a difference in many capital budgeting decisions; often, projects that appear attractive on a before-tax basis have to be rejected when income taxes are factored in. Income taxes typically affect both the amount and the timing of cash flows. Since net income, not cash inflows, is subject to tax, after-tax cash inflows are usually different from after-tax net income. Let us define:

$$S = \text{Sales}$$
$$E = \text{Cash operating expenses}$$
$$d = \text{Depreciation}$$
$$t = \text{Tax rate}$$

Then, before-tax cash inflows (or before-tax *cash savings*) $= S - E$ and net income $= S - E - d$.

By definition,

$$\text{After-tax cash inflows} = \text{Before-tax cash inflows} - \text{Taxes}$$
$$= (S - E) - (S - E - d)(t)$$

Rearranging gives the short-cut formula:

$$\text{After-tax cash inflows} = (S - E)(1 - t) + (d)(t)$$

Depreciation may be deducted from sales when you are computing net income subject to taxes. This reduces the company's income tax payments and thus serves as a tax shield.

$$\text{Tax shield} = \text{Tax savings on depreciation} = (d)(t)$$

EXAMPLE 10-9

Assume:

$$S = \$12,000$$
$$E = \$10,000$$
$$d = \$500 \text{ per year using the straight-line method}$$
$$t = 30\%$$

Then,

After-tax cash inflow
$$= (\$12,000 - \$10,000)(1 - .3) + (\$500)(.3)$$
$$= (\$2,000)(.7) + (\$500)(.3)$$
$$= \$1,400 + \$150$$
$$= \$1,550$$

Tax savings on depreciation
$$= (d)(t)$$
$$= (\$500)(.3)$$
$$= \$150$$

The higher the depreciation deduction, the higher the tax savings on depreciation. Therefore, using an accelerated depreciation method (such as double-declining balance) produces higher initial tax savings than the straight-line method. Accelerated methods produce higher present values for the tax savings, which may make a given investment more attractive.

EXAMPLE 10-10

The Shalimar Company estimates that it can save $2,500 a year in cash operating costs for the next ten years if it buys a special-purpose machine at a cost of $10,000. No salvage value is expected. Assume that the income tax rate is 30 percent and the after-tax cost of capital (minimum required rate of return) is 10 percent. Depreciation by straight-line is $10,000/10 = $1,000$ per year.

$$\text{Before-tax cash savings} = (S - E) = \$2,500$$

Thus,

$$
\begin{aligned}
\text{After-tax cash savings} &= (S - E)(1 - t) + (d)(t) \\
&= \$2,500(1 - .3) + \$1,000(.3) \\
&= \$1,750 + \$300 = \$2,050
\end{aligned}
$$

To see if this machine should be purchased, the net present value can be calculated.

$$\text{PV} = \$2,050 \; T_4(10\%, \; 10 \text{ years}) = \$2,050(6.145) = \$12,597.25$$

Thus,

$$\text{NPV} = \text{PV} - \text{I} = \$12,597.25 - \$10,000 = \$2,597.25$$

Since NPV is positive, the machine should be bought.

DEPRECIATION METHODS

The most commonly used depreciation methods are the straight-line method and two accelerated methods, sum-of-the-years'-digits (SYD) and the double-declining-balance (DDB).

Straight-Line Method

The easiest and most popular method of calculating depreciation, straight-line depreciation results in equal periodic depreciation deductions. This method is most appropriate when an asset's use is uniform from period to period, as is the case with furniture. The annual depreciation expense is calculated by using the following formula:

$$\text{Depreciation expense} = \frac{\text{Cost} - \text{salvage value}}{\text{number of years of useful life}}$$

EXAMPLE 10-11

An auto is purchased for $20,000 and has an expected salvage value of $2,000. The auto's estimated life is eight years. Its annual depreciation is calculated as follows:

$$\text{Depreciation expense} = \frac{\text{Cost} - \text{salvage value}}{\text{number of years of useful life}}$$

$$= \frac{\$20,000 - \$2,000}{8 \text{ years}}$$

$$= \$2,250/\text{year}$$

An alternative means of computation is to multiply the depreciable cost ($18,000) by the annual depreciation rate, which is 12.5 percent in this example. The annual rate is calculated by dividing the number of years of useful life into one (1/8 = 12.5%). The result is the same: $18,000 × 12.5% = $2,250.

Sum-of-the-Years'-Digits Method

This method uses a ratio in which the numerator is the number of years of life expectancy in reverse order, and the denominator is the sum of the digits. For example, if the life expectancy of a machine is eight years, write the numbers in reverse order: 8, 7, 6, 5, 4, 3, 2, 1. The sum of these digits is 36, or (8 + 7 + 6 + 5 + 4 + 3 + 2 + 1). Thus, the fraction for the first year is 8/36, while the fraction for the last year is 1/36. The sum of the eight fractions equals 36/36, or 1. Therefore, at the end of eight years, the machine is written down to its salvage value.

The following formula may be used to find the sum-of-the-years'-digits (S) quickly:

$$S = \frac{(N)(N + 1)}{2}$$

where N represents the number of years of expected life.

EXAMPLE 10-12

In Example 10-11, the depreciable cost is $18,000 ($20,000 − $2,000). Using the SYD method, the computation for each year's depreciation expense is

$$S = \frac{(N)(N + 1)}{2} = \frac{8(9)}{2} = \frac{72}{2} = 36$$

Year	Fraction ×	Depreciation Amount ($) =	Depreciation Expense
1	8/36	$18,000	$4,000
2	7/36	18,000	3,500
3	6/36	18,000	3,000
4	5/36	18,000	2,500
5	4/36	18,000	2,000
6	3/36	18,000	1,500
7	2/36	18,000	1,000
8	1/36	18,000	500
Total			$18,000

Double-Declining-Balance Method

In the double-declining-balance method, depreciation expense is highest in the early years of the asset's life and decreases in the later years. First, you determine a depreciation rate by doubling the straight-line rate. For example, if an asset has a life of 10 years, the straight-line depreciation rate is 1/10 or 10 percent, whereas the double-declining rate is 20 percent. Second, you calculate depreciation expense by multiplying the depreciation rate by the book value of the asset at the beginning of each year. Since book value declines over time, the depreciation expense decreases each successive period.

This method ignores salvage value. However, the book value of the fixed asset at the end of its useful life cannot be below its salvage value.

EXAMPLE 10-13

Assume the data in Example 10-11. Since the straight-line rate is 12.5 percent (1/8), the double-declining-balance rate is 25 percent (2 × 12.5%). The depreciation expense is computed as follows:

Year	Book Value at Beginning of Year	× Rate (%) =	Depreciation Expense	Year-end Book Value
1	$20,000	25%	$5,000	$15,000
2	15,000	25	3,750	11,250
3	11,250	25	2,813	8,437
4	8,437	25	2,109	6,328
5	6,328	25	1,582	4,746
6	4,746	25	1,187	3,559
7	3,559	25	890	2,669
8	2,669	25	667	2,002

If the original estimated salvage value had been $2,100, the depreciation expense for the eighth year would have been $569 ($2,669 − $2,100) rather than $667, since the asset cannot be depreciated below its salvage value.

Capital Budgeting Decisions and the Modified Accelerated Cost Recovery System

Although the traditional depreciation methods still can be used for computing depreciation for book purposes, 1981 saw a new way of computing depreciation deductions for tax purposes. The current rule is called the Modified Accelerated Cost Recovery System (MACRS) rule, as enacted by Congress in 1981 and then modified somewhat in 1986 under the Tax Reform Act of 1986. This rule is characterized as follows:

1. It abandons the concept of useful life and accelerates depreciation deductions by placing all depreciable assets into one of eight age property classes. It calculates deductions, based on an allowable percentage of the asset's original cost (see Tables 10-1 and 10-2).

    With a shorter asset tax life than useful life, the company would be able to deduct depreciation more quickly and save more in income taxes in the earlier years, thereby making an investment more attractive. The rationale behind the system is that this way the government encourages the company to invest in facilities and increase its productive capacity and efficiency. (Remember that the higher the d, the larger the tax shield (d)(t).)

2. Since the allowable percentages in Table 10-1 add up to 100 percent, there is no need to consider the salvage value of an asset when computing depreciation.

3. The company may elect the straight-line method. The straight-line convention must follow what is called the half-year convention. This means that the company can deduct only half of the regular straight-line depreciation amount in the first year. The reason for electing to use the MACRS optional straight-line method is that some firms may prefer to stretch out depreciation deductions using the straight-line method rather than to accelerate them. Those firms are the ones that just start out or have little or no income and wish to show more income on their income statements.

EXAMPLE 10-14

Assume that a machine falls under a three-year property class and costs $3,000 initially. The straight-line option under MACRS differs from the traditional straight-line method in that under this method the company would deduct only $500 depreciation in the first and fourth years ($3,000/3 years = $1,000; $1,000/2 = $500). The following table compares straight-line with half-year convention with MACRS.

ℓ Year	Straight-line (half-year) Depreciation	Cost	MACRS %	MACRS Deduction
1	$ 500	$3,000 ×	33.3%	$ 999
2	1,000	3,000 ×	44.5	1,335
3	1,000	3,000 ×	14.8	444
4	500	3,000 ×	7.4	222
	$3,000			$3,000

EXAMPLE 10-15

A machine costs $10,000. Annual cash inflows are expected to be $5,000. The machine will be depreciated using the MACRS rule and will fall under the 3-year property class. The cost of capital after taxes is 10%. The estimated life of the machine is 4 years. The salvage value of the machine at the end of the fourth year is expected to be $1,200. The tax rate is 30%.

The formula for computation of after-tax cash inflows $(S - E)(1 - t) + (d)(t)$ needs to be computed separately. The NPV analysis can be performed as follows:

	Present Value Factor @ 10%	Present Value
Initial investment: $10,000	1.000	$(10,000.00)
$\dfrac{(S - E)(1 - t)}{\$5,000(1 - .3)}$:		
= $3,500 for 4 years	3.170*	$11,095.00

* T_4 (10%, 4 years) = 3.170 (from Table 6-4).

(d)(t): Year	Cost	MACRS %	d	(d)(t)	Present Value @ 10%	Present Value
1	$10,000 ×	33.3%	$3,330	$ 999	.909[†]	908.09
2	$10,000 ×	44.5	4,450	1,335	.826[†]	1,102.71
3	$10,000 ×	14.8	1,480	444	.751[†]	333.44
4	$10,000 ×	7.4	740	222	.683[†]	151.63

Salvage value:	Present Value @ 10%	Present Value
$1,200 in year 4:		
$1,200 (1 − .3) = 840[‡]	.683[†]	573.72
Net present value (NPV)		$4,164.59

[†] T_3 values obtained from Table 6-3.

[‡] Any salvage value received under the MACRS rules is a *taxable gain* (the excess of the selling price over book value, $1,200 in this example), since the book value will be zero at the end of the life of the machine.

Since $NPV = PV - I = \$4,164.59$ is positive, the machine should be bought.

CHAPTER PERSPECTIVE

In this chapter, we have examined the process of evaluating investment projects. We have discussed five commonly used criteria for evaluating capital budgeting projects, including the net present value (NPV) and internal rate of return (IRR) methods. The problems that arise with mutually exclusive investments and capital rationing were addressed. Since income taxes often make a difference in whether a project is accepted, we examined the role of factors in financial decisions.

Although the traditional depreciation methods still can be used for computing depreciation for book purposes, since 1981 a new rule, called the Modified Accelerated Cost Recovery System (MACRS), has been available to businesses. The use of MACRS and an overview of the traditional depreciation methods were presented.

TABLE 10-1

MODIFIED ACCELERATED COST RECOVERY
SYSTEM CLASSIFICATION OF ASSETS

Property class

Year	3-year	5-year	7-year	10-year	15-year	20-year
1	33.3%	20.0%	14.3%	10.0%	5.0%	3.8%
2	44.5	32.0	24.5	18.0	9.5	7.2
3	14.8*	19.2	17.5	14.4	8.6	6.7
4	7.4	11.5*	12.5	11.5	7.7	6.2
5		11.5	8.9*	9.2	6.9	5.7
6		5.8	8.9	7.4	6.2	5.3
7			8.9	6.6*	5.9*	4.9
8			4.5	6.6	5.9	4.5*
9				6.5	5.9	4.5
10				6.5	5.9	4.5
11				3.3	5.9	4.5
12					5.9	4.5
13					5.9	4.5
14					5.9	4.5
15					5.9	4.5
16					3.0	4.4
17						4.4
18						4.4
19						4.4
20						4.4
21						2.2
Total	100.0%	100.0%	100.0%	100.0%	100.0%	100.0%

* Denotes the year of changeover to straight-line depreciation.

TABLE 10-2

MACRS TABLES BY PROPERTY CLASS

Property class

MACRS Property Class and Depreciation Method	Useful Life (ADR Midpoint Life*)	Examples of Assets
3-year property 200% declining balance	4 years or less	Most small tools are included; the law specifically *excludes* autos and light trucks from this property class.
5-year property 200% declining balance	More than 4 years to less than 10 years	Autos and light trucks, computers, typewriters, copiers, duplicating equipment, heavy general-purpose trucks, and research and experimentation equipment are included.
7-year property 200% declining balance	10 years or more to less than 16 years	Office furniture and fixtures and most items of machinery and equipment used in production are included.
10-year property 200% declining balance	16 years or more to less than 20 years	Various machinery and equipment, such as that used in petroleum distilling and refining and in the milling of grain, are included.
15-year property 150% declining balance	20 years or more to less than 25 years	Sewage treatment plants, telephone and electrical distribution facilities, and land improvements are included.
20-year property 150% declining balance	25 years or more	Service stations and other real property with an ADR midpoint life of less than 27.5 years are included.
27.5-year property Straight-line	Not applicable	All residential rental property is included.
31.5-year property Straight-line	Not applicable	All nonresidential real property is included.

---

* The term *ADR midpoint life* means the "useful life" of an asset in a business sense; the appropriate ADR midpoint lives for assets are designated in the tax *Regulations*.

Leverage and Capital Structure

INTRODUCTION AND MAIN POINTS

In Chapter 8 we developed an understanding of how securities are valued in the marketplace, and then, in Chapter 9, we presented various ways to measure the cost of funds to the company. The concepts to be covered in this chapter relate closely to those discussions of the valuation process and the cost of capital and extend to the crucial problem of determining the company's optimal capital structure. First, we discuss the concept of leverage and how it impacts on the company's profits; we then discuss how to build an appropriate financing mix.

Leverage is that portion of a company's fixed costs that represent a risk to the firm. Operating leverage, a measure of operating risk, refers to the fixed operating costs found in the income statement. Financial leverage, a measure of financial risk, refers to a long-term financing with fixed financing charges, of the company's assets. The higher the financial leverage, the higher the financial risk and therefore the higher the cost of capital. The optimal capital structure for any company depends to a great extent on the amount of leverage the company can tolerate and the resultant cost of capital.

In this chapter you will learn:

■ The basics of break-even analysis and operating leverage and how they relate to each other.

■ How to measure operating leverage and financial leverage and distinguish between them.

■ How to apply the EBIT-EPS approach to evaluate alternative financing plans.

■ How to determine the best capital structure.

BREAK-EVEN ANALYSIS, OPERATING LEVERAGE, AND FINANCIAL LEVERAGE

Break-even analysis, which is closely related to operating leverage, determines break-even sales—the financial crossover point at which revenues exactly match costs. Although this analysis does not show up in corporate earnings reports, financial officers find it an extremely useful measurement. Let us define:

$$S = \text{Sales (\$)}$$
$$x = \text{Sales volume in units}$$
$$p = \text{Selling price per unit}$$
$$v = \text{Unit variable cost}$$
$$VC = \text{Variable operating costs}$$
$$FC = \text{Fixed operating costs}$$

We also note the following important concepts.

■ *Contribution margin (CM)*—the excess of sales (S) over the variable costs (VC) of the product. It is the amount of money available to cover fixed costs (FC) and to generate profits. Symbolically, CM = S − VC.

■ *Unit CM*—the excess of the unit selling price (p) over the unit variable cost (v). Symbolically, unit CM = p − v.

EXAMPLE 11-1

To illustrate these concepts, consider the following data for company Z:

	Total	Per Unit	Percentage
Sales (1,500 units)	$37,500	$25	100%
Less: Variable costs	15,000	10	40
Contribution margin	$22,500	$15	60%
Less: Fixed costs	15,000		
Net income	$7,500		

From the data listed above, CM and unit CM are computed as:

$$CM = S - VC = \$37,500 - \$15,000 = \$22,500$$
$$\text{Unit CM} = p - v = \$25 - \$10 = \$15$$

Break-Even Point

The break-even point represents the level of sales revenue that equals the total of the variable and fixed costs for a given volume of output at a particular capacity use rate. Generally, the lower the break-even point, the higher the profits and the less the operating risk, other things being equal. You can determine the break-even point by setting sales just equal to the total of the variable costs plus the fixed costs:

$$S = VC + FC$$
$$px = vx + FC$$
$$(p - v)x = FC$$
$$x = \frac{FC}{(p - v)}$$

That is,

$$\text{Break-even point in units} = \frac{\text{Fixed costs}}{\text{Unit CM}}$$

EXAMPLE 11-2

Using the data from Example 11-1, in which unit CM $= \$25 - \$10 = \$15$, we get:

Break-even point in units $= \$15,000/\$15 = 1,000$ units
Break-even point in dollars $= 1,000$ units $\times \$25 = \$25,000$

Cash Break-Even Point

If a company has a small amount of available cash or if the opportunity cost of holding excess cash is too high, management may want to know the volume of sales necessary to cover all cash expenses during a period. This is known as the cash break-even point. Not all fixed operating costs involve cash payments; for example, depreciation expenses are noncash fixed charges. To find the cash break-even point, you must subtract noncash charges from fixed costs. As a result, the cash break-even point is usually lower than the break-even point. The formula is:

$$\text{Cash break-even point} = \frac{\text{Fixed costs} - \text{depreciation}}{\text{Unit CM}}$$

EXAMPLE 11-3

Assume from Example 11-1 that the total fixed costs of $15,000 include depreciation of $1,500. The cash break-even point is:

$$\frac{\$15,000 - \$1,500}{\$25 - \$10} = \frac{\$13,500}{\$15} = 900$$

Company Z has to sell 900 units to cover only its fixed cash costs of $13,500.

Operating Leverage Operating leverage, a measure of operating risk, arises from the company's use of fixed operating costs. A simple indication of operating leverage is the impact of a change in sales on earnings before interest and taxes (EBIT). The formula is:

$$\text{Operating leverage at a given level of sales (x)} = \frac{\text{Percent change in EBIT}}{\text{Percentage change in sales}}$$

$$= \frac{(p - v)x}{(p - v)x - FC}$$

where EBIT = Earnings before interest and taxes

= $(p - v)x - FC$

EXAMPLE 11-4

The Wayne Company manufactures and sells doors to home builders. The doors are sold for $25 each. Variable costs are $15 per door, and fixed operating costs total $50,000. Assume further that the Wayne Company is currently selling 6,000 doors per year. Its operating leverage is:

$$\frac{(p - v)x}{(p - v)x - FC} = \frac{(\$25 - \$15)(6,000)}{(\$25 - \$15)(6,000) - \$50,000}$$

$$= \frac{\$60,000}{10,000}$$

$$= 6$$

which means if sales increase by 10 percent, the company can expect its net income to increase by six times that amount, or 60 percent.

It's important to note that all types of leverage are two-edged swords. When sales decrease by some percentage, the impact on EBIT of that decrease will be an even larger percentage decline.

Financial Leverage

Financial leverage is a measure of financial risk that arises from the presence of debt and/or preferred stock in the company's capital structure. One way to measure financial leverage is to determine how earnings per share (EPS) is affected by a change in EBIT. When financial leverage is used, changes in EBIT translate into larger changes in EPS. If EBIT falls, a financially leveraged company will experience negative changes in EPS that are larger than the relative decline in EBIT. Again, leverage is a two-edged sword.

$$\text{Financial leverage at a given level of sales (x)} = \frac{\text{Percent change in EPS}}{\text{Percentage change in EBIT}}$$

$$= \frac{(p - v)x - FC}{(p - v)x - FC - I}$$

where EPS is earnings per share and I is fixed finance charges, such as interest expense or preferred stock dividends. [Preferred stock dividend must be adjusted for taxes, i.e., preferred stock dividend divided by $(1 - t)$.]

EXAMPLE 11-5

Using the data in Example 11-4, the Wayne Company has total financial charges of $2,000, half in interest expense and half in preferred stock dividends. The corporate tax rate is 40 percent. First, the fixed financial charges are:

$$I = \$1,000 + \frac{\$1,000}{(1 - 0.4)} = \$1,000 + \$1,667 = \$2,667$$

Therefore, Wayne's financial leverage is computed as follows:

$$\frac{(p - v)x - FC}{(p - v)x - FC - I} = \frac{(\$25 - \$15)(6,000) - \$50,000}{(\$25 - \$15)(6,000) - \$50,000 - \$2,667}$$

$$= \frac{\$10,000}{\$7,333}$$

$$= 1.36$$

which means that if EBIT increases by 10 percent, Wayne can expect its EPS to increase by 1.36 times, or by 13.6 percent.

Total Leverage

Total leverage is a measure of total risk. To measure total leverage, determine how EPS is affected by a change in sales.

$$\text{Total leverage at a given level of sales (x)} = \frac{\text{Percent in change in EPS}}{\text{Percent in change in sales}}$$

$$= \text{Operating leverage} \times \text{Financial leverage}$$

$$= \frac{(p - v)x}{(p - v)x - FC} \cdot \frac{(p - v)x - FC}{(p - v)x - FC - I}$$

$$= \frac{(p - v)x}{(p - v)x - FC - I}$$

EXAMPLE 11-6

From Examples 11-4 and 11-5, the total leverage for Wayne Company is:

$$\text{Operating leverage} \times \text{Financial leverage} = 6 \times 1.36 = 8.16$$

or

$$\frac{(p-v)x}{(p-v)x - FC - I} = \frac{(\$25 - \$15)(6,000)}{(\$25 - \$15)(6,000) - \$50,000 - \$2,667}$$

$$= \frac{\$60,000}{\$7,333}$$

$$= 8.16 \text{ (due to rounding error)}$$

TOOLS OF CAPITAL STRUCTURE MANAGEMENT

Capital structure management, which is closely related to cost of capital, is the mix of long-term funding sources used by the company. Its primary objective is to maximize the market value of the company. This mix, called the *optimal capital structure,* minimizes the overall cost of capital. However, not all financial managers believe that an optimal capital structure actually exists. Disputes over this question center on whether a business can, in reality, affect its valuation and its cost of capital by varying the mixture of the funds it uses.

The decision to use debt and/or preferred stock in capitalization results in two types of financial leverage effects. The first effect is an increased risk to earnings per share (EPS) caused by the use of fixed financial obligations. The second effect relates to the level of EPS at a given EBIT under a specific capital structure. *EBIT-EPS analysis* is used to measure this second effect.

EBIT-EPS Approach to Capital Structure Decisions

EBIT-EPS analysis is a practical tool that enables financial managers to evaluate alternative financing plans by investigating their effect on EPS for a range of EBIT levels. Its primary objective is to determine the EBIT break-even, or indifference, points at which the EPS will be the same regardless of the financing plan chosen by the financial manager.

This indifference point has major implications for capital structure decisions. At EBIT amounts in excess of the EBIT indifference level, a more heavily leveraged financing plan will generate a higher EPS. At EBIT amounts below the EBIT indifference level, however, the financing plan involving the least leverage will generate a higher EPS. Therefore, it is of critical importance for the financial manager to know the EBIT indifference level.

The indifference points between any two methods of financing can be determined by solving for EBIT in the following equation:

$$\frac{(EBIT - I)(1 - t) - PD}{S_1} = \frac{(EBIT - I)(1 - t) - PD}{S_2}$$

where

t = tax rate
PD = preferred stock dividends
S_1 and S_2 = number of shares of common stock outstanding after financing for plan 1 and plan 2, respectively.

EXAMPLE 11-7

Assume that ABC Company, with long-term capitalization consisting entirely of $5 million in stock, wants to raise $2 million for the acquisition of special equipment by (1) selling 40,000 shares of common stock at $50 each, (2) selling bonds at 10 percent interest, or (3) issuing preferred stock with an 8 percent dividend. The present EBIT is $800,000, the income tax rate is 50 percent, and 100,000 shares of common stock are now outstanding. To compute the indifference points, begin by calculating EPS at a projected EBIT level of $1 million.

	All Common	All Debt	All Preferred
EBIT	$1,000,000	$1,000,000	$1,000,000
Interest		200,000	
Earnings before taxes (EBT)	$1,000,000	$ 800,000	$1,000,000
Taxes	500,000	400,000	500,000
Earnings after taxes (EAT)	$ 500,000	$ 400,000	$ 500,000
Preferred stock dividend			160,000
Earnings available to common stockholders	$ 500,000	$ 400,000	$ 340,000
Number of shares	140,000	100,000	100,000
EPS	$3.57	$4.00	$3.40

Using Figure 11.1 as a model, connect the EPSs at the level of EBIT of $1 million with the EBITs for each financing alternative on the horizontal axis to obtain the EPS-EBIT graphs. Plot the EBIT necessary

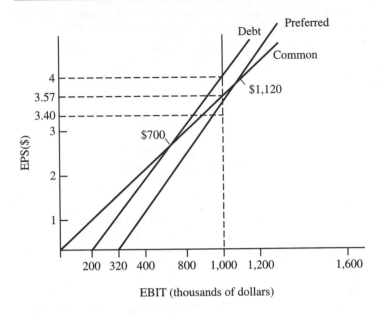

Figure 11.1 *EPS-EBIT Graph*

to cover all fixed financial costs for each financing alternative on the horizontal axis. The common stock plan has no fixed costs, so the intercept on the horizontal axis is zero. The debt plan calls for an EBIT of $200,000 to cover interest charges, so the horizontal axis intercept is at that point. The preferred stock plan requires an EBIT of $320,000 [$160,000/(1 − 0.5)] to cover $160,000 in preferred stock dividends at a 50 percent income tax rate; so $320,000 becomes the horizontal axis intercept. (See Figure 11.1.)

In this example, the indifference point between all common and all debt is:

$$\frac{(EBIT - I)(1 - t) - PD}{S_1} = \frac{(EBIT - I)(1 - t) - PD}{S_2}$$

$$\frac{(EBIT - 0)(1 - 0.5) - 0}{140,000} = \frac{(EBIT - 200,000)(1 - 0.5) - 0}{100,000}$$

Rearranging yields:

$$0.5(\text{EBIT})(100,000) = 0.5(\text{EBIT})(140,000)$$
$$-0.5(200,000)(140,000)$$
$$20,000 \text{ EBIT} = 14,000,000,000$$
$$\text{EBIT} = \$700,000$$

Similarly, the indifference point between all common and all preferred would be:

$$\frac{(\text{EBIT} - I)(1 - t) - PD}{S_1} = \frac{(\text{EBIT} - I)(1 - t) - PD}{S_2}$$
$$\frac{(\text{EBIT} - 0)(1 - 0.5) - 0}{140,000} = \frac{(\text{EBIT} - 0)(1 - 0.5) - 160,000}{100,000}$$

Rearranging yields:

$$0.5(\text{EBIT})(100,000) = 0.5(\text{EBIT})(140,000) - 160,000(140,000)$$
$$20,000 \text{EBIT} = 22,400,000,000$$
$$\text{EBIT} = \$1,120,000$$

Based on the preceding computations and observing Figure 11.1 we can draw the following conclusions.

1. At any level of EBIT, debt is better than preferred stock, since it gives a higher EPS.
2. At a level of EBIT above $700,000, debt is better than common stock. If EBIT is below $700,000, the reverse is true.
3. At a level of EBIT above $1,120,000, preferred stock is better than common. At or below that point, the reverse is true.

Financial leverage can magnify profits, but it can also increase losses. The EBIT-EPS approach helps financial managers examine the impact of financial leverage as a financing method.

Analysis of Corporate Cash Flows

A second tool of capital structure management is the *analysis of cash flows*. When considering the appropriate capital structure, it is important to analyze the company's cash flow in order to determine its ability to service fixed charges. The greater the dollar amount of debt and/or preferred stock the company issues and the shorter their maturity, the greater the fixed charges the company will have to bear. These charges include principal and interest payments on debt, lease payments, and preferred stock dividends. Before assuming additional fixed charges that will require cash outlays, the company should analyze its expected future cash flows, because the inability to meet these future charges, with the exception of preferred stock dividends, may result in insolvency. The greater and more stable the expected future cash flows of the company, the greater its debt capacity.

Coverage Ratios

A third tool for capital structure management is the calculation of *comparative coverage ratios*. Among the ways to gain insight into the debt capacity of a business is through the use of coverage ratios, which were introduced in Chapter 3. In the computation of these ratios, a corporate financial officer typically uses EBIT as a rough measure of the cash flow available to cover debt-servicing obligations. Perhaps the most widely used coverage ratio is *times interest earned,* which is simply:

$$\text{Times interest earned} = \frac{\text{EBIT}}{\text{Interest on debt}}$$

Assume that the most recent annual EBIT for a company was $4 million and that interest payments on all debt obligations were $1 million. Therefore, times interest earned would be four times. This indicates that even if EBIT drops by as much as 75 percent, the company will still be able to cover its interest payments out of earnings. However, a coverage of ratio of only 1.0 indicates that earnings are just sufficient to satisfy the interest burden. While it is difficult to generalize as to what is an appropriate interest coverage ratio, a financial officer usually is concerned when the ratio gets much below 3:1. However, the standard for this ratio can vary. In a highly stable industry, a relatively low times-interest-earned ratio may be acceptable, whereas it is not appropriate in a highly cyclical one.

Unfortunately, the times-interest-earned ratio reveals nothing about the company's ability to meet principal payments on its debt. The inability to meet a principal payment constitutes the same legal default as failure to meet an interest payment. Therefore, it is useful to compute the coverage ratio for the full debt-service burden. This ratio is

$$\text{Debt-service coverage} = \frac{\text{EBIT}}{\text{Interest} + \dfrac{\text{Principal payments}}{1 - \text{Tax rate}}}$$

Because EBIT represents earnings before taxes, principal payments are adjusted upward to compensate for the tax effect. Principal payments are not tax deductible; they must be paid out of after-tax earnings. Therefore, you should adjust principal payments so that they are consistent with EBIT. If EBIT equals $4 million, interest equals $1 million, principal payments equal $1.5 million, and the tax rate is 34 percent, the debt-service coverage ratio would be

$$\text{Debt-service coverage} = \frac{\$4 \text{ million}}{\$1 \text{ million} + \dfrac{\$1.5 \text{ million}}{1 - .34}} = 1.22$$

A coverage ratio of 1.22 means that EBIT can fall by only 22% before earnings coverage become insufficient to service the debt. Obviously, the closer the ratio is to 1.0, the worst things are, all other things being equal. However, even with a coverage ratio of less than 1.0, a company may still meet its obligations if it can refinance some of its debt when it comes due.

The financial risk associated with leverage should be analyzed on the basis of the company's ability to service total fixed charges. While lease financing is not debt per se, it has exactly the same impact on cash flows as the payment of interest and principal on a debt obligation. Therefore, annual lease payments should be added to the denominator of the formula in order to reflect the total cash-flow burden.

Coverage ratios can be used for two types of comparison. First, they can be compared with past and expected future ratios for the same company in order to determine if there has been an improvement or a deterioration in coverage over time. A second method for analyzing a company's capital structure is to evaluate the capital structure of other companies in the same industry. If a company is contemplating a capital structure that is significantly out of line with that of similar companies, potential investors will quickly notice the disparity. This is not to say, however, that the company's decision is wrong; other companies in the industry may be too conservative in their use of debt. The optimal capital structure for all companies in the industry may allow a higher proportion of debt to equity than the actual industry average; as a result, the company may well be able to justify more debt than the industry average. Because investment analysts and creditors tend to evaluate companies by industry, however, it should be able to justify its position if its capital structure is noticeably out of line in either direction.

Ultimately, financial officers want to be able to make generalizations about the appropriate amount of debt (and leases) for a company. Because, over the long run, the source of funds with which to service debt is earnings, coverage ratios are an important analytical tool. However, they are subject to certain limitations and consequently cannot be used as the sole means for determining the capital structure. For one thing, the fact that EBIT falls below the debt-service burden does not spell immediate doom for the company; often, alternative sources of funds, including renewal of a loan, are available, and these sources must be considered.

MAKING CAPITAL STRUCTURE DECISIONS IN PRACTICE

How do companies decide in practice which route to follow in raising capital? The decision is complex and is related to a company's balance sheet, market conditions, outstanding obligations, and a host of other factors.

Many financial managers believe that the following factors influence capital structure:

1. Growth rate and stability of future sales
2. Competitive structure in the industry
3. Asset makeup of the individual firm
4. The business risk to which the firm is exposed
5. Control status of owners and management
6. Lenders' attitudes toward the industry and the company

Surveys indicate that the majority of financial managers in large firms believe in the concept of an optimal capital structure, approximated by target debt ratios. The most frequently mentioned factor that affects the level of the target debt ratio is the company's ability to service fixed financing costs; other factors include (1) maintaining a desired bond rating, (2) providing an adequate borrowing reserve, and (3) exploiting the advantages of financial leverage.

CHAPTER PERSPECTIVE

The chapter discussed the process of arriving at an appropriate capital structure for the firm. Tools that can assist financial officers in this task were examined. We first discussed assessing the variability in earnings per share induced by operating leverage and financial leverage. This assessment built upon the principles of break-even analysis.

In deciding upon an appropriate capital structure, financial managers should consider a number of factors, including the relationship between earnings before interest and taxes and earnings per share for alternative methods of financing. In addition, the financial manager can learn much from a comparison of capital structure ratios and coverage ratios (such as times interest earned and debt-service coverage) for similar companies and over time for the company in question.

Using Working Capital Management Effectively

INTRODUCTION AND MAIN POINTS

Effective management of working capital (current assets less current liabilities) improves returns and minimizes the risk that the company will run short of cash. By optimally managing cash, receivables, and inventory, a company can maximize its rate of return and minimize its liquidity and business risk. The amount invested in each current asset may change daily and should be monitored carefully to ensure that funds are used in the most productive way possible. Large account balances may also indicate risk; for example, inventory may not be salable and/or accounts receivable may not be collectible. On the other hand, maintaining inadequate current asset levels may be costly; business may be lost if inventory is too low.

Cash refers to currency and demand deposits; excess funds may be invested in marketable securities. Cash management involves accelerating cash inflow and delaying cash outflow. Accounts receivable management involves selecting customers with good credit standing and speeding up customer collections. Inventory management involves having the optimal order size at the right time.

In this chapter, you will learn:
- How to accelerate cash receipts.
- How to delay cash payments.
- How to determine an optimal cash balance.
- The types of marketable securities.
- How to manage accounts receivable.
- What credit and discount policies may be advisable.
- How to manage inventory.
- Computing the carrying cost and ordering cost of inventory.
- How to determine how much inventory to order each time and when to order it.

EVALUATING WORKING CAPITAL

Working capital equals current assets less current liabilities. If current assets are $6,500,000 and current liabilities are $4,000,000, working capital equals $2,500,000. Managing working capital—regulating the various types of current assets and current liabilities—requires making decisions on how assets should be financed (e.g., by short-term debt, long-term debt, or equity); net working capital increases when current assets are financed through noncurrent sources.

Managing working capital is also evaluating the trade-off between return and risk. If funds are transferred from fixed assets to current assets, liquidity risk is reduced, greater ability to obtain short-term financing is enhanced, and the company has greater flexibility in adjusting current assets to meet changes in sales volume. However, it also receives reduced return, because the yield on fixed assets exceeds that of current assets. Financing with noncurrent debt carries less liquidity risk than financing with current debt because the former is payable over a longer time period. However, long-term debt often has a higher cost than short-term debt because of its greater uncertainty.

Liquidity risk may be reduced by using the *hedging* approach to financing, in which assets are financed by liabilities with similar maturity. When a company needs funds to purchase seasonal or cyclical inventory, it uses short-term financing, which gives it flexibility to meet its seasonal needs within its ability to repay the loan. On the other hand, the company's permanent assets should be financed with long-term debt. Because the assets last longer, the financing can be spread over a longer time, helping to ensure the availability of adequate funds with which to meet debt payments.

The less time it takes between purchase and delivery of goods, the less working capital is needed. For example, if the company can receive a raw material in two weeks, it can maintain a lower level of inventory than if two months' lead time is required. You should purchase material early if by doing so you can pay significantly lower prices and if the material's cost savings exceed inventory carrying costs.

CASH MANAGEMENT

The goal of cash management is to invest excess cash for a return and at the same time have adequate liquidity. A proper cash balance, neither excessive nor deficient, should exist; for example, companies with many bank accounts may be accumulating excessive balances. Proper cash forecasting is particularly crucial in a recession and is required to determine (1) the optimal time to incur and pay back debt and (2) the amount to transfer daily between accounts. A daily computerized listing of cash balances and transactions reporting can let you know the up-to-date cash balance so you can decide how best to use the funds. You should also assess the costs you are paying for banking services, looking at each account's cost.

When cash receipts and cash payments are highly synchronized and predictable, your company may keep a smaller cash balance; if quick liquidity is needed, it can invest in marketable securities. Any additional cash should be invested in income-producing securities with maturities structured to provide the necessary liquidity.

Financially strong companies that are able to borrow at favorable rates, even in difficult financial markets, can afford to keep a lower level of cash than companies that are highly leveraged or considered poor credit risks.

At a minimum, a company should hold in cash the greater of (1) compensating balances (deposits held by a bank to compensate it for providing services) or (2) precautionary balances (money held for emergency purposes) plus transaction balances (money to cover checks outstanding). It must also hold enough cash to meet its daily requirements.

A number of factors go into the decision on how much cash to hold, including the company's liquid assets, business risk, debt levels and maturity dates, ability to borrow on short notice and on favorable terms, and rate of return; economic conditions; and the possibility of unexpected problems, such as customer defaults.

Acceleration of Cash Inflow

To improve cash inflow, you should evaluate the causes of and take corrective action for delays in having cash receipts deposited. Ascertain the origin of cash receipts, how they are delivered, and how cash is transferred from outlying accounts to the main corporate account. Also investigate banking policy regarding availability of funds and the length of time lag between when a check is received and when it is deposited.

The types of delays in processing checks are: (1) "mail float," the time required for a check to move from debtor to creditor; (2) "processing float," the time needed for the creditor to enter the payment; and (3) "deposit collection float," the time it takes for a check to clear.

Figure 12.1 depicts the total float of a check.

You should try out all possible ways to accelerate cash receipts including the use of lockboxes, return envelopes, pre-authorized debits (PADs), wire transfers, and depository transfer checks.

■ *Lockbox.* A lockbox represents a way to place the optimum collection point near customers. Customer payments are mailed to strategic

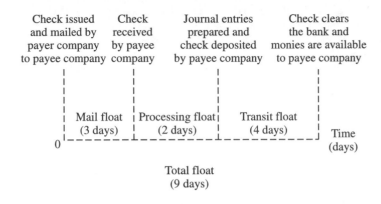

Figure 12.1 *Float on a Check Issued and Mailed by Payer to Payee*

post office boxes geographically situated to reduce mailing and depositing time. Banks make collections from these boxes several times a day and deposit the funds to the corporate account. They then prepare a computer listing of payments received by account and a daily total, which is forwarded to the corporation.

To determine the effectiveness of using a lockbox, you should determine the average face value of checks received, the cost of operations eliminated, reducible processing overhead, and the reduction in "mail float" days. Because per-item processing costs for lockboxes is typically significant, it makes the most sense to use one for low-volume, high-dollar collections. However, businesses with high-volume, low-dollar receipts are using them more and more as technological advances lower their per-item cost.

Wholesale lockboxes are used for checks received from other *companies*. As a rule, the average dollar cash receipts are large, and the number of cash receipts is small. Many wholesale lockboxes result in mail time reductions of no more than one business day and check-clearing time reductions of only a few tenths of one day. They are therefore most useful for companies that have gross revenues of at least several million dollars and that receive large checks from distant customers.

A *retail lockbox* is the best choice if the company deals with the *public* (retail customers as distinguished from companies). Retail lockboxes typically receive many transactions of nominal amounts. The lockbox reduces float and transfers workload from the company to the bank, resulting in improved cash flow and reduced expenses.

■ *Return Envelopes.* Providing return envelopes can accelerate customer remissions. On the return envelope, you can use bar codes, nine-digit code numbers, or post office box numbers. Another option is Accelerated Reply Mail (ARM), in which a unique "truncating" ZIP code is assigned to payments such as lockbox receivables. The coded remittances are removed from the postal system and processed by banks or third parties.

■ *Pre-Authorized Debits.* Cash from customers may be collected faster if you obtain permission from customers to have pre-authorized debits (PADs) automatically charged to the customers' bank accounts for repetitive charges. This is a common practice among insurance companies, which collect monthly premium payments via PADs. These debits may take the form of paper pre-authorized checks (PACs) or paperless automatic clearing house entries. PADs are cost-effective because they avoid the process of billing the customer, receiving and processing the payment, and depositing the check. Using PADs for variable payments is less efficient because the amount of the PAD must be changed each period and the customer generally must be advised by mail of the amount of the debit. PADs are most effective when used for constant, relatively nominal periodic payments.

■ *Wire Transfers.* To accelerate cash flow, you may transfer funds between banks by wire transfers through computer terminal and telephone. Such transfers should be used only for significant dollar amounts because wire transfer fees are assessed by both the originating and receiving banks. Wire transfers are best for intraorganization transfers, such as transfers to and from investments, deposits to an account made the day checks are expected to clear, and deposits made to any other account that requires immediate availability of funds. They may also be used to fund other types of checking accounts, such as payroll accounts. In order to avoid unnecessarily large balances in the account, you may fund it on a staggered basis. However, to prevent an overdraft, you should make sure balances are maintained in another account at the bank.

There are two types of wire transfers-preformatted (recurring) and free-form (nonrepetitive). Recurring transfers do *not* involve extensive authorization and are suitable for ordinary transfers in which the company designates issuing and receiving banks and provides its account number. Nonrecurring transfers require greater control, including written confirmations instead of telephone or computer terminal confirmations.

■ *Depository Transfer Checks (DTCs).* Paper or paperless depository checks may be used to transfer funds between the company's bank accounts. They do not require a signature, since the check is payable to the bank for credit to the company's account. DTCs typically clear in one day. *Manual* DTCs are preprinted checks that include all information except the amount and date; *automated* DTCs are printed as needed. It is usually best to use the bank's printer since it is not cost-effective for the company to purchase a printer. Automatic check preparation is advisable only for companies that must prepare a large number of transfer checks daily.

There are other ways to accelerate cash inflow. You can send bills to customers sooner than is your practice, perhaps immediately after the order is shipped. You can also require deposits on large or custom orders or submit progress billings as the work on the order progresses. You can charge interest on accounts receivable that are past due and offer cash discounts for early payment; you can also use cash-on-delivery terms. In any event, you should deposit checks immediately.

EXAMPLE 12-1

C Corporation obtains average cash receipts of $200,000 per day. It usually takes five days from the time a check is mailed until the funds are available for use. The amount tied up by the delay is:

$$5 \text{ days} \times \$200,000 = \$1,000,000$$

You can also calculate the return earned on the average cash balance.

EXAMPLE 12-2

A company's weekly average cash balances are as follows:

Week	Average Cash Balance
1	$12,000
2	17,000
3	10,000
4	15,000
Total	$54,000

The monthly average cash balance is:

$$\frac{\$54,000}{4} = \$13,500$$

If the annual interest rate is approximately 12 percent, the monthly return earned on the average cash balance is:

$$\$13,500 \times \frac{.12}{12} = \$135$$

If you are thinking of establishing a lockbox to accelerate cash inflow, you will need to determine the maximum monthly charge you will incur for the service.

EXAMPLE 12-3

It takes Travis Corporation about seven days to receive and deposit payments from customers. Therefore, it is considering establishing a lockbox system. It expects the system to reduce the float time to five days. Average daily collections are $500,000. The rate of return is 12 percent.

The reduction in outstanding cash balances arising from implementing the lockbox system is:

$$2 \text{ days } \times \$500,000 = \$1,000,000$$

The return that could be earned on these funds in a year is:

$$\$1,000,000 \times 0.12 = \$120,000$$

The maximum monthly charge the company should pay for this lockbox arrangement is therefore:

$$\frac{\$120,000}{12} = \$10,000$$

You should compare the return earned on freed cash to the cost of the lockbox arrangement to determine if using the lockbox is financially advantageous.

EXAMPLE 12-4

A company's financial officer is determining whether to initiate a lockbox arrangement that will cost $150,000 annually. The daily average collections are $700,000. Using a lockbox will reduce mailing and processing time by two days. The rate of return is 14 percent.

Annual return on freed cash	
($14\% \times 2 \times \$700,000$)	$196,000
Annual cost	150,000
Net advantage of lockbox system	$46,000

Sometimes you need to determine whether to switch banks in order to lower the overall costs associated with a lockbox arrangement.

EXAMPLE 12-5

You now have a lockbox arrangement in which Bank A handles $5 million a day in return for an $800,000 compensating balance. You are thinking of canceling this arrangement and further dividing your western region by entering into contracts with two other banks. Bank B will handle $3 million a day in collections with a compensating balance of $700,000, and Bank C will handle $2 million a day with a compensating balance of $600,000. Collections will be half a day quicker than they are now. Your return rate is 12 percent.

Accelerated cash receipts	
($5 million per day × 0.5 day)	$2,500,000
Increased compensating balance	500,000
Improved cash flow	$2,000,000
Rate of return	× 0.12
Net annual savings	$240,000

Delay of Cash Outlay

Delaying cash payments can help your company earn a greater return and have more cash available. You should evaluate the payees and determine to what extent you can reasonably stretch time limits without incurring finance charges or impairing your credit rating.

There are many ways to delay cash payments, including centralizing payables, having zero balance accounts, and paying by draft.

■ *Centralize Payables.* You should centralize your company's payables operation—that is, make one center responsible for making all payments—so that debt may be paid at the most profitable time and so that the amount of disbursement float in the system may be ascertained.

■ *Zero Balance Account (ZBA).* Cash payments may be delayed by maintaining zero balance accounts in one bank in which you maintain zero balances for all of the company's disbursing units, with funds being transferred in from a master account as needed. The advantages of ZBAs are that they allow better control over cash payments and reduced excess cash balances in regional banks. Using ZBAs is an aggressive strategy that requires the company to put funds into its payroll and payables checking accounts only when it expects checks to clear. However, watch out for overdrafts and service charges.

■ *Drafts.* Payment drafts are another strategy for delaying disbursements. With a draft, payment is made when the draft is presented for collection to the bank, which in turn goes to the issuer for acceptance. When the draft is approved, the company deposits the funds to the payee's account. Because of this delay, you can maintain a lower checking balance. Banks usually impose a charge for drafts, and you must endure the inconveniences of formally approving them before payment. Drafts can provide a measure of protection against fraud and theft because they must be presented for inspection before payment.

▬ *Delay in Mail.* You can delay cash payment by drawing checks on remote banks (e.g., a New York company might use a Texas bank), thus ensuring that checks take longer to clear. You may also mail checks from post offices that offer limited service or at which mail must go through numerous handling points. If you utilize the mail float properly, you can maintain higher actual bank balances than book balances. For instance, if you write checks averaging $200,000 per day and they take three days to clear, you will have $600,000 ($200,000 × 3) in your checking account for those three days, even though the money has been deducted in your records.

▬ *Check Clearing.* You can use probability analysis to determine the expected date for checks to clear. Probability is defined as the degree of likelihood that something will happen and is expressed as a percentage from 0 to 100. For example, it's likely that not all payroll checks are cashed on the payroll date, so you can deposit some funds later and earn a return until the last minute.

▬ *Delay Payment to Employees.* You can reduce the frequency of payments to employees (e.g., expense account reimbursements, payrolls); for example, you can institute a monthly payroll rather than a weekly one. In this way, you have the use of the cash for a greater time period. You can also disburse commissions on sales when the receivables are collected rather than when sales are made. Finally, you can utilize noncash compensation and remuneration methods (e.g., distribute stock instead of bonuses).

Other ways exist to delay cash payments. Instead of making full payment on an invoice, you can make partial payments. You can also delay payment by requesting additional information about an invoice from the vendor before paying it. Another strategy is to use a charge account to lengthen the time between when you buy goods and when you pay for them. In any event, never pay a bill before its due date.

EXAMPLE 12-6

Every two weeks the company disburses checks that average $500,000 and take three days to clear. You want to find out how much money can be saved annually if the transfer of funds is delayed from an interest-bearing account that pays 0.0384 percent per day (annual rate of 14 percent) for those three days.

$500,000 \times (0.000384 \times 3) = \$576$

The savings per year is $\$576 \times 26$ (yearly payrolls) $= \$14,976$

A cash management system is shown in Table 12-1.

CASH MODELS

A number of mathematical models have been developed to assist the financial manager in distributing a company's funds so that they provide a maximum return to the company. A model developed by William Baumol can determine the optimum amount of cash for a company to hold under conditions of certainty. The objective is to minimize the sum of the fixed costs of transactions and the opportunity cost (return forgone) of holding cash balances that do not yield a return. These costs are expressed as

$$F \cdot \frac{(T)}{C} + i \frac{(C)}{2}$$

where F = the fixed cost of a transaction
  T = the total cash needed for the time period involved
  i = the interest rate on marketable securities
  C = cash balance
  C* = optimal level of cash

The optimal level of cash is determined using the following formula:

$$C^* = \sqrt{\frac{2FT}{i}}$$

EXAMPLE 12-7

You estimate a cash need for $4,000,000 over a one-month period during which the cash account is expected to be disbursed at a constant rate. The opportunity interest rate is 6 percent per annum, or 0.5 percent for a one-month period. The transaction cost each time you borrow or withdraw is $100.

The optimal transaction size (the optimal borrowing or withdrawal lot size) and the number of transactions you should make during the month follow:

$$C^* = \sqrt{\frac{2FT}{i}} = \sqrt{\frac{2(100)(4,000,000)}{0.005}} = \$400,000$$

The optimal transaction size is $400,000.

TABLE 12-1

CASH MANAGEMENT SYSTEM

Acceleration of Cash Receipts	Delay of Cash Payments
Concentration Banking	Pay by Draft
Pre-Authorized Checks	Requisition More Frequently
Pre-Addressed Stamp	Disbursing Float
Envelopes	Make Partial Payments
Obtain Deposits on Large	Use Charge Accounts
Orders	Delay Frequency of Paying
Charge Interest on Overdue	Employees
Receivables	Lockbox System

The average cash balance is

$$\frac{C*}{2} = \frac{\$4,000,000}{2} = \$200,000$$

The number of transactions required is

$$\frac{\$4,000,000}{\$400,000} = 10 \text{ transactions during the month.}$$

There is also a model for cash management when cash payments are uncertain. The Miller-Orr model places upper and lower limits on cash balances. When the upper limit is reached, a transfer of cash to marketable securities is made; when the lower limit is reached, a transfer from securities to cash occurs. No transaction occurs as long as the cash balance stays within the limits.

Factors taken into account in the Miller-Orr model are the fixed costs of a securities transaction (F), assumed to be the same for buying as well as selling; the daily interest rate on marketable securities (i); and the variance of daily net cash flows (σ^2)—(σ is sigma). The objective is to meet cash requirements at the lowest possible cost. A major assumption of this model is the randomness of cash flows. The control limits in the Miller-Orr model are d dollars as an upper limit and zero dollars at the lower limit. When the cash balance reaches the upper level, d less z dollars (optimal cash balance) of securities are bought, and the new balance becomes z dollars. When the cash balance equals zero, z dollars of securities are sold and the new balance again reaches z. Of course, in practice the minimum cash balance is established at an amount greater than zero because of delays in transfer; the higher minimum in effect acts as a safety buffer.

The optimal cash balance z is computed as follows:

$$z = \sqrt[3]{\frac{3F\sigma^2}{4i}}$$

The optimal value for d is computed as 3z.

The average cash balance approximates $\frac{(z+d)}{3}$.

EXAMPLE 12-8

You wish to use the Miller-Orr model. The following information is supplied:

Fixed cost of a securities transaction	$10
Variance of daily net cash flows	$50
Daily interest rate on securities (10%/360)	0.0003

The optimal cash balance, the upper limit of cash needed, and the average cash balance follow:

$$z = \sqrt[3]{\frac{3(10)(50)}{4(0.0003)}} = \sqrt[3]{\frac{3(10)(5\sigma)}{0.0012}}$$

$$= \sqrt[3]{\frac{1,500}{0.0012}}$$

$$= \sqrt[3]{1,250,000}$$

$$= \$102$$

The optimal cash balance is $102; the upper limit is $306 (3 × $102); and the average cash balance is $136 $\left(\frac{\$102 + \$306}{3}\right)$.

When the upper limit of $306 is reached, $204 of securities ($306 − $102) will be purchased to bring the account to the optimal cash balance of $102. When the lower limit of zero dollars is reached, $102 of securities will be sold to again bring it to the optimal cash balance of $102.

BANKING RELATIONSHIPS

Before establishing a relationship with a bank, you should appraise its financial soundness by checking the ratings compiled by financial advisory services such as Moody's and Standard & Poor's. Your company may want to limit its total deposits at any one bank to no more than the amount insured by the Federal Deposit Insurance Corporation, especially if the bank is having difficulties.

You may also decide to use different banks for different services. In selecting a bank, consider location (which affects lockboxes and disbursement points), type and cost of services, and availability of funds.

You may undertake a bank account analysis by comparing the value of the company balance maintained at the bank to the service charges imposed. Banks will provide such analysis for you, if you wish, but you should scrutinize the bank's analysis closely to be sure it is accurate.

Most checks clear in one business day; clearing time of three or more business days is rare. Try to arrange for the financial institution to give same-day credit on deposits received prior to a specified cutoff time. If the deposit is made over the counter, the funds may not be immediately available; if the deposit is made early enough, especially through a lockbox, they may be.

INVESTING IN MARKETABLE SECURITIES

Cash management requires knowing the amount of funds the company has available for investment and the length of time for which they can be invested. Such investments earn a return for the company. Marketable securities include:

■ Time deposits—savings accounts that earn daily interest, long-term savings accounts, and certificates of deposit.

■ Money market funds—managed portfolios of short-term, high-grade debt instruments such as Treasury bills and commercial paper.

■ Interest—paying demand deposits.

■ U.S. Treasury securities.

Automatic short-term money market investments immediately deposit excess cash in money market securities in order to earn a return on the funds. Holding marketable securities serves as protection against cash shortages; companies with seasonal operations may purchase marketable securities when they have excess funds and then sell the securities when cash deficits occur. Companies may also invest in marketable securities when they are holding funds temporarily in expectation of short-term capital expansion. In selecting an investment portfolio, you should consider return, default risk, marketability, and maturity date.

You should monitor coupon and security collection to ensure that the company receives any interest it is entitled to and that securities that mature or are sold are properly collected and deposited.

MANAGEMENT OF ACCOUNTS RECEIVABLE

Accounts receivable management directly impacts the profitability of the firm. It includes determining discount policy and credit policy for marginal customers, investigating ways of speeding up collections and reducing bad debts, and setting terms of sale to assure ultimate collection.

As part of accounts receivable management, you should appraise order entry, billing, and accounts receivable activities to be sure that proper procedures are being followed from the time an order is received until ultimate collection. Among the points to consider is how the average time lag between completing the sales transaction and invoicing the customer can be reduced. You should also consider the opportunity cost of holding receivables, that is, the return lost by having funds tied up in accounts receivable instead of invested elsewhere.

Accounts receivable management involves two types of float-invoicing and mail. *Invoicing float* is the number of days between the time goods are shipped to the customer and the time the invoice is sent out. Obviously, the company should mail invoices on a timely basis. *Mail float* is the time between the preparation of an invoice and its receipt by the customer. Mail float may be reduced by decentralizing invoicing and mailing, coordinating outgoing mail with post office schedules, using express mail services for large invoices, enforcing due dates, and offering discounts for early payment.

Credit Policies

A key concern in accounts receivable management is determining credit terms to be given to customers, which affects sales volume and collections. For example, offering longer credit terms will probably increase sales. Credit terms have a direct bearing on the costs and revenue generated from receivables. If credit terms are tight, the company will have a lower investment in accounts receivable and incur fewer bad-debt losses, but it may also experience lower sales, reduced profits, and adverse customer reaction. On the other hand, if credit terms are lax, the company may enjoy higher sales and gross profit, but it risks increased bad debts and a higher opportunity cost of carrying the investment in accounts receivable because marginal customers take longer to pay. Receivable terms should be liberalized when you want to get rid of excessive inventory or obsolete items or if you operate in an industry in which products are sold in advance of retail seasons (e.g., swimsuits). If your products are perishable, you should impose short receivable terms and possibly require payment on delivery.

In evaluating a potential customer's ability to pay, consider the customer's integrity, financial soundness, and collateral. A customer's credit soundness may be appraised through quantitative techniques such as regression analysis, which examines the change in a dependent variable that occurs as an independent (explanatory) variable changes. Such techniques are particularly useful when you need to evaluate a large number of small customers. You should be able to estimate bad debt losses reliably if your company sells to many customers and has not changed its credit policies for a long time.

Keep in mind that extending credit involves additional expenses— the administrative costs of operating the credit department; computer services; and fees paid to rating agencies.

You may find it useful to obtain references from retail credit bureaus and professional credit reference services as part of your customer credit evaluation. Dun and Bradstreet (D&B) reports contain information about a company's nature of business, product line, management, financial statements, number of employees, previous payment history as reported by suppliers, current debts, including any past due, terms of sale, audit opinion, lawsuits, insurance coverage, leases, criminal proceedings, banking relationships and account information (e.g., current bank loans), location, and seasonal fluctuations, if applicable.

Monitoring Receivables

There are many ways to maximize profitability from accounts receivable and keep losses to a minimum. These include proper billing, factoring, and evaluating customers' financial health.

■ *Billing.* Cycle billing, in which customers are billed at different time periods, can smooth out the billing process. In such a system, customers with last names starting with A may be billed on the first of the month, those with last names beginning with B on the second day, and so on. Customer statements should be mailed within twenty-four hours of the close of the billing period.

To speed up collections, you can send invoices to customers when their order is processed at the warehouse instead of when the merchandise is shipped. You can also bill for services at intervals when work is performed over a period of time or charge a retainer, rather than receiving payment when the work is completed. In any event, you should bill large sales immediately.

When business is slow, seasonal datings, in which you offer delayed payment terms to stimulate demand from customers who are unable to pay until later in the season, can be used.

■ *Customer Evaluation Process.* Before giving credit, carefully analyze customer financial statements and obtain ratings from financial advisory services. Try to avoid high-risk receivables, such as customers who are in a financially troubled industry or region. Be careful of customers who have been in business less than one year since about 50 percent of businesses fail within the first two years. As a rule, consumer receivables carry a greater risk of default than do corporate receivables. You should modify credit limits and accelerate collections based on changes in a customer's financial health; you may want to withhold products or services until payments are made and ask for collateral in support of questionable accounts (the collateral value should equal or exceed the account balance). If necessary, you can use outside collection agencies to try to collect from recalcitrant customers.

You should age accounts receivable (that is, rank them by the time elapsed since they were billed) to spot delinquent customers and charge interest on late payments. After you compare current aged receivables to those of prior years, industry norms, and the competition's, you can prepare a Bad Debt Loss Report showing cumulative bad debt losses by customer, terms of sale, and size of account and then summarized by department, product line, and type of customer (e.g., industry). Bad debt losses are typically higher for smaller companies than for larger ones.

■ *Insurance Protection.* You may want to have credit insurance to guard against unusual bad debt losses. In deciding whether to acquire this protection, consider expected average bad debt losses, the company's financial ability to withstand the losses, and the cost of insurance.

■ *Factoring.* Factor (sell) accounts receivable if that results in a net savings. However, you should realize that confidential information may be disclosed in a factoring transaction. (Factoring is discussed in Chapter 13.)

Credit Policy

In granting trade credit, you should consider your competition and current economic conditions. In a recession, you may want to relax your credit policy in order to stimulate additional business. For example, the company may not rebill customers who take a cash discount even after the discount period has elapsed. On the other hand, you may decide to tighten credit policy in times of short supply, because at such times your company as the seller has the upper hand.

In offering a credit card, the seller will generate more sales and high interest income. However, there will be greater default risk.

DETERMINING THE INVESTMENT IN ACCOUNTS RECEIVABLE

To determine the dollar investment tied up in accounts receivable, use a computation that takes into account the annual credit sales and the length of time receivables are outstanding.

EXAMPLE 12-9

A company sells on terms of net/30, meaning payment is required within 30 days. The accounts are on average 20 days past due. Annual credit sales are $600,000. The investment in accounts receivable is:

$$\frac{50}{360} \times \$600,000 = \$83,333.28$$

The *investment* in accounts receivable represents the cost tied up in those receivables, including both the cost of the product and the cost of capital.

EXAMPLE 12-10

The cost of a product is 30 percent of selling price, and the cost of capital is 10 percent of selling price. On average, accounts are paid four months after sale. Average sales are $70,000 per month.

The investment in accounts receivable from this product is:

Accounts receivable (4 months × $70,000) $280,000

Investment in accounts receivable
$\left[\$280,000 \times (0.30 + 0.10)\right]$ 112,000

EXAMPLE 12-11

Accounts receivable are $700,000. The average manufacturing cost is 40% of the selling price. The before-tax profit margin is 10%. The carrying cost of inventory is 3% of selling price. The sales commission is 8% of sales. The investment in accounts receivable is:

$$\$700,000(0.40 + 0.03 + 0.08) = \$700,000(0.51) = \$357,000$$

The average investment in accounts receivable may be computed by multiplying the average accounts receivable by the cost/selling price ratio.

EXAMPLE 12-12

If a company's credit sales are $120,000, the collection period is 60 days, and the cost is 80 percent of sales price, what is (a) the average accounts receivable balance and (b) the average investment in accounts receivable?

$$\text{Accounts receivable turnover} = \frac{360}{60} = 6$$

$$\text{Average accounts receivable} = \frac{\text{Credit sales}}{\text{Turnover}}$$

$$= \frac{\$120,000}{6}$$

$$= \$20,000$$

Average investment in accounts receivable $\qquad \$20,000 \times 0.80 = \$16,000$

DISCOUNT POLICY

In order to determine if customers should be offered a discount for the early payment of account balances, the financial manager has to compare the return on freed cash resulting from customer's paying sooner to the cost of the discount.

EXAMPLE 12-13

The following data are provided:

Current annual credit sales	$14,000,000
Collection period	3 months
Terms	net/30
Minimum rate of return	15%

The company is considering offering a 3/10, net/30 discount (that is, if the customer pays within 10 days of the date of sale, the customer will receive a 3 percent discount. If payment is made after 10 days, no discount is offered. Total payment must be made within 30 days.) The company expects 25 percent of the customers to take advantage of the discount. The collection period will decline to two months.

The discount should be offered, as indicated in the following calculations:

Advantage of discount
Increased profitability:

Average accounts receivable balance before a change in policy

$$\frac{\text{Credit sales}}{\text{Accounts receivable turnover}} = \frac{\$14,000,000}{12 \div 3 = 4} = \$3,500,000$$

Average accounts receivable balance after change in policy

$$\frac{\text{Credit sales}}{\text{Accounts receivable turnover}} = \frac{\$14,000,000}{12 \div 2 = 6} = \underline{\$2,333,333}$$

Reduction in average accounts receivable balance	$1,116,667
Rate of return	× .15
Return	$ 175,000

Disadvantage of discount

Cost of the discount $0.30 \times 0.25 \times \$14,000,000$	$ 105,000
Net advantage of discount	$ 70,000

Changing Credit Policy

To decide whether the company should give credit to marginal customers, you need to compare the earnings on the additional sales obtained to the added cost of the receivables. If the company has idle capacity, the additional earnings is the contribution margin on the new sales, since fixed costs are constant. The additional cost of the receivables results from the likely increase in bad debts and the opportunity cost of tying up funds in receivables for a longer time period.

EXAMPLE 12-14

Sales price per unit	$120
Variable cost per unit	80
Fixed cost per unit	15
Annual credit sales	$600,000
Collection period	1 month
Minimum return	16%

If you liberalize the credit policy, you project that
- Sales will increase by 40%.
- The collection period on total accounts will increase to two months.
- Bad debts on the increased sales will be 5 percent.
Preliminary calculations:

Current units ($600,000/$120)	5,000
Additional units $(5,000 \times 0.4)$	2,000

Advantage of the change in policy
Additional profitability:

Incremental sales volume		2,000 units
× Contribution margin per unit		
(Selling price − Variable cost) $120 − $80		× $40
Incremental profitability		$80,000 units

Disadvantage of the change in policy
Incremental bad debts:

Incremental units × Selling price (2,000 × $120)	$240,000
Bad debt percentage	× 0.05
Additional bad debts	$12,000

The first step in determining the opportunity cost of the investment tied up in accounts receivable is to compute the new average unit cost as follows:

	Units	×	Unit Cost	=	Total Cost
Current units	5,000	×	$95	=	$475,000
Additional units	2,000	×	$80	=	160,000
Total	7,000				$635,000

$$\text{New average unit cost} = \frac{\text{Total cost}}{\text{Units}} = \frac{\$635,000}{7,000} = \$90.71$$

Note that at idle capacity, fixed cost remains constant; therefore, the incremental cost is only the variable cost of $80 per unit. Therefore, the average unit cost will drop.

We now compute the opportunity cost of funds placed in accounts receivable:

Average investment in accounts receivable after change in policy:

$$\frac{\text{Credit sales}}{\text{Accounts receivable turnover}} \times \frac{\text{Unit cost}}{\text{Selling price}}$$
$$= \frac{\$840,000@}{6} \times \frac{\$90.71}{\$120}$$
$$= \$105,828$$

@7,000 units ×$120 = $840,000.

Current average investment in accounts receivable:

$$\frac{\$600,000}{12} \times \frac{\$95}{\$120} = 39,583$$

Additional investment in accounts receivable	$66,245
Minimum return	× 0.16
Opportunity cost of funds tied up	$10,599

Net advantage of relaxation in credit standards:

Additional earnings		$80,000
Less:		
Additional bad debt losses	$12,000	
Opportunity cost	10,599	22,599
Net savings		$57,401

The company may have to decide whether to extend full credit to presently limited credit customers or no-credit customers. Full credit should be given only if net profitability occurs.

EXAMPLE 12-15

Category	Bad Debt Percentage	Collection Period	Credit Policy	Increase in Annual Sales if Credit Restrictions Are Relaxed
X	2%	30 days	Unlimited	$ 80,000
Y	5%	40 days	Restricted	600,000
Z	30%	80 days	No Credit	850,000

Gross profit is 25 percent of sales. The minimum return on investment is 12%.

	Category Y	Category Z

Gross profit $=$ Incremental sales rate $\times$ Gross profit rate

$\$600,000 \times .25$ $\$150,000$

$\$850,000 \times .25$ $\$212,500$

Less bad debts $=$ Incremental sales $\times$ Bad debt percentage

$\$600,000 \times .05$ $-(30,000)$

$\$850,000 \times .30$ $-(255,000)$

Incremental average investment in accounts receivable[*]

$\dfrac{40}{360} \times (0.75 \times \$600,000)$ $\$50,000$

$\dfrac{80}{360} \times (0.75 \times \$850,000)$ $\$141,667$

Opportunity cost of incremental investment in accounts receivable $\times 0.12$ $\times 0.12$

                                       $(6,000)$ $(17,000)$

Net earnings $\underline{\underline{\$114,000}}$

                                       $\underline{\underline{\$(59,500)}}$

Credit should be extended to category Y.

---

[*] $\dfrac{\text{Collection Period}}{\text{Days in the Year}} \times (\text{Cost of Sales} \times \text{Incremental sales})$

As you decide whether credit standards should be loosened, consider the gross profit on increased sales versus the opportunity cost associated with higher receivable balances and collection expenses.

EXAMPLE 12-16

You are considering liberalizing the credit policy to encourage more customers to purchase on credit. Currently, 80 percent of sales are on credit, and there is a gross margin of 30 percent. The return rate on funds is 10 percent. Other relevant data are:

	Currently	Proposal
Sales	$300,000	$450,000
Credit sales	240,000	360,000
Collection expenses	4% of credit sales	5% of credit sales
Accounts receivable turnover	4.5	3

An analysis of the proposal yields the following results:

Gross profit:

Expected increase in credit sales $360,000 − $240,000	$120,000
Gross profit rate	× .30
Increase in gross profit	$36,000

Opportunity cost:
Average accounts receivable balance
(credit sales/accounts receivable turnover)

Expected average accounts receivable $360,000/3	$120,000
Current average accounts receivable $240,000/4.5	53,333
Increase in average accounts receivable	$66,667
× Return rate	× 10%
Opportunity cost of funds tied up in accounts receivable	$6,667

Collection expenses:

Expected collection expenses 0.05 × $360,000	$18,000
Current collection expenses 0.04 × $240,000	9,600
Increase in collection expenses	$8,400

You would profit from a more liberal credit policy as follows:

Increase in gross profit	$36,000
Opportunity cost in accounts receivable	(6,667)
Increase in collection expenses	(8,400)
Net advantage	$20,933

To determine whether it is advantageous to engage in a sales campaign, you should consider the gross margin earned, the sales discount, and the opportunity cost of higher receivable balances.

EXAMPLE 12-17

The company is planning a sales campaign in which it will offer credit terms of 3/10, net/45. It expects the collection period to increase from 60 days to 80 days. Relevant data for the contemplated campaign follow:

	Percent of Sales Before Campaign	Percent of Sales During Campaign
Cash sales	40%	30%
Payment from (in days)		
1–10	25	55
11–100	35	15

The proposed sales strategy will probably increase sales from $8 million to $10 million. There is a gross margin rate of 30 percent. The rate of return is 14 percent. Sales discounts are given on cash sales.

	Without Sales Campaign		With Sales Campaign	
Gross margin				
(0.3 × $8,000,000)		$2,400,000	0.3× $10,000,000	$3,000,000
Sales subject to discount				
0.65 × $8,000,000	$5,200,000			
0.85 × $10,000,000			$8,500,000	
Sales discount	×0.03	– 156,000	×0.03	– 255,000
Investment in average accounts receivable				
$\frac{60}{360}$ × $8,000,000 × 0.7		$933,333		
$\frac{80}{360}$ × $10,000,000 × 0.7			$1,555,555	
Return rate	×0.14	– 130,667	×0.14	– 217,778
Net profit		$2,113,333		$2,527,222

The company should undertake the sales campaign, because earnings will increase by $413,889 ($2,527,222 – $2,113,333).

INVENTORY MANAGEMENT

The purpose of inventory management is to develop policies that will achieve an optimal inventory investment. This level varies among industries and among companies in a given industry. Successful inventory management minimizes inventory, lowers cost, and improves profitability.

As part of this process, you should appraise the adequacy of inventory levels, which depend on many factors, including sales, liquidity, available inventory financing, production, supplier reliability, delay in receiving new orders, and seasonality. In the event you have slow-moving products, you may wish to consider discarding them at lower prices to reduce inventory carrying costs and improve cash flow.

You should try to minimize the lead time in your company's acquisition, manufacturing, and distribution functions—that is, how long it takes to receive the merchandise from suppliers after an order is placed. Depending upon lead times, you may need to increase inventory or alter the purchasing pattern. Calculate the ratio of the value of outstanding orders to average daily purchases to indicate the lead time for receiving orders from suppliers; this ratio indicates whether you should increase the inventory balance or change your buying pattern.

You must also consider the obsolescence and spoilage risk of inventory. For example, technological, perishable, fashionable, flammable, and specialized goods usually have high salability risk, which should be taken into account in computing desired inventory levels.

Inventory management involves a trade-off between the costs of keeping inventory and the benefits of holding it. Different inventory items vary in profitability and the amount of space they take up, and higher inventory levels result in increased costs for storage, casualty and theft insurance, spoilage, property taxes for larger facilities, increased staffing, and interest on funds borrowed to finance inventory acquisition. On the other hand, an increase in inventory lowers the possibility of lost sales from stockouts and the production slowdowns caused by inadequate inventory. Additionally, large volume purchases result in greater purchase discounts.

Inventory levels are also affected by short-term interest rates. As short-term interest rates increase, the optimum level of holding inventory is reduced.

You may have to decide whether it is more profitable to sell inventory as is or to sell it after further processing. For example, assume inventory can be sold as is for $40,000 or for $80,000 if it is put into further processing costing $20,000. The latter should be selected because the additional processing yields a $60,000 profit, compared to $40,000 for the current sale.

Quality Discount

You may be entitled to a quantity discount when purchasing large orders. The discount reduces the cost of materials.

EXAMPLE 12-18

A company purchases 1,000 units of an item having a list price of $10 each. The quantity discount is 5 percent. The net cost of the item is:

Acquisition cost (1,000 × $10)	$10,000
Less: Discount (0.05 × $10,000)	500
Net cost	$ 9,500

Investment in Inventory

You should consider the average investment in inventory, which equals the average inventory balance times the per unit cost.

EXAMPLE 12-19

Savon Company places an order for 5,000 units at the beginning of the year. Each unit costs $10. The average investment is:

Average inventory[a]	2,500 units
Unit cost, $	× $10
Average investment	$25,000

---

[a] $\frac{\text{Quantity (Q)}}{2} = \frac{5,000}{2}$

To get an average, add the beginning balance and the ending balance and then divide by 2. This gives the mid-value.

The more frequently a company places an order, the lower the average investment.

Determining Carrying and Ordering Costs

You want to determine the costs for planning, financing, record keeping, and control associated with inventory. Once inventory costs are known, you can compute the amount of timeliness of financing.

Inventory carrying costs include warehousing, handling, insurance, property taxes, and the opportunity cost of holding inventory. A provisional cost for spoilage and obsolescence should also be included in the analysis. The more the inventory held, the greater the carrying cost. Carrying costs equals:

$$\text{Carrying cost} = \frac{Q}{2} \times C$$

where $\frac{Q}{2}$ represents average quantity and C is the carrying cost per unit.

A knowledge of inventory carrying costs will help you determine which items are worth storing.

Inventory ordering costs are the costs of placing an order and receiving the merchandise. They include freight and the clerical costs incurred in placing the order. To minimize ordering costs, you should enter the fewest number of orders possible. In the case of produced items, ordering cost also includes scheduling cost. Ordering cost equals:

$$\text{Ordering cost} = \frac{S}{Q} \times P$$

where S = total usage, Q = quantity per order, and P = cost of placing an order.

The total inventory cost is therefore:

$$\frac{QC}{2} + \frac{SP}{C}$$

A knowledge of ordering costs helps you decide how many orders you should place during the period to suit your needs.

A tradeoff exists between ordering and carrying costs. A large order quantity increases carrying costs but lowers ordering costs.

The economic order quantity (EOQ) is the optimum amount of goods to order each time to minimize total inventory costs. EOQ analysis should be applied to every product that represents a significant proportion of sales.

$$EOQ = \sqrt{\frac{2SP}{C}}$$

The EOQ model assumes:

▬ Demand is constant and known with certainty.

▬ Depletion of stock is linear and constant.

▬ No discount is allowed for quantity purchases.

▬ Lead time, the time interval between placing an order and receiving delivery, is a constant (that is, stockout is not possible).

The number of orders for a period is the usage (S) divided by the EOQ.

Figure 12.2 graphically shows the EOQ point.

In the next two examples, we compute for a product the EOQ, the number of orders, and the number of days that should elapse before the next order is placed.

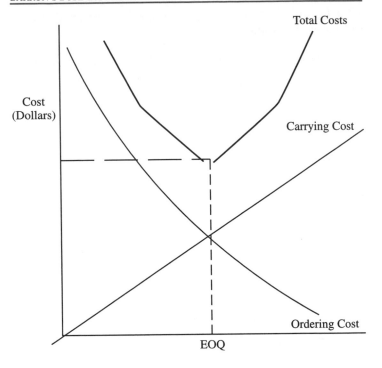

Figure 12.2   *EOQ Point*

EXAMPLE 12-20

You want to know how frequently to place orders to lower your costs. The following information is provided:

$$S = 500 \text{ units per month}$$
$$P = \$40 \text{ per order}$$
$$C = \$4 \text{ per unit}$$

$$EOQ = \sqrt{\frac{2SP}{C}} = \sqrt{\frac{2(500)(40)}{4}} = \sqrt{10,000} = 100 \text{ units}$$

The number of orders each month is:

$$\frac{S}{EOQ} = \frac{500}{100} = 5$$

Therefore, an order should be placed about every 6 days (31/5).

EXAMPLE 12-21

A company is determining its frequency of orders for product X. Each product X costs $15. The annual carrying cost is $200. The ordering cost is $10. The company anticipates selling 50 product Xs each month. Its desired average inventory level is 40.

$$S = 50 \times 12 = 600$$
$$P = \$10$$
$$C = \frac{\text{Purchase price} \times \text{carrying cost}}{\text{Average investment}} = \frac{\$15 \times \$200}{40 \times \$15} = \$5$$

$$\begin{aligned} \text{EOQ} = \sqrt{\frac{2SP}{C}} &= \sqrt{\frac{2(600)(10)}{5}} \\ &= \sqrt{\frac{12,000}{5}} \\ &= \sqrt{2,400} \\ &= 49 \text{ (rounded)} \end{aligned}$$

The number of orders per year is:

$$\frac{S}{\text{EOQ}} = \frac{600}{49} = 12 \text{ orders (rounded)}$$

The company should place an order about every thirty days (365/12).

The Reorder Point

The reorder point (ROP) is a signal that tells you when to place an order. Calculating the reorder point requires a knowledge of the lead time between order and receipt of merchandise. It may be influenced by the months of supply or total dollar ceilings on inventory to be held or inventory to be ordered.

Reorder point is computed as follows:

$$\text{ROP} = \text{lead time} \times \text{average usage per unit of time}$$

This reveals the inventory level at which a new order should be placed. If a safety stock is needed, add to the ROP.

You have to know at what inventory level you should place an order to reduce inventory costs and have an adequate stock of goods with which to satisfy customer orders.

EXAMPLE 12-22

A company needs 6,400 units evenly throughout the year. There is a lead time of one week. There are 50 working weeks in the year. The reorder point is:

$$1 \text{ week } \times \frac{6,400}{50 \text{ weeks}} = 1 \times 128 = 128 \text{ units}$$

When the inventory level drops to 128 units, a new order should be placed.

An optimal inventory level can be based on consideration of the incremental profitability resulting from having more merchandise compared to the opportunity cost of carrying the higher inventory balances.

EXAMPLE 12-23

The current inventory turnover is 12 times. Variable costs are 60 percent of sales. An increase in inventory balances is expected to prevent stockouts, thus increasing sales. Minimum rate of return is 18 percent. Relevant data include:

Sales	Turnover
$800,000	12
890,000	10
940,000	8
980,000	7

(1)	(2)	(3)	(4)	(5)	(6)
		[(1)(2)] Average Inventory Balance	Opportunity Cost of Carrying Incremental Inventory[a]	Increased Profitability[b]	[(5)−(4)] Net Savings
Sales	Turnover				
$800,000	12	$66,667	—	—	—
890,000	10	89,000	$4,020	$36,000	$31,980
940,000	8	117,500	5,130	20,000	14,870
980,000	7	140,000	4,050	16,000	11,950

[a] Increased inventory from column 3 × 0.18

[b] Increased sales from column 1 × 0.40

The optimal inventory level is $89,000, because it results in the highest net savings.

Using the ABC Inventory Control Method

ABC analysis focuses on the most critical items—gross profitability, sensitive price or demand patterns, and supply excesses or shortages.

The ABC method requires the classification of inventory into one of four groups—A, B, C, or D—according to the potential savings associated with a proper level of inventory control.

Perpetual inventory records should be maintained for Group A items, which require accuracy and frequent, often daily, attention. A items usually consist of about 70 percent of the dollar value of inventory. Group B items are less expensive than Group A items but are still important and require intermediate level control. Group C items include most of the inventory items. Since they are usually less expensive and less used, they receive less attention. There is usually a high safety stock level for Group C items. Blanket purchase orders should exist for A items and only "spot buys" for Bs and Cs. Group D items are the losers, items that have not been used for an extended time period (e.g., six months). D items should not be reordered unless special authorization is given. Items may be reclassified as need be. For instance, a "fragile" item or one that is frequently stolen can be reclassified from C to A.

To institute the ABC method:

1. Segregate merchandise into components based on dollar value.
2. Compute annual dollar usage by inventory type (anticipated annual usage times unit cost).
3. Rank inventory in terms of dollar usage, ranging from high to low (e.g., As in top 30 percent, Bs in next 50 percent, and Cs in last 20 percent). Tag inventory with the appropriate classification and record the classifications in the inventory records.

Figure 12.3 depicts an ABC inventory control system, while Table 12-2 illustrates an ABC distribution.

JUST-IN-TIME INVENTORY SYSTEM

The inventory control problem occurs in almost every type of organization. It exists whenever products are held to meet some expected future demand. In most industries, cost of inventory represents the largest liquid asset under the control of management. Therefore, it is very important to develop a production and inventory planning system that will minimize both purchasing and carrying costs. In recent years, the Japanese have demonstrated the ability to manage their production systems effectively. Much of their success has been attributed to what is known as the *Just-In-Time (JIT)* approach to production and inventory control, which has generated a great deal of interest among practitioners. The "Kanban" system—as they call it—has been a focal point of interest, with its dramatic impact on the inventory performance and productivity of the Japanese auto industry.

TABLE 12-2

ABC INVENTORY DISTRIBUTION

Inventory Classification	Population (Percent)	Dollar Usage (Percent)
A	20	80
B	30	15
C	50	5

The potential benefits of JIT are numerous. First, JIT practice reduces inventory levels, which means lower investments in inventories. Since the system requires only the smallest quantity of materials needed immediately, it reduces the overall inventory level substantially. In many Japanese companies that use the JIT concept, inventory levels have been reduced to the point that makes the annual working capital turnover ratio much higher than that experienced by U.S. counterparts. For instance, Toyota reported inventory turnover ratios of 41 to 63, whereas comparable U.S. companies reported inventory turnover ratios of 5 to 8.

Second, since purchasing under JIT requires a significantly shorter delivery lead time, lead time reliability is greatly improved. Reduced lead time and increased reliability also contribute to a significant reduction in safety stock requirements.

Third, reduced lead times and set-up times increase scheduling flexibility. The cumulative lead time, which includes both purchasing and production lead times, is reduced. Thus, the firm schedule within the production planning horizon is reduced. This results in a longer "look-ahead" time that can be used to meet shifts in market demand. The smaller lot size production made possible by reduced set-up time, adds flexibility.

Other financial benefits include:
- Lower investments in factory space for inventories and production
- Less obsolescence risk in inventories
- Reduction in scrap and rework
- Decline in paperwork
- Reduction in direct material costs through quantity purchases

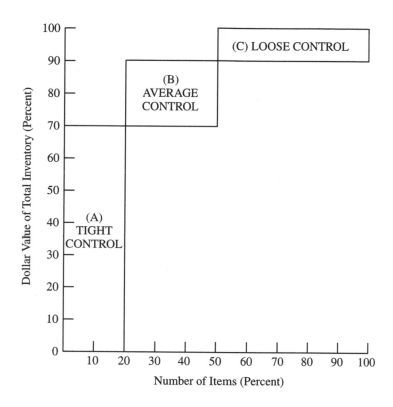

Figure 12.3 *ABC Inventory Control System*

CHAPTER PERSPECTIVE

To maximize cash flow, cash collections should be accelerated and cash payments delayed. Accounts receivable management requires decisions on whether to give credit and to whom, the amount to give, and the terms. The proper amount of investment in inventory may change daily and requires close evaluation. Improper inventory management occurs when funds tied up in inventory can be used more productively elsewhere. A buildup of inventory may carry risk, such as obsolescence. On the other hand, an excessively low inventory may result in reduced profit through lost sales. A JIT inventory system is designed to reduce inventory investment.

Short-Term and Intermediate-Term Financing

CHAPTER 13

INTRODUCTION AND MAIN POINTS

In this chapter we provide a broad picture of short-term financing (financing that will be repaid in one year or less). Examples of short-term financing are trade credit, short-term bank loans, commercial paper, and financing for receivables and inventory.

We also discuss intermediate-term financing, instruments with a maturity in excess of one year, such as some bank loans and leases. In deciding on a particular source of financing, managers should consider cost, risk, liquidity, and flexibility.

In this chapter, you will learn:

■ The different short-term financing instruments and when each one is most appropriate.

■ The advantages of trade credit.

■ The types of bank loans and how they work.

■ How to compute interest.

■ The attributes of commercial paper financing.

■ How to finance using receivables and inventory as collateral.

■ The differences between short-term and long-term financing.

■ The advantages and disadvantages of leasing.

SHORT-TERM FINANCING

Short-term financing may be used to meet seasonal and temporary fluctuations in funds position as well as to meet long-term needs. For example, short-term financing may be used to provide additional working capital, finance current assets (such as receivables and inventory), or provide interim financing for a long-term project (such as the acquisition of plant and equipment) until long-term financing is arranged. (Long-term financing may not always be appropriate because of perceived long-term credit risk or excessively high cost.)

When compared to long-term financing (see Chapter 14), short-term financing has several advantages. It is usually easier to arrange and less expensive and has more flexibility. The drawbacks of short-term financing are that it is subject to greater fluctuations in interest rates, refinancing is frequently required, there is greater risk of default because the loan comes due sooner, and any delinquency may damage the company's credit rating.

The sources of short-term financing include trade credit, bank loans, bankers' acceptances, finance company loans, commercial paper, receivable financing, and inventory financing. One particular source may be more appropriate than another in a given circumstance; some are more desirable than others because of interest rates or collateral requirements.

You should consider the merits of the different sources of short-term financing, focusing on:

- Cost.
- Effect on financial ratios.
- Effect on credit rating (some sources of short-term financing may negatively impact the company's credit rating, such as factoring accounts receivable).
- Risk (reliability of the source of funds for future borrowing). If your company is materially affected by outside forces, it will need more stable and reliable financing.
- Restrictions, such as requiring a minimum level of working capital.
- Flexibility.
- Expected money market conditions (e.g., future interest rates) and availability of future financing.
- Inflation rate.
- Company profitability and liquidity positions, both of which must be favorable if the company is to be able to pay its near-term obligations.
- Stability and maturity of operations.
- Tax rate.

If the company can predict that it will be short of cash during certain times, the financial manager should arrange for financing (such as a line of credit) in advance instead of waiting for an emergency.

Using Trade Credit

Trade credit (accounts payable) are balances owed by your company to suppliers. It is a spontaneous (recurring) financing source for creditworthy companies since it comes from normal operations. Trade credit is the least expensive form of financing inventory. Its benefits are that it is readily available, since suppliers want business; it requires no collateral; there is no interest charge or else a minimal one; it is convenient; and it is likely to be extended if the company gets into financial trouble. If the company has liquidity difficulties, it may be able to stretch (extend) accounts payable; however, the company will be required to give up any cash discount offered and accept a lower credit rating. The company should prepare a report analyzing accounts payable in terms of lost discounts, aged debit balances, aged unpaid invoices, and days to pay.

EXAMPLE 13-1

The company purchases $500 worth of merchandise per day from suppliers. The terms of purchase are net/60, and the company pays on time. The accounts payable balance is:

$$\$500 \text{ per day } \times 60 \text{ days } = \$30,000$$

The company should typically take advantage of a cash discount offered for early payment because failing to do so results in a high opportunity cost. The cost of not taking a discount equals:

$$\left(\frac{\text{Discount Lost}}{\substack{\text{Dollar proceeds you have use} \\ \text{of by not taking the discount}}} \right) \times \left(\frac{360}{\substack{\text{Number of days you have use of the} \\ \text{money by not taking the discount}}} \right)$$

EXAMPLE 13-2

The company buys $1,000 in merchandise on terms of 2/10, net/30. The company fails to take the discount and pays the bill on the thirtieth day. The cost of the discount is:

$$\frac{\$20}{\$980} \times \frac{360}{20} = 36.7\%$$

The company would be better off taking the discount even if it needed to borrow the money from the bank, since the opportunity cost is 36.7 percent. The interest rate on a bank loan would be far less.

Bank Loans

Even though other institutions, such as savings and loan associations and credit unions, provide banking services, most banking activities are conducted by commercial banks. Commercial banks allow the company to operate with minimal cash and still be confident of planning activities even in uncertain conditions.

Commercial banks favor short-term loans since they like to get their money back within one year. If the company is large, a group of banks may form a consortium to furnish the desired level of capital.

The prime interest rate is a benchmark for the short-term loan interest rate banks charge creditworthy corporate borrowers. Good companies with strong financial strength can get terms below prime. Your company's interest rate may be higher depending upon the risk the bank believes it is taking.

Bank financing may take the following forms:

■ Unsecured loans
■ Secured loans
■ Lines of credit
■ Letters of credit
■ Revolving credit
■ Installment loans

■ *Unsecured Loans.* Most short-term unsecured (uncollateralized) loans are self-liquidating. This kind of loan is recommended if the company has an excellent credit rating. It is usually used to finance projects having quick cash flows and is appropriate if the company has immediate cash and can either repay the loan in the near future or quickly obtain longer-term financing. Seasonal cash shortfalls and desired inventory buildups are among the reasons to use an unsecured loan. The disadvantages of this kind of loan are that it carries a higher interest rate than a secured loan since there is no collateral and that a lump-sum payment is required.

■ *Secured Loans.* If the company's credit rating is deficient, the bank may lend money only on a secured basis. Collateral can take many forms, including inventory, marketable securities, or fixed assets. Even if the company is able to obtain an unsecured loan, it may be better off taking a collateralized loan at a lower interest rate.

■ *Lines of Credit.* Under a line of credit, the bank agrees to lend money up to a specified amount on a recurring basis. The bank typically charges a commitment fee on the amount of the unused credit line. Credit lines are typically established for a one-year period and may be renewed annually. You can determine if the preferred line of credit is adequate for your company's present and immediate future needs by considering the current and expected cash requirements of the business.

The advantages of a line of credit are that it offers easy and immediate access to funds during tight money market conditions and it enables the company to borrow only as much as it needs and to repay immediately when cash is available. You should use a line of credit if the company is working on large individual projects for a long time period and will obtain minimal or no payments until the job is completed. The disadvantages of lines of credit relate to the collateral requirements and the additional financial information that must be presented to the bank. Banks also may place restrictions on the company, such as setting a ceiling on capital expenditures or requiring a minimum level of working capital.

When the company borrows under a line of credit, it may be required to maintain a compensating balance (a noninterest-bearing account) with the bank. The compensating balance is stated as a percentage of the loan and effectively increases the cost of the loan. A compensating balance may also be placed on the unused portion of a line of credit, in which case the interest rate is reduced.

EXAMPLE 13-3

The company borrows $200,000 and is required to keep a 12 percent compensating balance. It also has an unused line of credit of $100,000, for which a 10 percent compensating balance is required. The minimum balance that must be maintained is:

$$(\$200,000 \times .12) + (\$100,000 \times .10) = \$24,000 + \$10,000$$
$$= \$34,000$$

A line of credit is typically decided upon prior to the actual borrowing. In the days between the arrangement for the loan and the actual borrowing, interest rates may change. Therefore, the agreement will stipulate the loan is at the prime interest rate prevailing when the loan is extended plus a risk premium. (The prime interest rate will not be known until you actually borrow the money since market interest rates may change from the time you contract for a loan and the time you receive the funds.)

The bank may test the company's financial capability by requiring it to "clean up," that is, repay the loan for a brief time during the year (e.g., for one month). The payment shows the bank that the loan is actually seasonal rather than permanent. If the company is unable to repay a short-term loan, it should probably finance with long-term funds.

■ *Letters of Credit.* A letter of credit is a document issued by a bank guaranteeing the payment of a customer's drafts up to a specified amount for a designated time period. In effect, the bank's credit is substituted for that of the buyer, minimizing the seller's risk. Payment may be made on submission of proof of shipment or other performance. Letters of credit are used primarily in international trade.

There are different types of letters of credit. A *commercial letter of credit* is typically drawn in favor of a third party. A *confirmed letter of credit* is provided by a correspondent bank and guaranteed by the issuing bank.

The advantages of letters of credit are that the company does not have to pay cash in advance of shipment, using funds that could be used elsewhere in the business.

■ *Revolving Credit.* A revolving credit is an agreement between the bank and the borrower in which the bank contracts to make loans up to a specified ceiling within a prescribed time period. With revolving credit, notes are short term (typically ninety days). When part of the loan is paid, an amount equal to the repayment may again be borrowed under the terms of the agreement. Advantages are the readily available credit and few restrictions compared to line-of-credit agreements. A major disadvantage may be restrictions imposed by the bank.

■ *Installment Loans.* An installment loan requires monthly payments of interest and principal. When the principal on the loan decreases sufficiently, you may be able to refinance at a lower interest rate. The advantage of this kind of loan is that it may be tailored to satisfy seasonal financing needs.

Interest

Interest on a loan may be paid either at maturity (ordinary interest) or in advance (discounting the loan). When interest is paid in advance, the loan proceeds are reduced and the effective (true) interest rate is increased.

EXAMPLE 13-4

The company borrows $30,000 at 16 percent interest per annum and repays the loan one year later. The interest is $30,000 \times .16 = \$4,800$. The effective interest rate is 16 percent ($4,800/$30,000).

EXAMPLE 13-5

Assume the same facts as in the prior example, except the note is discounted. The effective interest rate increases as follows:

$$\text{Proceeds} = \text{Principal} - \text{Interest} = \$30,000 - \$4,800 = \$25,200$$

$$\text{Effective interest rate} = \frac{\text{Interest}}{\text{Proceeds}} = \frac{\$4,800}{\$25,000} = 19\%$$

A compensating balance will increase the effective interest rate.

EXAMPLE 13-6

The effective interest rate for a one-year, $600,000 loan that has a nominal interest rate of 19 percent with interest due at maturity and requiring a 15 percent compensating balance is:

Effective interest rate (with compensating balance) equals:

$$\frac{\text{Interest rate} \times \text{principal}}{\text{Proceeds, \%} \times \text{principal}} = \frac{.19 \times \$600,000}{(1.00 - .15) \times \$600,000}$$

$$= \frac{\$114,000}{\$510,000}$$

$$= 22.4\%$$

EXAMPLE 13-7

Assume the same facts as in the prior example, except that the loan is discounted. The effective interest rate is:

Effective interest rate (with discount) equals:

$$\frac{\text{Interest rate} \times \text{principal}}{(\text{Proceeds, \%} \times \text{principal}) - \text{interest}}$$

$$= \frac{.19 \times \$600,000}{(0.85 \times \$600,000) - \$114,000}$$

$$= \frac{\$114,000}{\$396,000} = 28.8\%$$

EXAMPLE 13-8

The company has a credit line of $400,000, but it must maintain a compensating balance of 13 percent on outstanding loans and a compensating balance of 10 percent on the unused credit. The interest rate on the loan is 18 percent. The company borrows $275,000. The effective interest rate on the loan is calculated as follows.

The required compensating balance is:

$$
\begin{array}{lrr}
.13 & \times & \$275,000 & \$35,750 \\
.10 & \times & 125,000 & \underline{12,500} \\
& & & \$48,250 \\
\end{array}
$$

Effective interest rate (with line of credit) equals:

$$\frac{\text{Interest rate (on loan)} \times \text{principal}}{\text{Principal} - \text{compensating balance}} = \frac{.18 \times \$275,000}{\$275,000 - \$48,250}$$

$$= \frac{\$49,500}{\$226,750}$$

$$= 21.8\%$$

On an installment loan, the effective interest rate computation is illustrated below. Assuming a one-year loan payable in equal monthly installments, the effective rate is based on the average amount outstanding for the year. The interest is computed on the face amount of the loan.

EXAMPLE 13-9

The company borrows $40,000 at an interest rate of 10 percent to be paid in 12 monthly installments. The average loan balance is $40,000/2 = $20,000. Divide by 2 to obtain an average (the beginning balance is $40,000 and the ending balance is 0, so the average is beginning plus ending divided by 2). The effective interest rate is

$$\frac{\text{Interest}}{\text{Average loan balance}} = \frac{\$40,000 \times 10\%}{\$20,000} = \frac{\$4,000}{\$20,000} = 20\%$$

EXAMPLE 13-10

Assume the same facts as in the prior example, except that the loan is discounted. The interest of $4,000 is deducted in advance so the proceeds received are $40,000 − $4,000 = $36,000. The average loan balance is $36,000/2 = $18,000. The effective interest rate is $4,000/$18,000 = 22.2 percent.

The effective interest cost computation may be more complicated when installment payments vary. The true interest cost of an installment loan is the internal rate of return of the applicable cash flows converted on an annual basis (if desired).

EXAMPLE 13-11

The company borrows $100,000 and will repay it in three monthly installments of $25,000, $25,000, and $50,000. The interest rate is 12 percent.

Amount of borrowing equals:

Installment loan	$100,000
Less: Interest on first installment ($25,000 × .12)	3,000
Balance	$97,000

We now compute the effective interest cost on the installment loan as follows:

$$0 = -\$97,000 + \$25,000/(1 + \text{Cost}) + \$25,000/(1 + \text{Cost})2$$
$$+\$50,000/(1 + \text{Cost})3$$
$$= 1.37\% \text{ on monthly basis}$$
$$= 1.37\% \times 12 = 16.44\% \text{ on annual basis}$$

This shows that the effective annual interest rate on the installment loan is 16.44 percent.

Dealing with the Banker

Banks are eager to lend money to meet self-liquidating, cyclical business needs. A short-term bank loan is an inexpensive way to obtain funds to satisfy working capital requirements during the business cycle. But the financial officer must be able to explain what the company's needs are in an intelligent manner.

Commercial Finance Loans

When credit is unavailable from a bank, the company may have to go to a commercial finance company, which typically charges a higher interest rate than the bank and requires collateral. Typically, the value of the collateral is greater than the balance of the loan and may consist of accounts receivable, inventories, and fixed assets. Commercial finance companies also finance the installment purchases of industrial equipment. A portion of their financing is sometimes obtained through commercial bank borrowing at wholesale rates.

Commercial Paper

Commercial paper is a short-term unsecured obligation with a maturity ranging from 2 to 270 days, issued by companies to investors with temporarily idle cash. Commercial paper can be issued only if the company possesses a very high credit rating; therefore, the interest rate is less than that of a bank loan, typically one-half percent below the prime interest rate. Commercial paper is sold at a discount (below face value), with the interest immediately deducted from the face of the note by the creditor; however, the company pays the full face value. Commercial paper may be issued through a dealer or directly placed to an institutional investor (a dealer is a company that buys securities and then sells them out of its own inventory, while an institutional investor is an entity that buys large volumes of securities, such as banks and insurance companies).

The benefits of commercial paper are that no security is required, the interest rate is typically less than that required by banks or finance companies, and the commercial paper dealer often offers financial advice. The drawbacks are that commercial paper can be issued only by large, financially sound companies and that commercial paper dealings are impersonal. Commercial paper is usually backed by a bank letter of credit.

We now look at an example that determines whether the amount of commercial paper issued by a company is excessive.

EXAMPLE 13-12

A company's balance sheet appears below.

ASSETS	
Current assets	$ 540,000
Fixed assets	800,000
Total assets	$1,340,000

LIABILITIES AND STOCKHOLDERS' EQUITY	
Current liabilities:	
Notes payable to banks	$ 100,000
Commercial paper	650,000
Total current liabilities	$ 750,000
Long-term liabilities	260,000
Total liabilities	$1,010,000
Stockholders' equity	330,000
Total liabilities and stockholders' equity	$1,340,000

The amount of commercial paper issued by the company is a high percentage of both its current liabilities, 86.7% ($650,000/$750,000), and its total liabilities, 64.4% ($650,000/$1,010,000). Because bank loans are minimal, the company may want to do more bank borrowing and less commercial paper financing. In the event of a money market squeeze, the company may find it advantageous to have a working relationship with a bank.

EXAMPLE 13-13

The company issues $500,000 of commercial paper every two months at a 13 percent rate. There is a $1,000 placement cost each time. The percentage cost of the commercial paper is:

Interest ($500,000 × .13)	$65,000
Placement cost ($1,000 × 6)	6,000
Cost	$71,000

$$\text{Percentage cost of commercial paper } = \frac{\$71,000}{\$500,000} = 14.2\%$$

EXAMPLE 13-14
Ajax Corporation issues $300,00 worth of 18 percent, 90-day commercial paper. However, the funds are needed for only 70 days. The excess funds can be invested in securities earning 17 percent. The brokerage fee associated with the commercial paper transaction is 1.5 percent. The dollar cost to the company in issuing the commercial paper is:

Interest expense [0.18 × $300,000 × (90/360)]	$13,500
Brokerage fee (0.015 × $300,000)	4,500
Total cost	$18,000
Less: Return on marketable securities	
[0.17 × $300,000 × (20/360)]	2,833
Net cost	$15,167

EXAMPLE 13-15
The company needs $300,000 for the month of November. Its options are:
1. Obtaining a one-year line of credit for $300,000 with a bank. The commitment fee is 0.5 percent, and the interest charge on the used funds is 12 percent.
2. Issuing two-month commercial paper at 10 percent interest. Because the funds are needed only for one month, the excess funds ($300,000) can be invested in 8 percent marketable securities for December. The total transaction fee for the marketable securities is 0.3 percent.

The line of credit costs:

Commitment fee for unused period	
(0.005) (300,000) (11/12)	$1,375
Interest for one month (0.12) (300,000) (1/12)	3,000
Total cost	$4,375

The commercial paper costs:	
Interest charge (0.10) (300,000) (2/12)	$5,000
Transaction fee (0.003) (300,000)	900
Less interest earned on marketable securities	
(0.08) (300,000) (1/12)	(2,000)
Total cost	$3,900

Since $3,900 is less than $4,375, the commercial paper arrangement is the better option.

Using Receivables for Financing

In accounts receivable financing, the accounts receivable serve as security for the loan as well as the source of repayment.

Financing backed by accounts receivable generally takes place when:

- Receivables are at least $25,000.
- Sales are at least $250,000.
- Individual receivables are at least $100.
- Receivables apply to selling merchandise rather than rendering services.
- Customers are financially strong.
- Sales returns are low.
- The buyer receives title to the goods at shipment.

Receivable financing has several advantages. It eliminates the need to issue bonds or stock to obtain a recurring cash flow. Its drawback is the high administrative costs of monitoring many small accounts.

Accounts receivable may be financed under either a factoring agreement or an assignment (pledging) arrangement. *Factoring* is the outright sale of accounts receivable to a bank or finance company without recourse; the purchaser takes all credit and collection risks. The proceeds received by the seller are equal to the face value of the receivables less the commission charge, which is usually 2 to 4 percent higher than the prime interest rate. The cost of the factoring arrangement is the factor's commission for credit investigation, interest on the unpaid balance of advanced funds, and a discount from the face value of the receivables if there is high credit risk. Remissions by customers are made directly to the factor.

The advantages of factoring are that it offers immediate cash, it reduces overhead because the credit examination function is no longer needed, it provides financial advice, it allows for receipt of advances as required on a seasonal basis, and it strengthens the company's balance sheet position.

The disadvantages of factoring include both the high cost and the negative impression left with customers as a result of the change in ownership of the receivables. Factors may also antagonize customers by their demanding methods of collecting delinquent accounts.

In an *assignment* (pledging) arrangement, ownership of the accounts receivable is not transferred. Instead, receivables are given to a finance company with recourse. The finance company usually advances between 50 and 85 percent of the face value of the receivables in cash; your company is responsible for a service charge, interest on the advance, and any resulting bad debt losses, and continues to receive customer remissions.

The assignment of accounts receivable has the advantages of providing immediate cash, making cash advances available on a seasonal basis, and avoiding negative customer feelings. The disadvantages include the high cost, the continuing of administrative costs, and the bearing of all credit risk.

Financial managers must be aware of the impact of a change in accounts receivable policy on the cost of financing receivables. When accounts receivable are financed, the cost of financing may rise or fall. For example, when credit standards are relaxed, costs rise; when recourse for defaults is given to the finance company, costs decrease; and when the minimum invoice amount of a credit sale is increased, costs decline.

The financial officer should compute the costs of accounts receivable financing and select the least expensive alternative.

EXAMPLE 13-16

A factor will purchase the company's $120,000 per month accounts receivable. The factor will advance up to 80 percent of the receivables for an annual charge of 14 percent and a 1.5 percent fee on receivables purchased. The cost of this factoring arrangement is:

Factor fee [0.015 × ($120,000 × 12)]	$21,600
Cost of borrowing [0.14 × ($120,000 × 0.8)]	13,440
Total cost	$35,040

EXAMPLE 13-17

A factor charges a 3 percent fee per month. The factor lends the company up to 75 percent of receivables purchased for an additional 1 percent per month. Credit sales are $400,000 per month. As a result of the factoring arrangement, the company saves $6,500 per month in credit costs and a bad debt expense of 3 percent of credit sales.

XYZ Bank has offered an arrangement to lend the company up to 75 percent of the receivables. The bank will charge 2 percent per month interest plus a 4 percent processing charge on receivable lending.

The collection period is 30 days. If the company borrows the maximum per month, should it stay with the factor or switch to XYZ Bank?

Cost of factor:	
Purchased receivables (0.03 × $400,000)	$12,000
Lending fee (0.01 × .75 × $400,000)	3,000
Total cost	$15,000

Cost of bank financing:	
Interest (0.02 × .75 × $400,000)	$6,000
Processing charge (0.04 × $300,000)	12,000
Additional cost of not using the factor:	
Credit costs	6,500
Bad debts (0.02 × $400,000)	8,000
Total Cost	$32,500

Since $15,000 is less than $32,500, the company should stay with the factor.

EXAMPLE 13-18

A company needs $250,000 and is weighing the alternatives of arranging a bank loan or going to a factor. The bank loan terms are 18 percent interest, discounted, with a compensating balance of 20 percent. The factor will charge a 4 percent commission on invoices purchased monthly; the interest rate on the purchased invoices is 12 percent, deducted in advance. By using a factor, the company will save $1,000 monthly credit department costs, and avoid uncollectible accounts estimated at 3 percent of the factored accounts. Which is the better alternative for the company?

The bank loan which will net the company its desired $250,000 is:

$$\frac{\text{Proceeds}}{(100\% - \text{ proceeds deducted})} = \frac{\$250,000}{100\% - (18\% + 20\%)}$$

$$= \frac{\$250,000}{1.0 - 0.38}$$
$$= \frac{\$250,000}{0.62}$$
$$= \$403,226$$

The effective interest rate of the bank loan is:

$$\text{Effective interest rate } = \frac{\text{interest rate}}{\text{proceeds, \%}} = \frac{.18}{.62} = 29.0\%$$

We must briefly switch to the factor arrangement in order to determine the $8,929 below as a bank cost.

The amount of accounts receivable that should be factored to net the firm $250,000 is:

$$\frac{\$250,000}{1.0 - 0.12 - .04} = \frac{\$250,000}{0.84} = \$297,619$$

The total annual cost of the bank arrangement is:

Interest ($250,000 × 0.29)	$72,500
Additional cost of not using a factor:	
Credit costs ($1,000 × 12)	12,000
Uncollectible accounts ($297,619 × 0.03)	8,929
Total cost	$93,429

The effective interest rate of factoring accounts receivable is:

$$\text{Effective interest rate } = \frac{\text{interest rate}}{\text{proceeds, \%}} = \frac{12\%}{100\% - (12\% + 4\%)}$$
$$= \frac{0.12}{0.84}$$
$$= 14.3\%$$

The total annual cost of the factoring alternative is:

Interest ($250,000 × 0.143)	$35,750
Factoring ($297,619 × 0.04)	11,905
Total cost	$47,655

Factoring should be used since it will cost almost half as much as the bank loan.

Before looking at the next example on factoring, we should discuss several items that were mentioned in that example. Reserve on accounts receivable is the amount retained by the factor against problem receivables, which reduces the proceeds received by the company. Average accounts receivable is the average balance held for the period and is the basis for the factor's commission at the time the receivables are purchased by the factor.

EXAMPLE 13-19

A company is considering a factoring arrangement. The company's sales are $2,700,000, accounts receivable turnover is 9 times, and a 17 percent reserve on accounts receivable is required. The factor's commission charge on average accounts receivable payable at the point of receivable purchase is 2.0 percent. The factor's interest charge is 16 percent of receivables after subtracting the commission charge and reserve. The interest charge reduces the advance. The annual effective cost under the factoring arrangement is computed below.

$$\text{Average accounts receivable} = \frac{\text{credit sales}}{\text{turnover}} = \frac{\$2,7000,000}{9}$$
$$= \$300,000$$

The company will receive the following amount by factoring its accounts receivable:

Average accounts receivable	$300,000
Less: Reserve ($300,000 × 0.17)	-51,000
Commission ($300,00 × 0.02)	-6,000
Net prior to interest	$243,000
Less: Interest ($243,000 × 16%/9)	4,320
Proceeds received	$238,680

The annual cost of the factoring arrangement is:

Commission ($300,000 × 0.02)	$6,000
Interest ($243,000 × 16%/9)	4,320
Cost each 40 days (360/9)	$10,320
Turnover	× 9
Total annual cost	$92,880

The annual effective cost under the factoring arrangement based on the amount received is:

$$\frac{\text{Annual cost}}{\text{Average amount received}} = \frac{\$92,880}{\$238,680} = 38.9\%$$

Using Inventories for Financing

Financing inventory, which typically takes place when the company has completely used its borrowing capacity on receivables, requires the existence of marketable, nonperishable, and standardized goods that have quick turnover and that are not subject to rapid obsolescence. Good collateral inventory can be easily sold. However, you should consider the price stability of the merchandise and the costs of selling it when deciding on a course of action.

The cash advance for financed inventory is high when there is marketable inventory. In general, the financing of raw materials and finished goods is about 75 percent of their value; the interest rate is approximately 3 to 5 points over the prime interest rate.

The drawbacks of inventory financing include the high interest rate and the restrictions it places on inventory.

Types of inventory financing include floating (blanket) liens, warehouse receipts, and trust receipts. With a *floating lien,* the creditor's security lies in the aggregate inventory rather than in its components. Even though the company sells and restocks, the lender's security interest continues. With a *warehouse receipt,* the lender receives an interest in the inventory stored at a public warehouse; the fixed costs of this arrangement are high. There may be a field warehouse arrangement in which the warehouser sets up a secured area directly at the company's location; the company has access to the goods but must continually account for them. With a *trust receipt* loan, the creditor has title to the goods but releases them to the company to sell on the creditor's behalf; as goods are sold, the company remits the funds to the lender. The drawback of the trust receipt arrangement is that a trust receipt must be given for specific items.

A collateral certificate guaranteeing the existence of pledged inventory may be issued by a third party to the lender. The advantage of a collateral certificate is its flexibility; merchandise need not be segregated or possessed by the lender.

EXAMPLE 13-20

The company wants to finance $500,000 of inventory. Funds are required for three months. A warehouse receipt loan may be taken at 16 percent with a 90 percent advance against the inventory's value. The warehousing cost is $4,000 for the three-month period. The cost of financing the inventory is:

Interest $[0.16 \times 0.90 \times \$500,000 \times (3/12)]$	$18,000
Warehousing cost	4,000
Total cost	$22,000

EXAMPLE 13-21

The company shows growth in operations but is experiencing liquidity difficulties. Six large financially sound companies are customers and account for 75 percent of sales. On the basis of the following financial information for 20X1, should the financial manager borrow on receivables or inventory?

Balance sheet data follow:

Balance Sheet

ASSETS
Current Assets

Cash	$ 27,000	
Receivables	380,000	
Inventory (consisting of 55% of work-in-process)	320,000	
Total Current Assets		$ 727,000
Fixed Assets		250,000
Total Assets		$ 977,000

LIABILITIES AND STOCKHOLDERS' EQUITY
Current Liabilities

Accounts Payable	$ 260,000	
Loans Payable	200,000	
Accrued Expenses	35,000	
Total Current Liabilities		$ 495,000
Noncurrent Liabilities		
Bonds Payable		110,000
Total Liabilities		$ 605,000
Stockholders' Equity		
Common Stock	$ 250,000	
Retained Earnings	122,000	
Total Stockholders' Equity		372,000
Total Liabilities and Stockholders' Equity		$ 977,000

Selected income statement information follows:

Sales	$1,800,000
Net income	130,000

Receivable financing is the expected choice, since a high percentage of sales are made to only six large and financially strong companies. Receivables thus are highly collectible. It is also easier to control a few large customer accounts.

Inventory financing is not likely because of the high percentage of partially completed items. Lenders are reluctant to finance inventory when a large work-in-process balance exists, since it will be hard for them to process and sell the goods.

Financing with Other Assets

Assets other than inventory and receivables may be used as security for short-term bank loans. Possibilities include real estate, plant and equipment, cash surrender value of life insurance policies, and securities. Lenders are also usually willing to advance a high percentage of the market value of bonds or to make loans based on a third-party guaranty.

Table 13-1 presents a summary of the major features of short-term financing sources.

Short-term financing is easier to arrange, has lower cost, and is more flexible than long- term financing. However, short-term financing leaves the borrower more vulnerable to interest rate swings, requires more frequent refinancing, and requires earlier payment. As a rule, you should use short-term financing to provide additional working capital, to finance short-lived assets, or to serve as interim financing on long-term projects. Long-term financing is more appropriate for the financing of long-term assets or construction projects.

INTERMEDIATE-TERM FINANCING: TERM LOANS AND LEASING

We now consider the use of intermediate-term loans, primarily through banks and leases, to meet corporate financing needs. Examples are bank loans, insurance company term loans, and equipment financing.

Purposes of Intermediate-term Bank Loans

Intermediate-term loans are loans with a maturity of more than one year but less than five years. They are appropriate when short-term unsecured loans are not, such as when a business is acquired, new fixed assets are purchased, or long-term debt is retired. If a company wants to float long-term debt or issue common stock but market conditions are unfavorable, it may seek an intermediate loan to bridge the gap until conditions improve. A company may use extendable debt when it will have a continuing financing need, reducing the time and cost required for repeated debt issuance.

The interest rate on intermediate-term loans is typically higher than that for short-term loans because of the longer maturity period and varies with the amount of the loan and the company's financial strength. The interest rate may be either fixed or variable.

TABLE 13-1

SUMMARY OF MAJOR SHORT-TERM FINANCING SOURCES

Type of Financing	Source	Cost or Terms	Features
A. Spontaneous sources			
Accounts payable	Suppliers	No explicit cost but there is an opportunity cost if a cash discount for early payment is not taken. Companies should take advantage of the discount offered.	The main source of short-term financing typically on term of 0 to 120 days.
Accrued expenses	Employees and tax agencies	None	Expenses incurred but not yet paid (e.g., accrued wages payable, accrued taxes payable
B. Unsecured sources			
Bank loans 1. Single-payment note	Commercial banks	Prime interest rate plus risk premium. The interest rate may be fixed or variable. Unsecured loans are less costly than secured loans.	A single-payment loan to satisfy a funds shortage to last a short time period.
2. Lines of credit	Commercial banks	Prime interest rate plus risk premium. The interest rate may be fixed or variable. A compensating balance is typically required. The line of credit must be "cleaned up" periodically.	An agreed-upon borrowing limit for funds to satisfy seasonal needs.

Commercial paper	Commercial banks, insurance companies, other financial institutions, and other companies	A little less than the prime interest rate.	Unsecured, short-term note of financially strong companies.

C. Secured sources

Accounts receivable as collateral			
1. Pledging	Commercial banks and finance companies	2% to 5% above prime plus fees (usually 2%–3%). Low administrative costs. Advances typically ranging from 60% to 85%.	Qualified accounts receivable accounts serve as collateral. Upon collection of the account, the borrower remits to the lender. Customers are not notified of the arrangement. With recourse meaning that the risk of nonpayment is borne by the company.
2. Factoring	Factors, commercial banks, and commercial finance companies	Typically a 2%–3% discount from the face value of factored receivables. Interest on advances of almost 3% over prime. Interest on surplus balances held by factor of about $\frac{1}{2}\%$ per month. Costs with factoring are higher than with pledging.	Certain accounts receivable are sold on a discount basis without recourse. Customers are notified of the arrangement. The factor provides more services than is the case with pledging.

Inventory collateral

1. Floating liens	Commercial banks and commercial finance companies	About 4% above prime. Advance is about 40% of collateral value.	Collateral is all the inventory. There should be a stable inventory with many inexpensive items.
2. Trust receipts (floor planning)	Commercial banks and commercial finance companies	About 3% above prime. Advances ranging from 80% to 100% of collateral value.	Collateral is specific inventory that is typically expensive. Borrower retains collateral. Borrower remits proceeds to lender upon sale of the inventory.
3. Warehouse receipts	Commercial banks and commercial finance companies	About 4% above prime plus about 2% warehouse fee. Advance of about 80% of collateral value.	Collateralized inventory is controlled by lender. A warehousing company issues a warehouse receipt held by the lender. The warehousing company acts as the lender's agent.

Ordinary intermediate-term loans are payable in periodic equal installments except for the last payment, which may be higher (a balloon payment). The schedule of loan payments should be based on the company's cash flow position to satisfy the debt. The periodic payment in a term loan equals:

$$\text{Periodic Payment} = \frac{\text{Amount of loan}}{\text{Present value factor}}$$

EXAMPLE 13-22

The company contracts to repay a term loan in five equal year-end installments. The amount of the loan is $150,000 and the interest rate is 10 percent. The payment each year is:

$$\frac{\$150,000}{3.791^{(a)}} = \$39,567.40$$

---

[a] Present value of annuity for five years at 10%, T_4(10%, 5 years) (see Table 6-4 in Chapter 6).

The total interest on the loan is:

Total payments (5 × $39,567.40)	$197,837
Principal	150,000
Interest	$ 47,847

EXAMPLE 13-23

The company takes out a term loan in twenty year-end annual installments of $2,000 each. The interest rate is 12 percent. The amount of the loan is:

$$\$2,000 = \frac{\text{Amount of loan}}{7.469^{(a)}}$$
$$\text{Amount of loan} = \$2,000 \times 7.469$$
$$= \$14,938$$

---

[a] Present value of annuity for twenty years at 12%, T_4(12%, 12 years) (see Table 6-4).

The amortization schedule for the first two years is:

Year	Payment	Interest[a]	Principal	Balance
0				$14,938.00
1	$2,000	$1,792.56	$207.44	14,730.56
2	2,000	1,767.67	232.33	14,498.23

---

[a] 12 percent times the balance of the loan at the beginning of the year.

Restrictions may be placed on the company by the lender in an intermediate-term loan agreement in order to protect the lender's interest. Typical restrictions include:

■ Working capital requirements and cash dividend limitations, such as requiring a minimum amount of working capital or limiting dividend payment to no more than 20 percent of net income.

■ Routine (uniform) provisions employed universally in most agreements, such as the payment of taxes and the maintenance of proper insurance to assure maximum lender protection.

■ Specific provisions tailored to a particular situation, such as limiting future loans and requiring adequate life insurance for executives.

The advantages of intermediate-term loans are:

■ Flexibility—terms may be altered as the company's financing requirements change.

■ Confidentiality—no public issuance (offering to the investment public after registering with the Securities and Exchange Commission) is involved, so no information about the company's finances need be made public.

■ Speed—the loan may be arranged quickly, compared to preparing a public offering.

■ Security—avoids the possible nonrenewal of a short-term loan.

■ Low cost—eliminates public flotation (issuance) costs.

The disadvantages of intermediate-term loans are these:

■ Collateral and restrictive covenants are usually required.

■ Budgets and financial statements may have to be submitted periodically to the lender.

■ "Kickers" or "sweeteners," such as stock warrants or a share of the profits, are sometimes requested by the bank.

Insurance Company Term Loans

Insurance companies and other institutional lenders such as commercial finance companies may be sources of intermediate-term loans. Insurance companies typically accept loan maturity dates exceeding 10 years, but their rate of interest is often higher than that of bank loans. Insurance companies do not require compensating balances but usually impose a prepayment penalty, which is typically not true with a bank loan. A company may opt for an insurance company loan when it desires a longer maturity range.

Equipment-backed Financing

Equipment may serve as collateral for a loan, with the advance based on the market value of the equipment. The more marketable the equipment and the lower the cost of selling it, the higher the advance will be. The repayment schedule is designed so that the market value of the equipment at any given time is in excess of the unpaid loan principal.

Equipment financing may be obtained from banks, finance companies, and manufacturers of equipment and is secured by a chattel mortgage or a conditional sales contract. A *chattel mortgage* serves as a lien on property, except for real estate. In a *conditional sales contract,* the seller of the equipment keeps title to it until the buyer has satisfied the terms; otherwise the seller can repossess the equipment. Conditional sales contracts are generally used by small companies with low credit ratings.

Equipment trust certificates may be issued to finance the purchase of readily salable equipment, preferably equipment that is general purpose and easily movable. A trust is formed by the lessor to buy the equipment and lease it to the user; the trust issues the certificates to finance 75 to 85 percent of the purchase price and holds title to the equipment until *all* the certificates have been fully repaid, at which time the title passes to the lessee.

Advantages of Leasing

The parties in a lease are the *lessor,* who legally owns the property, and the *lessee,* who uses it in exchange for making rental payments. Of course, your company is the *lessee.*

There are several types of leases:

1. *Operating (service) lease.* This type of lease includes both financing and maintenance services. The company leases property that is owned by the lessor, who may be the manufacturer of the asset or a leasing company that buys assets from the manufacturer to lease to others. The lease payments under the contract are typically not adequate to recover the full cost of the property. Operating leases usually contain a cancellation clause that allows the lessee to return the property prior to the expiration date of the agreement. The life of the contract is less than the economic life of the property.

2. *Financial (capital) lease.* This type of lease usually does not provide for maintenance services. It is noncancellable, and the rental payments equal the full price of the leased property. The life of the contract approximates the life of the property.

3. *Sale and leaseback.* With this lease arrangement, the company sells an asset to another (usually a financial institution) and then leases it back. This allows the company to obtain cash from the sale and still have the use of the property.

4. *Leveraged lease.* In a leveraged lease, a third party serves as the lender. The lessor borrows a significant portion of the purchase price (usually up to 80 percent) to buy the asset and provides the balance of the purchase price as his equity investment. The property is then leased to the lessee. As security for the loan, the lessor grants the long-term lender a mortgage on the asset and assigns the lease contract to the lender. Leverage leasing is a cost-effective

alternative to debt financing when the lessee cannot use the full tax benefits of asset ownership.

Leasing has a number of advantages:

▬ No immediate cash outlay is required.

▬ It is a satisfactory way to meet temporary equipment needs and provides flexibility in operations.

▬ Usually there is a purchase option that allows the company to obtain the property at a bargain price at the expiration of the lease. This allows the flexibility to make a purchase decision based on the value of the property at the termination date.

▬ The lessor's expert service is available.

▬ Leasing typically imposes fewer financing restrictions than are imposed by lenders.

▬ The company's obligation for future rental payment need not be reported on the balance sheet if the lease is considered an operating lease. However, capital leases must be stated in financial statements.

▬ Leasing allows the company, in effect, to depreciate land, which is not allowed if land is purchased.

▬ Lessors may claim a maximum of three years' lease payments in the event of bankruptcy or reorganization, whereas creditors have a claim for the total amount of the unpaid financing.

▬ Leasing eliminates equipment disposal.

Leasing may be more attractive than buying when a business cannot use all of the tax deductions and tax credits associated with purchasing the assets.

Drawbacks to leasing are these:

▬ It carries a higher cost in the long run than purchasing the asset; the lessee does not build equity.

▬ The interest cost of leasing is typically higher than the interest cost on debt.

▬ If the property reverts to the lessor at termination of the lease, the lessee must cither sign a new lease or buy the property at higher current prices. Also, the salvage value of the property is realized by the lessor.

▬ The lessee may have to retain property it no longer needs or wants (i.e., obsolete equipment).

▬ The lessee cannot make improvements to the leased property without the permission of the lessor.

Examples 13-24 to 13-26 require the use of the present value of annuity table (Table 6-4), discussed in Chapter 6.

EXAMPLE 13-24

The company enters into a lease for a $100,000 machine. It is to make ten equal annual payments at year-end. The interest rate on the lease is 14 percent. The periodic payment equals:

$$\frac{\$100,000}{5.216^{(a)}} = \$19,171.78$$

---

[a] The present value of an ordinary annuity factor = T_4(14%, 10 years) = 5.216 (see Table 6-4).

EXAMPLE 13-25

Assume the same facts as in Example 13-24, except that now the annual payments are to be made at the beginning of each year. The periodic payment equals:

Year	Factor
0	1.0
1-9	4.9464
	5.9464

$$\frac{\$100,000}{5.946} = \$16,818.03$$

The interest rate associated with a lease agreement can also be computed by dividing the value of the leased property by the annual payment to obtain the factor, which is then used to find the interest rate with the help of a present value of annuity table.

EXAMPLE 13-26

The company leased $300,000 of property and is to make equal annual payments at year-end of $40,000 for 11 years. The interest rate associated with the lease agreement is:

$$\frac{\$300,000}{\$40,000} = 7.5$$

Going to the present value of annuity table and looking across 11 years to a factor nearest to 7.5, we find 7.499 at a 7% interest rate. Thus, the interest rate in the lease agreement is 7%.

Lease-Purchase Decision

The lease-purchase decision is one commonly confronting firms considering the acquisition of new assets. It is a hybrid capital budgeting decision that forces a company to compare the leasing and purchasing alternatives. To make an intelligent decision, an after-tax, cash out-flow, present value comparison is needed. There are special steps to take when making this comparison. When considering a lease, take the following steps:

1. Find the annual lease payment. Since the annual lease payment is typically made in advance, the formula used is:

$$\text{Amount of lease} = A + A \cdot T_4(i, n - 1)$$

or

$$A = \frac{\text{Amount of lease}}{1 + T_4(i, n - 1)}$$

Notice that we use $n - 1$ rather than n.

2. Find the after-tax cash outflows.
3. Find the present value of the after-tax cash outflows.

When considering a purchase, take the following steps:
1. Find the annual loan amortization by using:

$$A = \frac{\text{Amount of loan for the purchase}}{T_4(i, n - 1)}$$

The step may not be necessary since this amount is usually available.

2. Calculate the interest. The interest is segregated from the principal in each of the annual loan payments because only the interest is tax-deductible.
3. Find the cash outflows by adding interest and depreciation (plus any maintenance costs), and then compute the after-tax outflows.
4. Find the present value of the after-tax cash outflows, using Table 6-3.

EXAMPLE 13-27

A firm has decided to acquire an asset costing $100,000 that has an expected life of 5 years, after which the asset is not expected to have any residual value. The asset can be purchased by borrowing, or it can be leased. If leasing is used, the lessor requires a 12 percent return. As is customary, lease payments are to be made in advance, that is, at the end of the year prior to each of the 10 years. The tax rate is 50 percent, and the firm's cost of capital, or after-tax cost of borrowing, is 8 percent.

To summarize:

	Lease Proposal	Purchase Proposal
Cost of machine	$ 100,000	$ 100,000
Terms of payment	5 years	5 years
Interest rate	12%	10%
Down payment		
Monthly lease payment at the end of the year	$ 23,216	
Monthly loan payment		$ 26,381
Depreciation		Straight line
Residual purchase price	0%	0%
Corporate tax bracket	50%	50%
After-tax cost of capital.	8%	8%

First, compute the present value of the after-tax cash outflows associated with the leasing alternative.

Begin by finding the annual lease payment:

$$A = \frac{\text{Amount of lease}}{1 + T_4(i, n - 1)} = \frac{\$100,000}{1 + T_4(12\%, 4 \text{ ycars})}$$
$$= \frac{\$100,000}{1 + 3.3073}$$
$$= \frac{\$100,000}{4.3073}$$
$$= \$23,216 \text{ (rounded)}$$

Steps 2 and 3 can be done in the same schedule, as follows:

	(1)	(2)	(3) = (1) − (2)	(4)	(5) = (3) × (4)
Year	Lease Payment ($)	Tax Savings ($)	After-Tax Cash Outflow ($)	PV at 8%	PV of Cash Outflow ($ rounded)
0	23,216		23,216	1.000	23,216
1–4	23,216	11,608[a]	11,608	3.3121[b]	38,447
5		11,608	(11,608)	0.6806[c]	(7,900)
					53,763

---

[a] $23,216 × 50%

[b] From Table 6-4.

[c] From Table 6-3.

If the asset is purchased, the firm is assumed to finance it entirely with a 10 percent unsecured term loan. Straight-line depreciation is used with no salvage value. Therefore, the annual depreciation is $20,000 ($100,000/5 years). In this alternative, first find the annual loan payment by using:

$$A = \frac{\text{Amount of loan}}{T_4(i, n)} = \frac{\$100,000}{T_4(10\%, 5 \text{ years})}$$
$$= \frac{\$100,000}{3.7906}$$
$$= \$26,381 \text{ (rounded)}$$

Then, calculate the interest by setting up a loan amortization schedule.

	(1)	(2)	(3) = (2)(10%)	(4) = (1) – (3)	(5) = (2) – (4)
Yr	Loan Payment ($)	Beginning-of-Year Principal ($)	Interest ($)	Principal ($)	End-of-Year Principal ($)
1	26,381	100,000	10,000	16,381	83,619
2	26,381	83,619	8,362	18,019	65,600
3	26,381	65,600	6,560	19,821	45,779
4	26,381	45,779	4,578	21,803	23,976
5	26,381	23,976[a]	2,398	23,983[a]	

[a] Because of rounding errors, there is a slight difference between (2) and (4).

Steps 3 (cash outflows) and 4 (present values of those outflows) can be done as shown in Figure 13.1.

The sum of the present values of the cash outflows for leasing and purchasing by borrowing shows that purchasing is preferable because the PV of borrowing is less than the PV of leasing ($52,008 versus $53,763). The incremental savings is $1,675.

TABLE 13-2

BUY VERSUS LEASE EVALUATION REPORT

Year	Loan Payments (1)	Interest Expense (2)	Depreciation Expense (3)	Net After-Tax Cash Flow (4) = (1) − {.5[(2) + (3)]}	Present Value Factor (5)	Discounted Cash Flow Buy (6) = (4) × (5)
1	$26,381	$10,000	$ 20,000	$11,381	0.9259	10,538
2	26,381	8,362	20,000	12,200	0.8573	10,459
3	26,381	6,560	20,000	13,101	0.7938	10,400
4	26,381	4,578	20,000	14,092	0.735	10,358
5	26,381	2,398	20,000	15,182	0.6806	10,333
	$131,905	$31,898	$100,000	$65,956		$52,087

CHAPTER PERSPECTIVE

When seeking short-term financing, you should select the best financing vehicle available to meet the company's objectives. The choice of a particular financing instrument depends on the company's particular circumstances and such factors as cost, risk, restrictions, stability of operations, and tax rate. Sources of short-term financing include trade credit, bank loans, bankers' acceptances, finance company loans, commercial paper, receivable financing, and inventory financing.

Intermediate-term financing has a maturity between one and five years and includes multi-year bank or insurance company loans and leases. Fixed assets may serve as collateral. Some advantages of intermediate-term financing are its flexibility and its lower flotation costs.

Long-Term Debt Financing

INTRODUCTION AND MAIN POINTS

Long-term financing generally refers to financing with a maturity of more than five years. This chapter discusses the what, why, and how-to of long-term debt financing. Long-term debt financing consists primarily of bonds. Long-term financing is often used to finance long-lived assets, such as land or equipment, or construction projects. The more capital-intensive the business, the more it should rely on long-term debt and equity.

A company's mix of long-term funds is referred to as its *capital structure*. The ideal capital structure maximizes the total value of the company and minimizes the overall cost of capital. Managers charged with formulating an appropriate capital structure should take into account the nature of the business and industry, the company's strategic business plan, its current and historical capital structure, and its planned growth rate.

In this chapter, you will learn:
- The types of bonds that can be issued.
- The advantages of using bonds for long-term financing.
- How bond interest is calculated and paid.
- How to decide if a bond issue should be refunded before maturity.

TYPES OF LONG-TERM DEBT

Different types of debt instruments are appropriate in different circumstances. The amount of debt a company may have depends largely on its available collateral. Sources of long-term debt include mortgages and bonds.

Mortgages

Mortgages are notes payable that are secured by real assets and that require periodic payments. Mortgages can be issued to finance the purchase of assets, the construction of plant, or the modernization of facilities. Banks require that the value of the property exceed the mortgage on that property and usually lend up to between 70 percent and

90 percent of the value of the collateral. Mortgages may be obtained from a bank, life insurance company, or other financial institution. As a rule, it is easier to obtain mortgage loans for multiple-use real assets than for single-use real assets.

There are two types of mortgages: *senior* mortgages, which have first claim on assets and earnings, and *junior* mortgages, which have subordinate liens.

A mortgage may have a closed-end provision that prevents the company from issuing additional debt of the same priority against the specific property. If the mortgage is open-ended, the company can issue additional first-mortgage bonds against the property.

Mortgages have a number of advantages, including favorable interest rates, fewer financing restrictions than bonds, extended maturity dates for loan repayment, and easy availability.

Bonds

Long-term corporate debt usually takes the form of bonds payable and loans payable. A *bond* is a certificate indicating that the company has borrowed money and agrees to repay it. A written agreement, called an *indenture,* describes the features of the bond issue (e.g., payment dates, call prices should the issuer decide to reacquire the bonds, conversion privileges, and any restrictions).

The indenture is a contract between the company, the bondholder, and the trustee, who makes sure that the company meets the terms of the bond contract (in many instances, the trustee is the trust department of a commercial bank). Although the trustee is an agent for the bondholder, it is selected by the issuing company prior to the issuance of the bonds. If a provision of the indenture is violated, the bonds are in default. (Covenants in the indenture should be flexible enough to allow companies to respond quickly to changes in the financial world.) The indenture may also have a negative pledge clause, which precludes the issuance of new debt that takes priority over existing debt in the event of liquidation. The clause can apply to assets currently held as well as to assets that may be purchased in the future.

The price of a bond depends on several factors, including its maturity date, interest rate, and collateral. In selecting a maturity period for long-term debt, you should structure the debt repayment schedule so that not all of the debt comes due close together. It is best to spread out the payments to avoid the possibility that the cash flow will be inadequate to meet the debt payment. Also, if you expect your company's credit rating to improve in the near term, you should issue short-term debt and then refinance later at a lower interest rate.

Bond prices and market interest rates are inversely related. As market interest rates increase, the price of existing bonds falls because investors can invest in new bonds paying higher interest rates. The price of a bond on the open market depends on several factors such as its maturity value, interest rate, and collateral.

Interest. Bonds are issued in $1,000 denominations; many have maturities of 10 to 30 years. The interest payment to the bondholder is called *nominal interest,* which is the interest on the face of the bond and which is equal to the coupon (nominal) interest rate times the face value of the bond. Although the interest rate is stated on an annual basis, interest on a bond is usually paid seminannually. Interest expense incurred by the issuer is tax deductible.

EXAMPLE 14-1
A company issues a 20 percent, 20-year bond. The tax rate is 46 percent. The annual after-tax cost of the debt is:

$$20\% \times 54\% = 10.8\%$$

EXAMPLE 14-2
A company issues a $100,000, 12 percent, 10-year bond. The semi-annual interest payment is:

$$\$100,000 \times 12\% \times 6/12 = \$6,000$$

Assuming a tax rate of 30 percent, the after-tax semiannual interest is:

$$\$6,000 \times 70\% = \$4,200$$

A bond sold at face value ($1,000) is said to be sold at 100. If a bond is sold below its face value, it is being sold at less than 100 and is issued at a discount. If a bond is sold above face value, it is being sold at more than 100, that is, at a premium. A bond is likely to be sold at a discount when the interest rate on the bond is below the prevailing market interest rate for that type of security, when the issuing company is risky, or when it carries a long maturity period. A bond is sold at a premium when the opposite conditions exist.

Bond issue costs are also tax deductible.

EXAMPLE 14-3
Travis Corporation issues a $100,000, 14 percent, 20-year bond at 94. The maturity value of the bond is $100,000. The annual interest payment is:

$$14\% \times \$100,000 = \$14,000$$

The proceeds from the issuance of the bond is:

$$94\% \times \$100,000 = \$94,000$$

The amount of the discount is:

$$\$100,000 - \$94,000 = \$6,000$$

EXAMPLE 14-4

A bond having a face value of $100,000 with a 25-year life was sold at 102. The tax rate is 40 percent. The bond was sold at a premium since it was issued above face value. The total premium is $2,000 ($100,000 \times 0.02$).

Types of Bonds. Companies may issue various types of bonds:

■ *Debentures.* Because debentures are unsecured (have no collateral) debt, they can be issued only by large, financially strong companies with excellent credit ratings. Note, however, that most "junk bonds" are debentures of large companies that do not have good credit ratings.

■ *Subordinated Debentures.* The claims of the holders of these bonds are subordinated to those of senior creditors. Debt that has a prior claim over the subordinated debentures is set forth in the bond indenture. Typically, in the event a company is liquidated, subordinated debentures are paid off after short-term debt.

■ *Mortgage Bonds.* These are bonds secured by real assets. The first-mortgage claim must be met before a distribution is made to a second-mortgage claim. There may be several mortgages for the same property.

■ *Collateral Trust Bonds.* The collateral for these bonds is the company's security investments in other companies (bonds or stocks), which are held by a trustee for safekeeping.

■ *Convertible Bonds.* These bonds may be converted to stock at a later date based on a specified conversion ratio. Convertible bonds are typically issued in the form of subordinated debentures. Convertible bonds are more marketable and are typically issued at a lower interest rate than are regular bonds because they offer the right to *conversion* to common stock. Of course, if bonds are converted to stock, the debt is not repaid. A convertible bond is a quasi-equity security because its market value is tied to its value if converted to stock rather than as a bond. Chapter 17 discusses convertible bonds in detail.

■ *Income Bonds.* These bonds pay interest only if the company makes a profit. The interest may be cumulative, in which case it accumulates regardless of earnings and if bypassed must be paid in a later year when adequate earnings exist, or noncumulative. Income bonds are appropriate for companies with large fixed capital investments and large fluctuations in earnings or for emerging companies that expect low earnings in the early years.

■ *Guaranteed Bonds.* These are debt issued by one party and guaranteed by another.

■ *Serial Bonds.* These bonds are issued with different maturities available. At the time serial bonds are issued, a schedule is prepared to show the yields, interest rates, and prices for each maturity. The interest rate on the shorter maturities is lower than the interest rate on the longer maturities because there is less uncertainty about the near future.

■ *Deep Discount Bonds.* These bonds have very low interest rates and thus are issued at substantial discounts from face value. The return to the holder comes primarily from appreciation in price rather than from interest payments. The bonds are volatile in price.

■ *Zero Coupon Bonds.* These bonds do not pay interest; the return to the holder is in the form of appreciation in price. Lower interest rates may be available for zero coupon bonds (and deep discount bonds) because they cannot be called.

■ *Variable-Rate Bonds.* The interest rates on the bonds are adjusted periodically to reflect changes in money market conditions (e.g., prime interest rate). These bonds are popular when future interest rates and inflation are uncertain.

■ *Eurobonds.* Eurobonds are issued outside the country in whose currency the bonds are denominated. Dollar-denominated Eurobonds cannot be sold by U.S. issuers to U.S. investors but may be sold only to foreign investors, because they are not registered with the SEC. The bonds are typically in bearer form, meaning the securities are not registered on the books of the issuing corporation and thus are payable to whoever possesses them. A bearer bond has coupons attached, which the bondholder sends in or presents on the interest date to receive payment. If you are considering a bond issue, check to see if the Eurodollar market will give the company a lower cost option than the U.S. market. Eurobonds typically can only be issued by high-quality borrowers.

Small companies with unproven track records may have to issue what is commonly referred to as "junk bonds" (high-yielding risky bonds rated by Standard & Poor's as B+ or below or by Moody's Investors Service as B-1 or below). These are considered low-quality bonds.

A summary of the characteristics and priority claims associated with bonds appears in Table 14-1.

TABLE 14-1

SUMMARY OF CHARACTERISTICS AND PRIORITY CLAIMS OF BONDS

Bond Type	Characteristics	Priority of Lender's Claim
Debentures	Available only to financially strong companies. Convertible bonds are typically debentures.	General creditor.
Subordinated Debentures	Comes after senior debt holders.	General creditor.
Mortgage Bonds	Collateral is real property or buildings.	Paid from the proceeds from the sale of the mortgaged assets. If any deficiency exists, general creditor status applies.
Collateral Trust Bonds	Secured by stock and (or) bonds owned by the issuer. Collateral value is usually 30% more than bond value.	Paid from the proceeds of stock and (or) bond that is collateralized. If there is a deficiency, general creditor status applies.
Income Bonds	Interest is only paid if there is net income. Often issued when a company is in reorganization because of financial problems.	General creditor.
Deep Discount and Zero Coupon Bonds	Issued at very low or no (zero) coupon rates. Issued at prices significantly below face value. Usually callable at par value.	Unsecured or secured status may apply depending on the features of the issue.
Variable-rate Bonds	Coupon rate changes within limits based on changes in money or capital market rates. Appropriate when uncertainty exists regarding inflation and future interest rates. Because of the automatic adjustment to changing market conditions, the bonds sell near face value.	Unsecured or secured status may apply depending on the features of the issue.

Bond Ratings. Financial advisory services, such as Standard & Poor's and Moody's, rate publicly traded bonds according to their risk of default. An inverse relationship exists between the quality of a bond and its yield; low-quality bonds have a higher yield than high-quality bonds. Hence, a risk-return trade-off exists for the bondholder. Bond ratings are important because they influence marketability and the cost associated with the bond issue.

Advantages and Disadvantages to Debt Refinancing

Among the advantages of long-term debt are these:

▬ Interest is tax-deductible, while dividends paid to stockholders are not.

▬ Bondholders do not participate in earnings growth of the company.

▬ Debt is repaid in cheaper dollars during inflationary periods.

▬ Company control remains undiluted.

▬ Financing flexibility can be achieved by including a call provision allowing the company to pay the debt before the expiration date of the bond in the bond indenture. However, the issuer pays a price for this advantage in the form of the higher interest rates that callable bonds require.

▬ It may safeguard the company's future financial stability if used in times of tight money markets when short-term loans are not available.

The disadvantages of issuing long-term debt are these:

▬ Interest charges must be met regardless of the company's earnings.

▬ Debt must be repaid at maturity.

▬ Higher debt implies greater financial risk, which may increase the cost of financing.

▬ Indenture provisions may place stringent restrictions on the company.

▬ Overcommitments may arise from errors in forecasting future cash flow.

To investors, bonds have the following advantages:

▬ They pay a fixed interest payment each year.

▬ They are safer than equity securities.

However, investors should consider these disadvantages:

▬ Bonds carry interest rate risk, the chance that principal will be lost if interest rates rise and the bond drops in value.

▬ Bonds do not participate in corporate profitability.

▬ Bondholders have no voting rights and therefore no say in how the company is run.

The proper mixture of long-term debt and equity depends on company organization, credit availability, and the after-tax cost of financing.

If the company already has a high level of debt, it should take steps to minimize other corporate risks.

Long-term debt financing is appropriate when:

■ The interest rate on debt is less than the rate of return that can be earned on the money borrowed. For example, a company may borrow at 10 percent interest but earn a return of 18 percent by investing that money in the business. Through the use of other people's money (OPM), the company can increase its after-tax profit. (Stockholders will have made an extra profit with no extra investment!)

■ The company's revenue and earnings are stable, so that the company will be able to meet interest and principal in both good and bad years. However, cyclical factors should not scare a company away from having any debt. The important thing is to accumulate no more interest and principal repayment obligations that can reasonably be satisfied in bad times as well as good.

■ There is a satisfactory profit margin so that earnings are sufficient to meet debt obligations.

■ The liquidity and cash flow positions are good.

■ The debt/equity ratio is low so the company can handle additional obligations.

■ The risk level of the firm is low.

■ Stock prices are currently depressed so that it does not pay to issue common stock at the present time.

■ Control considerations are a primary factor (if common stock was issued, greater control might fall into the hands of a potential corporate raider).

■ The firm is mature, meaning it has been in business for a long time.

■ The inflation rate is expected to rise, so that debt can be paid back in cheaper dollars.

■ There is a lack of competition (e.g., entry barriers exist in the industry, such as stringent governmental regulations).

■ The markets for the company's products are expanding and the company is growing.

■ The tax rate is high so that the company will benefit by deducting interest payments from its taxes.

■ Bond indenture restrictions are not burdensome.

■ Money market trends are favorable and any necessary financing is available.

Project financing is tied to particular projects and may be suitable for large, self-contained undertakings, perhaps involving joint ventures.

If your company is experiencing financial difficulties, it may wish to refinance short-term debt on a long-term basis, perhaps by extending the maturity dates of existing loans. This may alleviate current liability and cash flow problems. As the default risk of your company becomes higher, so will the interest rate lenders demand to compensate for the greater risk.

When a high degree of debt (financial leverage) exists, you should try to reduce other risks (e.g., product risk) so that total corporate risk is controlled. The threat of financial distress or even bankruptcy is the ultimate limitation on leverage. If the company's debt is beyond a reasonable limit, the tax savings on interest expense will be offset by the increased interest rate demanded by creditors to compensate for the increased risk. Excessive debt also lowers the market price of stock because of the greater risk associated with the company.

Small companies with thinly traded stocks (little market activity) often issue debt and equity securities together in the form of *units*. A company may elect to issue units instead of convertible debt if it desires to increase its common equity immediately.

Bond Refunding. Companies may refund bonds before maturity by either issuing a serial bond or exercising a call privilege on a straight bond. The issuance of serial bonds allows the company to refund the debt over the life of the issue; calling the bond enables the company to retire it before the expiration date.

When future interest rates are expected to drop, it is wise for the company to exercise the call provision. It can buy back the higher-interest bond and then issue one at lower interest. The timing for the refunding depends on expected future interest rates. The call price typically exceeds the face value of the bond; the resulting call *premium* equals the difference between the call price and the maturity value. The call premium is usually equal to one year's interest if the bond is called in the first year; it declines at a constant rate each year thereafter. Also involved in selling a new issue are flotation costs (e.g., brokerage commissions, printing costs).

A bond with a call provision typically has a lower offering price and is issued at an interest rate higher than one without the call provision. Investors prefer not to have a situation in which the company can buy back the bond at its option prior to maturity; they would obviously prefer to hold onto a high-interest bond when prevailing interest rates are low.

EXAMPLE 14-5

A $100,000 issue of 8 percent, 10-year bonds is priced at 94 percent.
The call price is 103 percent. Three years after the issue, the bonds are
called. The call premium is equal to:

Call price	$103,000
Face value of bond	100,000
Call premium	$3,000

EXAMPLE 14-6

A company issues $40,000 of callable bonds. The call price is 104. The
tax rate is 35 percent. The after-tax cost of calling the issue is:

$$\$40,000 \times 0.04 \times 0.65 = \$1,040$$

EXAMPLE 14-7

Your company has a $20 million, 10 percent bond issue outstanding that
has 10 years to maturity. The call premium is 7 percent of face value.
New 10-year bonds in the amount of $20 million can be issued at an 8
percent interest rate. Flotation costs of the new issue are $600,000.

Refunding of the original bond issue should occur as shown here.

Old interest payments ($20,000,000 x 0.10)	$2,000,000
New interest payments ($20,000,000 x 0.08)	1,600,000
Annual Savings	$400,000
Call premium ($20,000,000 x 0.07)	$1,400,000
Flotation cost	600,000
Total cost	$2,000,000

Year	Calculation		Present Value
0	−$2,000,000	×1	−$2,000,000
1–10	$400,000	×6.71[a]	2,684,000
	Net present value		$684,000

---

[a] Present value of annuity factor for i = 8%, n = 10

Sinking Fund. Bond issues may require a sinking fund, into which the company puts aside money with which to buy and retire part of a bond issue each year. Usually, a mandatory fixed amount must be retired, but occasionally the amount is tied to the company's sales or profit for the year. If a sinking fund payment is not made, the bond issue may be in default.

In many instances, the company can handle the sinking fund in one of the following two ways:

▬ It can call a given percentage of the bonds at a specified price each year, for instance, 10 percent of the original amount at a price of $1,070.

▬ It can buy its own bonds on the open market.

The least costly of these alternatives should be selected. If interest rates have increased, the price of the bonds will have decreased and the open market option should be employed. If interest rates have decreased, bond prices will have increased; thus calling the bonds is less costly.

EXAMPLE 14-8

Your company has to reduce bonds payable by $300,000. The call price is 104. The market price of the bonds is 103. The company will opt to buy back the bonds on the open market because it is less expensive, as indicated below:

Call price ($300,000 × 104%)	$312,000
Purchase on open market ($300,000 × 103%)	309,000
Advantage of purchasing bonds on the open market	$3,000

CHAPTER PERSPECTIVE

This chapter has discussed the kinds of bonds a company uses in long-term financing. We have explained when to use bond financing and have discussed the advantages and disadvantages of using bonds. We have shown how bond interest is calculated and paid and we have showed you how to decide if bonds should be refunded before maturity. The next chapter covers stockholders' equity, the other source of long-term capital.

Long-Term Equity Financing

INTRODUCTION AND MAIN POINTS

All stock issued by a company is either preferred stock or common stock, regardless of what name the issue of stock may be given. And, although some companies may describe several different types or classes, there is (except in very rare cases) only one class of common stock. All other classes of stock, regardless of name, are preferred in some way over the one class of common stock. This chapter discusses the advantages and disadvantages of the different kinds of stock and other equity securities a company can issue. We will discuss the role of the investment banker and the difference between a public and private placement of securities.

After studying the material in this chapter:

■ You will understand the advantages and disadvantages of the different kinds of stock and other equity securities.

■ You will understand the characteristics of the different classes of stock.

■ You will understand the role of the investment banker.

■ You will see the importance of making wise capital structure decisions.

■ You will know the difference between a private and public placement of securities.

ISSUING EQUITY SECURITIES

The sources of equity financing are preferred stock and common stock. There are advantages and disadvantages associated with issuing preferred and common, and each is the issue of choice in certain circumstances.

Preferred Stock

Preferred stock is a hybrid of bonds and common stock. Preferred stock comes after debt but before common stock in the event of liquidation and in the distribution of earnings. The optimal time to issue preferred stock is when the company has excessive debt and an issue of common stock might encourage a corporate raider to try to take control of the company. Issuing preferred stock is a more expensive way to raise capital than issuing bonds because dividend payments are not tax deductible.

Preferred stock may be cumulative or noncumulative. If any prior year's dividend payments to holders of cumulative preferred stock have been missed, they must be made up before dividends can be paid to common stockholders. If preferred dividends are in arrears for a long time, the company may find it difficult to resume its dividend payments to common stockholders. The company need not pay missed preferred dividends to holders of noncumulative preferred stock. Most preferred stock is cumulative; dividends are limited to a specified rate, which is based on the total par value of the outstanding shares.

EXAMPLE 15-1

As of December 31, 20X6, Ace Company has 6,000 shares of $15 par value, 14 percent, cumulative preferred stock outstanding. Dividends have not been paid in 20X4 and 20X5. Assuming the company has been profitable in 20X6, the amount of the dividend to be distributed is:

Par value of stock $= 6,000$ shares $\times \$15 = \$90,000$

Dividends in arrears ($90,000 \times 14\% \times 2$ years)	$25,200
Current year dividend ($90,000 \times 14\%$)	12,600
Total dividend	$37,800

If dividends exceed the amount typically given to preferred stockholders and common stockholders, the preferred and common stockholders will participate in the excess dividends; in such cases, the preferred stock is referred to as participating preferred stock. Unless stated otherwise, the distribution of the excess dividends will be based on the relative total par values. Nonparticipating preferred stock does *not* participate with common stock in excess dividends. Most preferred stock is nonparticipating. Dividend policy is discussed further in Chapter 16.

Preferred stock may be callable. This provision is advantageous to the company when interest rates decline, since the company has the option of discontinuing payment of dividends at a rate that has become excessive by buying back outstanding preferred stock. Unlike bonds, preferred stock rarely has a maturity date; however, preferred stock that has a sinking fund associated with it in effect has a maturity date for repayment.

There are several forms of preferred stock issues. *Limited life preferred stock* has a specified maturity date or can be redeemed at the holder's option. *Perpetual preferred stock* automatically converts to common stock at a given date. There is also preferred stock with *"floating rate" dividends,* which keep the preferred stock at par by altering the dividend rate.

In the event of a corporate bankruptcy, preferred stockholders are paid after creditors and before common stockholders. In such a case, preferred stockholders receive the par value of their shares, dividends in arrears, and the current year's dividend. Any asset balance then goes to the common stockholders.

The cost of preferred stock usually follows changes in interest rates and is likely to be low when interest rates are low. When the cost of common stock is high, preferred stock may be issued at a lower cost.

A preferred stock issue has the following advantages:

■ Preferred dividends do not have to be paid (important during periods of financial distress). Interest on debt must be paid.

■ Preferred stockholders cannot force the company into bankruptcy.

■ Preferred shareholders do not share in unusually high profits because the common stockholders are the real owners of the business.

■ A growth company can generate better earnings for its original owners by issuing preferred stock having a fixed dividend rate than by issuing common stock.

■ Preferred stock issuance does not dilute the ownership interest of common stockholders in terms of earnings participation and voting rights.

■ No sinking fund is required.

■ The company does not have to collateralize its assets as it may have to do if bonds are issued.

■ The debt to equity ratio is improved.

A preferred stock issue does have some disadvantages:

■ Preferred stock must offer a higher yield than corporate bonds because it carries greater risk (since preferred stock comes after bonds in corporate liquidation).

■ Preferred dividends are not tax deductible.

■ Preferred stock has higher flotation costs than bonds.

To an investor, a preferred stock offers the following:

■ Preferred stock usually provides a constant return in the form of a fixed dividend payment.

■ Preferred stockholders come before common stockholders in the event of corporate bankruptcy.

■ Preferred dividends are subject to an 80 percent dividend exclusion for corporate investors. For example, if a company holds preferred stock in another company and receives dividends of $10,000, only 20 percent (or $2,000) is taxable. On the other hand, interest income received on bonds is fully taxable.

The disadvantages of preferred stock to an investor are:

■ Return is limited because of the fixed dividend rate.

■ Prices of preferred stock fluctuate more than those of bonds because there is no maturity date on the stock.

■ Preferred stockholders cannot require the company to pay dividends if the firm has inadequate earnings.

Common Stock Issues

Common stock is the residual equity ownership in the business; it does not involve fixed charges, maturity dates, or sinking fund requirements. Holders of common stock have voting power but come after preferred stockholders in receiving dividends and in liquidation.

Common stockholders enjoy the following rights:

■ The right to receive dividends.

■ The right to receive assets if the business dissolves.

■ The right to vote.

■ The preemptive right to buy new shares of common stock prior to their sale to the general public, thus allowing them to maintain proportionate percentage ownership in the company.

■ The right to a stock certificate which evidences ownership in the firm. The stock certificate may then be sold by the holder to another investor in the secondary security market, exchanges and over-the-counter markets in which securities are bought and sold after their original issuance. Proceeds of secondary market sales go to the dealers or investors, not to the company which originally issued the securities.

■ The right to inspect the company's books.

Companies may occasionally issue different classes of common stock. Class A is stock issued to the public that has no dividends but does usually have voting rights (although these are insufficient to obtain control of the company). Class B stock, which is typically kept by the company's organizers, does not pay dividends until the company has generated adequate earnings; it provides majority voting rights in order for current management to maintain control. Having two classes of stock enables the founders or management of the company to keep control by holding majority voting rights.

Authorized shares represent the maximum amount of stock the company can issue according to the corporate charter. *Issued shares* represents the number of authorized shares that have been sold by the firm. *Outstanding shares* are the issued shares actually being held by the investing public; *treasury stock* is stock that has been reacquired by the company. Outstanding shares are therefore equal to the issued shares less the treasury shares; dividends are based on the outstanding shares.

The *par value* of a stock is a stated amount of value per share as specified in the corporate charter. The company usually cannot sell stock at a price below par value since stockholders would then be liable to creditors for the difference between par value and the amount received if the company were to fail.

The price of common stock moves in opposition to market interest rates. For example, if market interest rates increase, stock prices fall as investors transfer funds out of stock into higher-yielding money market instruments and bank accounts. Further, higher interest rates raise the cost of borrowing, lowering profits and thus stock prices. Common stock is generally issued in one of the following ways:

■ *Broad syndication.* In a broad syndication, many investment bankers distribute corporate securities. This method is most common, because it gives the issuer the greatest control over distribution and thus probably achieves the highest net price. It also provides the widest public exposure. Its drawbacks are that it may take longer and has high transaction costs.

■ *Limited distribution.* In a limited distribution, a limited number of underwriters are involved in the issuance of the company's securities. As a result, the stock receives less public exposure. However, the issuing company may choose to work with only those investment bankers it believes are best qualified or who have the widest contacts.

■ *Sole distribution.* In a sole distribution, only one underwriter is used, possibly resulting in unsold shares. The company has less control in this set up than in a broad syndication, but incurs lower transaction costs. Sole distribution is also fast.

■ *Dribble-out.* In this method, the company periodically issues stock at different prices depending on market conditions. This approach is *not* recommended because of the high associated costs, and because it depresses stock price because of the constant issuance of shares.

In timing a public issuance of common stock, you should consider the following:

■ Do not offer shares near the expiration date for options on the company's shares, since the option-related transaction may affect share price. (An option is the right to buy stock at a specified price within a given time period. If the right is not exercised within the specified time period, the option expires.)

■ Offer higher yielding common stock just before the ex-dividend date to attract investors. Ex-dividend is a term used to indicate that a stock is selling without a recently declared dividend. The ex-dividend date is four business days before the date of record.

■ Issue common stock when there is little competition from other recent issues in the industry.

■ Issue shares in bull markets (a rising stock market) and refrain from issuing them in bear markets (declining markets).

You may need to determine the number of shares that must be issued to raise funds required to satisfy your capital budget.

EXAMPLE 15-2

Your company currently has 650,000 shares of common stock outstanding. The capital budget for the upcoming year is $1.8 million.

Assuming new stock may be issued for $16 a share, the number of shares that must be issued to provide the necessary funds to meet the capital budget are:

$$\frac{\text{Funds needed}}{\text{Market price per share}} = \frac{\$1,800,000}{\$16} = 112,500 \text{ shares}$$

EXAMPLE 15-3

Your company wants to raise $3 million in its first public issue of common stock. After its issuance, the total market value of stock is expected to be $7 million. Currently, there are 140,000 outstanding shares that are closely held (that is, held by a few shareholders). The shares held by the controlling group are not considered likely to be available for purchase.

We want to compute the number of new shares that must be issued to raise the $3 million.

The new shares will constitute 3/7 ($3 million/$7 million) of the outstanding shares after the stock issuance, and current stockholders will be holding 4/7 of the shares.

$$140,000 \text{ shares} = 4/7 \text{ of the total shares}$$
$$\text{Total shares} = \frac{140,000}{4/7}$$
$$\text{Total shares} = 245,000$$
$$\text{New shares} = 3/7 \times 245,000 = 105,000 \text{ shares}$$

After the stock issuance, the expected price per share is:

$$\text{Price per share} = \frac{\text{Market value}}{\text{Shares outstanding}} = \frac{\$7,000,000}{245,000} = \$28.57$$

A company that is about to make its first public offering of stock is referred to as "going public." The estimated price per share to sell the securities is equal to:

$$\frac{\text{Anticipated market value of the company}}{\text{Total outstanding shares}}$$

The anticipated market value of the company is based on a valuation model.

For an established company, the market price per share can be determined as follows:

$$\frac{\text{Expected dividend}}{\text{Cost of capital} - \text{growth rate in dividends}}$$

EXAMPLE 15-4

Your company expected the dividend for the year to be $10 a share. The cost of capital is 13 percent. The growth rate in dividends is expected to be constant at 8 percent. The price per share is:

$$
\begin{aligned}
\text{Price per share} &= \frac{\text{Expected dividend}}{\text{Cost of capital} - \text{growth rate in dividends}} \\
&= \frac{\$10}{0.13 - 0.08} \\
&= \frac{\$10}{0.05} \\
&= \$200
\end{aligned}
$$

Another approach to pricing the share of stock for an existing company is through the use of the price/earnings (P/E) ratio, which is equal to:

$$\frac{\text{Market price per share}}{\text{Earnings per share}}$$

EXAMPLE 15-5

Your company's earnings per share is $7. It is expected that the company's stock should sell at eight times earnings. (This expectation is usually based on what the stock of similar companies sells for in the market.)

The market price per share is therefore:

$$\text{P/E} = \frac{\text{Market price per share}}{\text{Earnings per share}}$$

$$\text{Market price per share} = \text{P/E multiple} \times \text{Earnings per share}$$
$$= 8 \times 7$$
$$= \$56$$

You may want to determine the market value of your company's stock. There are a number of different ways to accomplish this.

EXAMPLE 15-6
Assuming an indefinite stream of future dividends of \$300,000 and a required return rate of 14 percent, the market value of the stock equals:

$$\text{Market value} = \frac{\text{Expected dividends}}{\text{Rate of return}} = \frac{\$300,000}{0.14} = \$2,142,857$$

If there are 200,000 shares, the market price per share is:

$$\text{Market value} = \frac{\$2,142,857}{200,000} = \$10.71$$

EXAMPLE 15-7
Your company is considering a public issue of its securities. The average price/earnings multiple in the industry is 15. The company's earnings are \$400,000. There will be 100,000 shares outstanding after the issue. The expected price per share is:

$$\text{Total market value} = \text{Net income} \times \text{Price/earnings multiple}$$
$$= \$400,000 \times 15$$
$$= \$6,000,000$$

$$\text{Price per share} = \frac{\text{Market value}}{\text{Shares}}$$
$$= \frac{\$6,000,000}{100,000}$$
$$= \$60$$

If your company has significant debt, it will be better off financing with an equity issue to lower overall financial risk.

Financing with common stock has the following advantages:

■ The company is not required to pay fixed charges such as interest or dividends.

■ There is no repayment date or sinking fund requirement.

■ A common stock issue improves the company's credit rating compared to a bond issue. For example, it improves the debt-equity ratio.

Financing with common stock has disadvantages:

■ Dividends are not tax deductible.

■ Ownership interest is diluted. The additional voting rights might vote to remove the current ownership group from power.

■ Earnings and dividends must be spread over more shares outstanding.

■ The flotation costs of a common stock issue are higher than those for preferred stock and debt financing.

It is always cheaper to finance operations from internally generated funds because such financing involves no flotation costs. Retained earnings may be used as equity funding if the company believes its stock price is lower than the true value of its assets or if transaction costs for external financing are high.

The company may make use of dividend reinvestment plans, in which stockholders reinvest their dividends into the company by buying more shares, and employee stock option plans, which allow employees to buy company stock at an option price typically below what the market price of the stock will be when the option is exercised. Such plans allow the company to raise financing and avoid issuance costs and the market impact of a public offering.

An employee stock ownership plan (ESOP) is a program encouraging employees to invest in the employer's stock as a motivation tool for workers and a way for the company to raise funds.

A summary comparison of bonds and common stocks is presented in Exhibit 15-1.

Stock Rights

Stock rights—options to buy securities at a specified price at a later date—are a good source of common stock financing. *Preemptive rights* provide existing stockholders with the first option to buy additional shares. Exercising this right permits investors to maintain voting control and protects against dilution in ownership and earnings.

Financial management decides on the life of the right (typically about two months), its price (typically below the current market price), and the number of rights needed to buy a share.

In a rights offering, a date of record indicates the last day that the receiver of the right must be the legal owner as reflected in the company's stock ledger. To compensate for bookkeeping lags, stocks are often sold *ex rights* (without rights) four business days before the record date; prior to this point, the stock is sold *rights on,* which means the purchasers receive the rights and can exercise them, sell them, or let them expire.

EXHIBIT 15-1

SUMMARY COMPARISON OF BONDS AND COMMON STOCK

Bonds	Common Stock
Bondholders are creditors.	Stockholders are owners.
No voting rights exist.	Voting rights exist.
There is a maturity date.	There is no maturity date.
Bondholders have prior claims on profits and assets in bankruptcy.	Stockholders have residual claims on profits and assets in bankruptcy.
Interest payments represent fixed charges.	Dividend payments do not constitute fixed charges.
Interest payments are deductible on the tax return.	There is no tax deductibility for dividend payments.
The rate of return required by bondholders is typically lower than that required by stockholders.	The rate of return required by stockholders is typically greater than that required by bondholders.

Since stock rights are transferable, many are traded on the stock exchange and over-the-counter markets. They may be exercised for a given period of time at a *subscription price,* which is set somewhat below the prevailing market price. After the subscription price has been determined, financial management must ascertain the number of rights necessary to purchase a share of stock. The total number of shares that must be sold equals:

$$\text{Shares to be sold} = \frac{\text{Amount of funds to be obtained}}{\text{Subscription price}}$$

The number of rights needed to acquire one share equals:

$$\text{Rights per share} = \frac{\text{Total shares outstanding}}{\text{Shares to be sold}}$$

EXAMPLE 15-8

Your company wants to obtain $800,000 by a rights offering. There are presently 100,000 shares outstanding. The subscription price is $40 per share. The shares to be sold equal:

$$\text{Shares to be sold} = \frac{\text{Amount of funds to be obtained}}{\text{Subscription price}}$$
$$= \frac{\$800,000}{\$40}$$
$$= 20,000 \text{ shares}$$

The number of rights to acquire one share equals:

$$\text{Rights per share} = \frac{\text{Total shares outstanding}}{\text{Shares to be sold}} = \frac{100,000}{20,000} = 5$$

Thus, five rights will buy one new share at $40. Each right enables the holder to buy $\frac{1}{5}$ of a share of stock.

Value of a Right. The value of a right should, theoretically, be the same whether the stock is selling with rights on or with ex rights.

When stock is selling with rights on, the value of a right equals:

$$\frac{\text{Market value of stock with rights on } - \text{ subscription price}}{\text{Number of rights needed to buy one share } + 1}$$

EXAMPLE 15-9

Your company's common stock sells for $55 a share with rights on. Each stockholder is given the right to buy one new share at $35 for every four shares held. The value of each right is:

$$\frac{\$55 - \$35}{4 + 1} = \frac{\$20}{5} = \$4$$

When stock is traded ex rights, the market price is expected to decline by the value of the right. The market value of stock trading ex rights should theoretically equal:

$$\begin{array}{ccc} \text{Market value of stock} & & \text{Value of a right when} \\ \text{with rights on} & - & \text{stock is selling rights on} \end{array}$$

The value of a right with stock is selling ex rights equals:

$$\frac{\text{Market value of a stock trading ex rights } - \text{ subscription price}}{\text{number of rights needed to buy one new share}}$$

EXAMPLE 15-10

Assuming the same information as in Example 15-9, the value of the company's stock trading ex rights should equal:

Market value of stock with rights on — Value of a right when stock is selling rights on

or

$$\$55 - \$4 = \$51$$

The value of a right when stock is selling ex rights is:

$$\frac{\text{Market value of a stock trading ex rights} - \text{subscription price}}{\text{number of rights needed to buy one new share}}$$

$$= \frac{\$51 - \$35}{4}$$

$$= \frac{\$16}{4}$$

$$= \$4$$

The theoretical value of the right is identical when the stock is selling rights on or ex rights.

GOVERNMENTAL REGULATION

When securities are issued publicly, they must conform to federal and state regulations. The major federal laws are the Securities Act of 1933 and the Securities Exchange Act of 1934. State rules are referred to as *blue sky laws.*

The financial manager must be familiar with these laws for several reasons. First, a violation of the laws makes the manager subject to personal legal liability. Second, governmental regulation impacts the availability and costs of financing. Third, regulations apply to the money and capital markets in which the company's shares are traded. Fourth, the laws serve as safeguards to investors.

The Securities Act of 1933 deals with the regulation of new security issues. Its purpose is to ensure full disclosure of financial information about the company's affairs and to furnish a record of representations. The Act applies to interstate offerings to the public in amounts exceeding $1.5 million. Securities must be registered with the Securities and Exchange Commission (SEC) at least twenty days before they are publicly offered. Prior to the issuance of a new security issue, the company must prepare a prospectus for investors which contains a condensed version of the registration statement filed with the SEC, including accounting, financial, and legal information about the company. The SEC may delay or cease a public offering if information contained in the registration statement is erroneous, misleading, or incomplete. If the SEC-approved registration statement or prospectus is later found to contain misrepresentations, an investor who suffers losses can sue the issuing company and its officers for damages.

The Securities Exchange Act of 1934 applies to existing securities transactions. It requires full and accurate disclosure of financial information. Companies whose securities are listed on securities exchanges must file registration statements and periodic financial reports with both the SEC and the listing stock exchange. "Insider transactions" are monitored; officers and major stockholders of the company must prepare monthly reports of their holdings in the company's stock and changes therein. (An insider is defined as an officer, director, or stockholder of the company who controls 10 percent or more of equity shares.) The SEC also monitors trading practices in the stock exchanges and is empowered to monitor and punish manipulative activities affecting the company's stock. The voting process for corporate elections, particularly proxy voting (power of attorney by which the holder of stock transfers the voting right to another party), is also subject to SEC scrutiny; margin requirements regulating the purchase of securities on credit are regulated by the Federal Reserve System.

State blue sky laws are designed to protect investors from being defrauded. Companies issuing securities must register their offerings with the state in which they are incorporated, and furnish relevant financial information.

SELECTING A FINANCING METHOD

Some companies obtain most of their funds by issuing stock and from earnings retained in the business. Other companies borrow as much as possible and raise additional money from stockholders only when they can no longer borrow. Most companies are somewhere in the middle.

Financial managers are concerned with selecting the best possible source of financing based on the company's situation. They must consider the following:

▬ The cost and risk of alternative financing strategies.

▬ Future trends in market conditions and their impact on future fund availability and interest rates. For example, if interest rates are expected to go up, the company will be better off financing with long-term debt at the currently lower interest rates. If stock prices are high, equity issuance may be preferred over debt.

▬ The current debt-to-equity ratio. A very high ratio, for example, indicates financial risk, so additional funds should come from equity sources.

■ The maturity dates of present debt instruments. For example, the company should avoid having all debt come due at the same time; in an economic downturn, it may not have adequate funds to meet required debt payments.

■ The restrictions in loan agreements. For instance, a restriction may place a cap on the allowable debt-equity ratio.

■ The type and amount of collateral required by long-term creditors.

■ The company's ability to change financing strategy to adjust to changing economic conditions. For example, a company subject to large cyclical variations should have less debt because it may not be able to meet principal and interest at the low point of the cycle. If earnings are unstable and/or there is a highly competitive environment, more emphasis should be given to equity financing.

■ The amount, nature, and stability of internally generated funds. If earnings are stable, the company will be better able to meet debt obligations.

■ The adequacy of present lines of credit to meet current and future needs.

■ The inflation rate, since debt is repaid in cheaper dollars.

■ The earning power and liquidity position of the company. For example, a liquid company is able to meet debt payments.

■ The nature and risk of assets. High-quality assets in terms of cash realizability allow for greater debt.

■ The nature of the product line. A company, for example, that faces obsolescence risk in its product line (e.g., computers) should refrain from overusing debt.

■ The uncertainty of large expenditures. If huge cash outlays may be required (e.g., for a lawsuit or the acquisition of another company), additional debt capacity should be available.

■ The tax rate. For example, a higher tax rate makes debt more attractive because interest expense is tax deductible.

You have to select the best possible source of financing based on the facts.

EXAMPLE 15-11

Your company is considering issuing either debt or preferred stock to finance the purchase of a plant costing $1.3 million. The debt position is currently very high. The interest rate on the debt is 15 percent. The dividend rate on the preferred stock is 10 percent. The tax rate is 34 percent.

The annual interest payment on the debt is:

$$15\% \times \$1,300,000 = \$195,000$$

The annual dividend on the preferred stock is:

$$10\% \times \$1,300,000 = \$130,000$$

The required earnings before interest and taxes to meet the dividend payment is:

$$\frac{\$130,000}{(1 - 0.34)} = \$196,970$$

If your company anticipates earning $196,970 or more, it should issue the preferred stock because of its currently excessive debt position.

EXAMPLE 15-12

Your company has sales of $30 million a year. It needs $6 million in financing for capital expansion. The debt/equity ratio is 68 percent, which is considered quite high in the industry. Your company is in a risky industry, and net income is not stable. The common stock is selling at a high P/E ratio compared to competition. The company is considering either a common stock or a debt issue.

Because your company is in a high-risk industry and has a high debt/equity ratio and unstable earnings, issuing debt may be costly, restrictive, and potentially dangerous to the company's future financial health. A common stock issue is recommended.

EXAMPLE 15-13

Your company is a mature one in its industry. It has limited ownership. The company has vacillating sales and earnings. The debt/equity ratio is 70 percent, compared to the industry standard of 55 percent. The after-tax rate of return is 16 percent. Since your company is in a seasonal business, there are certain times during the year when its liquidity position is inadequate. Your company is unsure of the best way to finance.

Preferred stock is one possible means of financing. Debt financing is not recommended because of the already high debt/equity ratio, the fluctuation in profit, the seasonal nature of the business, and the deficient liquidity posture. Because of the limited ownership, common stock financing may not be appropriate because it would dilute the ownership.

EXAMPLE 15-14

A new company is established and plans to raise $15 million in funds. The company expects to obtain contracts that will provide $1,200,000 a year in before-tax profits. The company is considering whether to issue bonds only or an equal amount of bonds and preferred stock. The interest rate on AA corporate bonds is 12 percent. The tax rate is 50 percent.

The company will probably have difficulty issuing $15 million of AA bonds because the interest cost of $1,800,000 (13% × $15,000,000) on these bonds is greater than estimated earnings before interest and taxes. The issuance of debt by a new company is a risky alternative.

Financing with $7.5 million in debt and $7.5 million in preferred stock is also not recommended. While some debt may be issued, it is not practical to finance the balance with preferred stock. If $7.5 million of AA bonds were issued at the 12 percent rate, the company would be required to pay $900,000 in interest. A forecasted income statement would look as follows:

Earnings before interest and taxes	$1,200,000
Interest	900,000
Taxable income	$ 300,000
Taxes	150,000
Net income	$ 150,000

The amount available for the payment of preferred dividends is only $150,000. Hence, the maximum rate of return that could be paid on $7.5 million of preferred stock is .02 ($150,000/$7,500,000), too low to attract investors.

The company should consider financing with common stock.

EXAMPLE 15-15

Your company wants to construct a plant that will take about $1\frac{1}{2}$ years to construct. The plant will be used to produce a new product line, for which your company expects a high demand. The new plant will materially increase corporate size. The following costs are expected:
1. The cost to build the plant, $800,000
2. Funds needed for contingencies, $100,000
3. Annual operating costs, $175,000

The asset, debt, and equity positions of your company are similar to industry standards. The market price of the company's stock is less than it should be, taking into account the future earning power of the new product line. What would be an appropriate means to finance the construction?

Because the market price of stock is less than it should be and considering the potential of the product line, convertible bonds and installment bank loans might be appropriate means of financing, since interest expense is tax deductible. Additionally, issuing convertible bonds might not require repayment, since the bonds are likely to be converted to common stock because of the company's profitability. Installment bank loans can be paid off gradually as the new product generates cash inflow. Funds needed for contingencies can be obtained through open bank lines of credit.

If the market price of the stock were not depressed, financing through equity would be an alternative financing strategy.

EXAMPLE 15-16

Your company wants to acquire another business but has not determined an optimal means to finance the acquisition. The current debt/equity position is within the industry guideline. In prior years, financing has been achieved through the assistance of short-term debt.

Profit has shown vacillation; as a result, the market price of the stock has fluctuated. Currently, however, the market price of stock is strong.

Your company's tax bracket is low.

The purchase should be financed through the issuance of equity securities for the following reasons:

- The market price of stock is currently at a high level.
- Issuing long-term debt will cause greater instability in earnings, because of high fixed interest charges. Consequently, the stock price will become even more volatile.
- Issuing debt will result in a higher debt/equity ratio relative to the industry norm, negatively impacting the company's cost of capital and availability of financing.
- Short-term debt would have to be paid before the company receives a return from the acquired business and is therefore not advisable.

INVESTMENT BANKING

Investment banking is the underwriting of a securities issue by a firm that serves as an intermediary between the issuing company and the investing public.

The direct underwriting responsibilities of the investment banking firm may include preparing the SEC registration statement, assisting in pricing the issue, forming and managing a group of underwriters, and stabilizing the price of the issue during the offering and distribution period. When a client-relationship exists, the underwriter provides counseling and may have a seat on the board of directors of the company.

Investment bankers conduct the following activities:

■ *Underwriting.* The investment banker buys a new security issue, pays the issuer, and markets the securities. The underwriter's compensation is the difference between the price at which the securities are sold at to the public and the price paid to the issuing company.

■ *Distributing.* The investment banker markets the company's security issue.

■ *Advice.* The investment banker advises the company on the best way to obtain funds. The investment banker is knowledgeable about alternative sources of long-term funds, debt and equity markets, and SEC regulations.

■ *Providing Funds.* The investment banker provides funds to the company during the distribution period.

A *syndicate* is a group of several investment bankers who have come together to market a particularly large or risky issue. One investment banker (originating house) in the group will be selected to manage the syndicate and underwrite the major amount of the issue. The syndicate makes one bid for the issue, but the terms and features of the issue are set by the company.

The distribution channels for a new security issue are illustrated in Figure 15.1.

In another approach to investment banking, the investment banker may agree to sell the company's securities on a best-efforts basis, or to an agent. Here, the investment banker does not act as underwriter but instead sells the stock and receives a sales commission. Depending on the agreement, the agent may exercise an option to buy enough shares to cover its sales to the public, or the agent may cancel the incompletely sold issue altogether. Investment bankers may insist on this type of arrangement if they have reservations about the likelihood of success of the offering, such as with speculative securities issued by new and financially weak companies. A best-efforts arrangement involves risks and delays to the issuing company.

In selecting an investment banker for a new issue of securities, you should look for the following:

■ Low spread. Spread is the difference between the price paid to the issuing company by the investment banker and the resale price to the investor.

■ Good references, meaning other issuing companies were satisfied

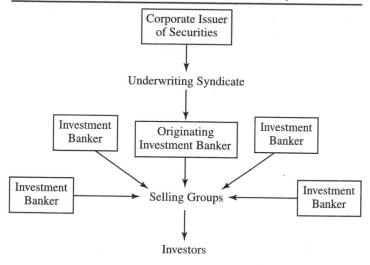

Figure 15.1 *Distribution Channels for a New Security Issue*

with the investment banker's performance.
- Ability to float many shares at a good price.
- Institutional (corporate) and retail (individual) clientele.
- Good after-market performance, meaning securities do well after issuance.
- Wide geographic distribution.
- Attractive secondary markets for resale.
- Knowledge of market, regulations, industry, and company.

Public vs. Private Placement

Equity and debt securities may be issued either publicly or privately. In a public issuance, the shares are bought by the general public; in a private placement, the company issues securities directly to either one or a few large investors, usually financial institutions such as insurance companies, pension plans, and commercial banks.

Private placement has the following advantages compared to public issuance:
- The flotation cost is less. The flotation cost for common stock exceeds that for preferred stock and, expressed as a percentage of gross proceeds, is higher for smaller issues than for larger ones.

▬ It avoids SEC filing requirements.

▬ It avoids the need for disclosure of information to the public.

▬ It reduces the time lag for obtaining funds.

▬ It offers greater flexibility.

▬ It may be the only avenue available to small companies planning small issues that would not be sufficiently profitable to attract the interest of investment bankers.

▬ If the company's credit rating is low, private investors with limited funds may not be interested in purchasing the securities.

The drawbacks of private placement compared to public issuance are these:

▬ Private placement often requires a higher interest rate because of a reduced resale market.

▬ Private placements usually have a shorter maturity period than public issues.

▬ It is more difficult to obtain significant amounts of money in private placements than in public ones.

▬ Large private investors typically use stringent credit standards and require the company to be in strong financial condition. In addition, they impose more restrictive terms.

▬ Large institutional investors may watch the company's activities more closely than smaller investors in a public issue.

▬ Large institutional investors are more capable of obtaining voting control of the company, assuming they hold a large amount of stock.

Most private placements involve debt securities; in fact, only about 2 percent of common stock is placed privately. The private market is more receptive to smaller issues (e.g., those up to several million dollars). Small and medium-sized companies typically find it cheaper to place debt privately than publicly, especially when the issue is $5 million or less.

CHAPTER PERSPECTIVE

Your company may finance long-term with debt or equity (preferred stock and common stock) funds. Each has its own advantages and disadvantages. The facts of a situation have to be examined to determine which type is best under the circumstances. For example, a rapidly growing company needs flexibility in its capital structure. While a high debt position may be needed to sustain growth, it is important that periodic additions to equity are made.

INTRODUCTION AND MAIN POINTS

Corporate earnings that are distributed to stockholders are referred to as dividends. Dividends are paid in either cash or stock, usually on a quarterly basis, and may be paid only out of retained earnings, not from invested capital. Generally, the more stable a company's profitability, the more regular its issuance of dividends. Types of dividend policies include stable dividends per share, constant dividend payout ratio, and residual dividends. The factors that determine the amount of money available for dividends include corporate growth rate, restrictive covenants, profitability, earnings stability, degree of debt, and tax factors.

In this chapter, you will learn:
- The effect of a company's dividend policy on its cash flow and the market price of its stock.
- The different dividend dates.
- The types of dividend policies, advantages and disadvantages.
- The financial and operating factors that affect the amount of dividends paid.
- The difference between stock dividends and stock splits.
- The reasons a company might reacquire its stock and the financial effects of such an action.

DIVIDEND POLICY

Dividend policy is important for the following reasons:
- It influences investor attitudes. Stockholders look negatively on companies that cut dividends, since they associate such cutbacks with financial difficulties. In establishing a dividend policy, a financial manager must determine and fulfill the owners' objectives; otherwise, the stockholders may sell their shares, in turn driving down the market price of the stock. Stockholder dissatisfaction raises the possibility that control of the company may be seized by an outside group.

■ It impacts the financing program and capital budget of the company.

■ It affects the company's cash flow. A company with a poor liquidity position may be forced to restrict its dividend payments.

■ It lowers stockholders' equity, since dividends are paid from retained earnings. This results in a higher debt to equity ratio.

If a company's cash flow and investment requirements are volatile, the company should not establish a high regular dividend. It is preferable to establish a low regular dividend that can be met even in bad years.

DIVIDEND DATES

A number of dividend dates are important to understand:

■ *Declaration date*—the date on which the board of directors declares the dividend. On this date, the payment of the dividend becomes a legal liability to the corporation.

■ *Date of record*—the date on which the stockholder is entitled to receive the dividend.

■ *Ex-dividend date*—the date on which the right to the dividend leaves the shares. The right to a dividend stays with the stock until four days before the date of record; that is, on the fourth day before the record date, the right to the dividend is no longer with the shares, and the seller, rather than the buyer, of the stock is the one who will receive the dividend. The market price of the stock takes into account the fact that it has gone ex-dividend and decreases by approximately the amount of the dividend.

■ *Date of payment*—the date on which the company distributes its dividend checks to its stockholders.

Dividends are usually paid in cash and are expressed in dollars and cents per share. However, the dividend on preferred stock is sometimes expressed as a percentage of par value.

EXAMPLE 16-1

The date of record for the dividend declared by the ABC Company is October 20. Mr. H sells Ms. J his 100 shares on October 18. Mr. H, not Ms. J, will receive the dividend.

EXAMPLE 16-2

On November 15, 20X1, a cash dividend of $1.50 per share was declared on 10,000 shares of $10 par value common stock. The amount of the dividend paid by the company is $15,000 (10,000 × $1.50).

EXAMPLE 16-3

J Corporation has 20,000 shares of $10 par value, 12 percent preferred stock outstanding. On October 15, 20X1, a cash dividend was declared to holders of record as of December 15, 20X1. The amount of dividend to be paid by J Corporation is equal to:

20,000 shares $\times$ $10 par value $= $200,000 \times 12\% = $24,000$

Some companies allow stockholders to reinvest their dividends automatically in corporate shares rather than receive cash. The advantage to the stockholders is that they avoid the brokerage fees associated with buying new shares. However, they receive no tax advantage since they must still pay ordinary income taxes on the dividend received.

TYPES OF DIVIDEND POLICIES

A financial manager's dividend policy objectives are to maximize owner wealth while providing adequate financing for the company. An increase in a company's earnings does not automatically raise the dividend; there is generally a time lag between increased earnings and the payment of a higher dividend. Only when the financial manager is optimistic that the increased earnings will be sustained should he or she increase the dividend. Once dividends are increased, they should continue at the higher rate because stockholders get used to it and react unfavorably to decreased payments.

Different types of dividend policies include:

■ *Stable dividend-per-share policy.* Many companies use a stable dividend-per-share policy, since such a policy is favored by investors. Dividend stability implies a low-risk company; even in a year when the company shows a loss, it should maintain its dividend to avoid repercussions among current and prospective investors, who are then more likely to see the loss as temporary. Some stockholders rely on the receipt of stable dividends for income. A stable dividend policy is also necessary for a company to be considered for investment by major financial institutions, such as pension funds and insurance companies. Being on such a list provides greater marketability for corporate shares.

■ *Constant dividend-payout ratio (dividends per share/earnings per share).* Companies following this policy pay out a constant percentage of earnings in dividends. Because net income fluctuates, dividends also vary. The problem this policy causes is that if the company's earnings fall drastically or if there is a loss, dividends will be significantly reduced or nonexistent. This policy does not maximize market price per share, since most stockholders do not want variability in their dividend receipts.

■ *A compromise policy.* One compromise between the policies of a stable dollar amount and a percentage amount of dividends is for a company to pay a stable lower dollar amount per share plus a percentage increment in good years. While this policy gives flexibility, it also creates uncertainty in the minds of investors as to the amount of dividends they are likely to receive. Stockholders typically do not like such uncertainty. However, this policy may be appropriate if earnings vary considerably over the years. The percentage, or extra, portion of the dividend should not be paid regularly; otherwise, it becomes meaningless.

■ *Residual-dividend policy.* When a company's investment opportunities are not stable, its financial managers may wish to consider a vacillating dividend policy. With this type of policy the amount of earnings retained depends on the availability of investment opportunities in a given year. Dividends are drawn from the *residual* earnings after the company's investment needs are met.

EXAMPLE 16-4

Company A and company B are identical in every respect except for their dividend policies. Company A pays out a constant percentage of its net income (60 percent dividends), while company B pays out a constant dollar dividend. Company B's market price per share is higher than that of company A because the stock market looks favorably upon stable dollar dividends. They reflect less investor uncertainty about the company.

EXAMPLE 16-5

Most Corporation had a net income of $800,000 in 20X1. Earnings have grown at an 8 percent annual rate. Dividends in 20X1 were $300,000. In 20X2, the net income was $1,100,000. This was much higher than the typical 8 percent annual growth rate. It is expected that profits will be back to the 8 percent rate in future years. The investment in 20X2 was $700,000.

Assuming a stable dividend payout ratio of 25 percent, the dividends to be paid in 20X2 will be $275,000 ($1,100,000 × 25%).

If a stable dollar dividend policy is maintained, the 20X2 dividend payment will be $324,000 ($300,000 × 1.08).

Assuming a residual dividend policy is maintained and 40 percent of the 20X2 investment is financed with debt, the 20X2 dividend will be:

Equity needed $= \$700,000 × 60\% = \$420,000$

Because net income exceeds the equity needed, all of the $420,000 of equity investment will be derived from net income.

$$\text{Dividend} = \$1,100,000 - \$420,000 = \$680,000$$

If the investment for 20X2 is to be financed with 80 percent debt and 20 percent retained earnings and any net income not invested is paid out in dividends, then the dividends will be:

$$\text{Earnings retained} = \$700,000 \times 20\% = \$140,000$$
$$\text{Dividend} = \text{Net income} - \text{Earnings retained}$$
$$\$960,000 = \$1,100,000 - \$140,000$$

Theoretically, a company should retain earnings rather than distribute them when the corporate return exceeds the return investors can obtain on their money elsewhere. In addition, if the company obtains a return on its profits that exceeds the cost of capital, the market price of its stock will be maximized. On the other hand, a company should not keep funds for investment if it earns a lower return than its investors can earn elsewhere. If the owners have better investment opportunities outside the company, the company should pay a high dividend.

Although theoretical considerations from a financial perspective should be taken into account when establishing dividend policy, the *practicality* of the situation is that investors expect to be paid dividends. Psychological factors come into play and may adversely impact the market price of a stock that does not pay dividends.

FACTORS THAT AFFECT DIVIDEND POLICY

A company's dividend policy depends on many variables, some of which have been already mentioned. Other factors to be considered are:

■ *Company growth rate.* A rapidly growing business, even if profitable, may have to restrict dividends to keep funds within the company to invest for growth.

■ *Restrictive covenants.* Sometimes there is a restriction in a credit agreement that limits the dividends that may be paid.

■ *Profitability.* Dividend distribution is keyed to the profitability of the company.

■ *Earnings stability.* A company with stable earnings is more likely to distribute a higher percentage of its earnings than one with unstable earnings.

■ *Maintenance of control.* Financial managers who are reluctant to issue additional common stock because they fear diluting control of the business will retain a higher percentage of its earnings. Internal financing enables the company to maintain its control.

■ *Degree of financial leverage.* A company with a high debt-to-equity ratio is more likely to retain profits to ensure that it will have the funds to pay interest and principal on debt.

■ *Ability to finance externally.* A company that is capable of entering the capital markets easily can afford to have a higher dividend payout ratio. If access to external sources of funds is limited, the company will retain more earnings to meet planned financial needs.

■ *Uncertainty.* Payment of dividends reduces the uncertainty in stockholders' minds about the company's financial health.

■ *Age and size.* The age and size of the company bear upon its ease of access to capital markets. A mature, large company is typically deemed to be more secure than a young company.

■ *Tax penalties.* A desire to avoid possible tax penalties for excess accumulation of retained earnings may result in high dividend payouts.

■ *Tax position of investors.* Under current tax law, dividends are fully taxed to individual investors, but long-term capital gains are capped at 20 percent. For example, an individual in the 31 percent tax bracket would have to pay 31 percent in taxes on dividends but only 20 percent on long-term capital gains.

There is an ongoing controversy about the impact of dividend policy on a company's financial well-being. A number of authors have taken positions on this issue.

Many believe that cash flows of a company having a low dividend payout will be capitalized at a lower rate. They argue that investors will consider capital gains resulting from earnings retention to be more risky than dividends, because there is more uncertainty in depending on appreciation in market price of stock than in receiving a fixed dividend.

A change in dividends impacts the price of the stock, since investors consider such a change as being a statement about expected future profits. They believe that investors are generally indifferent to dividends or capital gains.

The choice of dividend policy varies with the particular characteristics of the company and its owners, including the tax bracket and income needs of stockholders and corporate investment opportunities.

STOCK DIVIDENDS

A stock dividend is an additional share of stock issued to stockholders. Such dividends may be declared when the cash position of the company is inadequate to support a cash dividend and/or when the company wishes to prompt increased trading in its stock by reducing its market price. Stock dividends increase the number of shares held, but the proportion of the company owned by each stockholder remains the same. In other words, if a stockholder has a 2 percent interest in the company prior to a stock dividend, he or she will continue to have a 2 percent interest after the stock dividend.

EXAMPLE 16-6

Mr. J owns 200 shares of N Corporation. There are 10,000 shares outstanding; therefore, Mr. J holds a 2 percent interest in the company. The company issues a stock dividend of 10 percent. Mr. J will then have 220 shares out of 11,000 shares issued. His proportionate interest remains at 2 percent (220/11,000).

STOCK SPLITS

A stock split is the issuance of a substantial amount of additional shares, thereby reducing the par value of the stock on a proportionate basis. A stock split is often prompted by a desire to reduce the market price per share, making it easier for small investors to buy shares.

EXAMPLE 16-7

S Corporation has 1,000 shares of $20 par value common stock out-standing. The total par value is $20,000. A 4-for-1 stock split is issued. After the split, 4,000 shares at $5 par value will be outstanding. The total par value thus remains at $20,000. Theoretically, the market price per share of the stock should drop to one-fourth of what it was before the split.

STOCK DIVIDEND VERSUS STOCK SPLIT

The differences between a stock dividend and stock split are as follows:
1. With a stock dividend, a company reduces its retained earnings and distributes shares on a pro rata basis to stockholders. A stock split increases the shares outstanding but does not lower retained earnings.
2. The par value of stock remains the same after a stock dividend is paid but is proportionally reduced in a stock split.

Stock dividends and stock splits are similar in that:
1. Cash is not paid.
2. Shares outstanding increase.
3. Stockholders' equity remains the same.

STOCK REPURCHASES

Companies may purchase treasury stock as an alternative to paying dividends. Since outstanding shares will be fewer after such a purchase, earnings per share will increase (assuming net income is constant). The increase in earnings per share may result in a higher market price per share.

EXAMPLE 16-8

A company earned $2.5 million in 20X1. Of this amount, it decided that 20 percent would be used to buy treasury stock. Currently, there are 400,000 shares outstanding. Market price per share is $18. The company can use $500,000 (20% × $2.5 million) to buy back 25,000 shares through a tender offer to stockholders of $20 per share. The offer price of $20 is higher than the current market price of $18 because the company feels its buyback will drive up the price of existing shares as a function of the law of supply and demand.

Current earnings per share is:

$$\text{EPS} = \frac{\text{Net income}}{\text{Outstanding shares}} = \frac{\$2,500,000}{400,000} = \$6.25$$

The current P/E multiple is:

$$\frac{\text{Market price per share}}{\text{Earnings per share}} = \frac{\$18}{\$6.25} = 2.88 \text{ times}$$

Earnings per share after treasury stock is acquired becomes:

$$\frac{\$2,500,000}{400,000 - 25,000} = \frac{\$2,500,000}{375,000} = 6.67$$

The expected market price, assuming the P/E ratio (multiple) remains the same, is:

$$\text{P/E multiple} \times \text{New earnings per share} = \text{Expected market price}$$
$$2.88 \times \$6.67 = \$19.21$$

To stockholders, stock repurchases have the advantage of increasing the market price per share, since fewer shares will be outstanding.

To the company, the benefits of a stock repurchase include the following:

1. It is a way of using excess temporary cash without paying higher dividends that may not be able to be maintained.
2. Treasury stock can be used for future acquisitions or used as a basis for stock options.

3. Treasury stock can be resold in the market if additional funds are needed.

To stockholders, the disadvantages of treasury stock acquisitions include the following:
1. The market price of stock may benefit more from a dividend than from a stock repurchase.
2. Treasury stock may be bought at an excessively high price to the detriment of the remaining stockholders. A higher price may be paid for treasury stock when share activity is limited or when the company wishes to reacquire a significant number of shares.

To the company, the disadvantages of treasury stock acquisition are these:
1. Market price may drop if investors believe that the company is engaging in a repurchase plan because its management does not have good alternative investment opportunities. However, this is not always the case.
2. The company risks an SEC investigation if it appears that the reacquisition of stock is in an effort to manipulate the company's stock price. Further, if the Internal Revenue Service (IRS) concludes that the repurchase is designed to avoid paying tax on dividends, tax penalties may be imposed because of the improper accumulation of earnings.

CHAPTER PERSPECTIVE

Companies may declare two types of dividends—cash and stock. A company's dividend policy affects its cash flow and the market price of its stock. Important dividend dates are declaration date, date of record, and payment date. Companies may select from different dividend policies, including stable dividends per share and constant dividend payout ratio. A company's dividend policy may be based on many factors such as growth rate, earnings, liquidity, restrictive convenants, and operating risk. A company may issue a stock split or reacquire its shares depending on its financial objectives.

Warrants and Convertibles

INTRODUCTION AND MAIN POINTS

Warrants and convertibles are unique among securities because they may be converted into common stock. This chapter discusses the valuation of warrants and convertibles, presents their advantages and disadvantages, and discusses when their issuance is most appropriate.

In this chapter, you will learn:

■ What warrants are and how to value them.

■ The positive and negative aspects of warrants.

■ The features of convertible securities and how to value them.

■ The positive and negative aspects of convertible securities.

■ The role of warrants and convertibles in a company's financing strategy.

■ The difference between warrants and convertibles.

WARRANTS

A *warrant* is an option to purchase a given number of shares of stock at a specified price. A warrant can be either detachable or nondetachable. A *detachable* warrant may be sold separately from the bond with which it is associated, allowing the holder to exercise the warrant without redeeming the bond; a *nondetachable* warrant is sold with its bond to be exercised by the bondholder simultaneously with the convertible bond.

A company may sell warrants separately or in combination with other securities.

To obtain common stock, the holder must surrender the warrant and pay a sum called the *exercise price*. Although warrants typically expire on a given date, some are perpetual. A holder of a warrant may exercise it by buying the stock, sell it on the market to other investors, or continue to hold it. An investor may wish to hold a warrant rather than exercise or sell it because there exists a possibility of achieving a high rate of return as the market price of the related common stock appreciates. But there are several drawbacks to warrants, including a high risk of losing money, the absence of voting rights, and the lack of dividends.

The company cannot force the exercise of a warrant. However, the company may vary the exercise price associated with a warrant.

If a stock split or stock dividend is declared before the warrant is exercised, the option price of the warrant is usually adjusted to reflect the effect of the action.

Warrants can provide additional funds for the issuer. When a bond is issued with a warrant, the warrant price is typically set between 10 percent and 20 percent above the stock's market price. If the company's stock price goes above the option price, the warrants will, of course, be exercised at the option price. The closer the warrants are to their expiration date, the greater the chance that they will be exercised, assuming the stock has reached the exercise price.

Valuing a Warrant

The theoretical value of a warrant may be computed by a formula; however, the formula value is usually less than the market price of the warrant. The reason for this difference is that the speculative appeal of a warrant allows investors to obtain a good degree of personal leverage because, with a relatively small investment, they have a chance to obtain a significant gain.

Value of a warrant = (Market price per share − Exercise price)
                                          × Number of shares that may be bought

EXAMPLE 17-1

A warrant for XYZ company's stock gives the owner the right to buy one share of common stock at $25 a share. The market price of the common stock is $53. The formula price of the warrant is $28 [($53 − $25) × 1].

If the owner had the right to buy three shares of common stock with one warrant, the theoretical value of the warrant would be $84 [($53 − $25) × 3].

If the stock is selling for an amount below the option price, the warrant's value will be negative. Since this is illogical, we use a formula value of zero.

EXAMPLE 17-2

Assume the same facts as in Example 17-1, except that the stock is selling at $21 a share. The formula amount is −$4 [($21 − $25) × 1]. (However, a value of zero will be assigned.)

Warrants do not have an investment value because they pay neither interest nor dividends and carry no voting rights. Hence, the market value of a warrant derives solely from its convertibility value into common stock. But the market price of a warrant, referred to as the *premium* on the warrant, is usually more than its theoretical value. The lowest amount that a warrant will sell for is its theoretical value.

The value of a warrant depends on the remaining life of the option, dividend payments on the common stock, the variability in price of the common stock, whether the warrant is listed on the exchange, and the opportunity cost of funds for the investor. Warrants generally have a high value when their life is long, the dividend payment on common stock is small, the stock price is volatile, the warrant is listed on the exchange, and the value of funds to the investor is great (since the warrant requires a smaller investment).

EXAMPLE 17-3

ABC stock currently has a market value of $50. The exercise price of the warrant is also $50. Therefore, the theoretical value of the warrant is $0. However, the warrant will sell at a premium (positive price) provided there is the possibility that the market price of the common stock will exceed $50 before the expiration of the warrant. The further into the future the expiration date, the greater the premium, since there is a longer period for possible price appreciation.

Of course, the lower the market price compared to the exercise price, the smaller the premium.

EXAMPLE 17-4

Assume the same facts as in Example 17-3, except that the current market price of the stock is $35. The warrant's premium in this instance will be much lower, since it would take a long time for the stock's price to increase to above $50 a share. If investors anticipate that the stock price will not increase above $50 at any time in the future, the warrants will be valued at $0.

If the market price of ABC stock rises above $50, the market price of the warrant will increase and the premium will decrease. In other words, when the stock price exceeds the exercise price, the market price of the warrant approximately equals the theoretical value, causing the premium to disappear. The reduction in the premium arises because of the reduced value of owning the warrant relative to exercising it.

Advantages and Disadvantages of Warrants

The advantages of issuing warrants include the following:

■ They permit the issuance of debt at a lower interest rate.

■ The company receives additional cash when the warrants are exercised.

The disadvantages of issuing warrants include the following:

■ When exercised, warrants dilute common stock, possibly reducing the market price of stock.

■ The warrants may be exercised at a time when the business has no need for additional capital.

Warrants vs. Stock Rights

There is a difference between a warrant and a *stock right*. A stock right is given free to current stockholders, who may either exercise them by buying new shares or sell them in the market. Stock rights also have shorter durations than warrants.

CONVERTIBLE SECURITIES

A *convertible security* is one that may be exchanged for common stock by the holder or, in some cases, the issuer, according to agreed-upon terms. Examples are convertible bonds and convertible preferred stock. A specified number of shares of stock are received by the holder of the convertible security at the time of the exchange; the number is determined by the *conversion ratio,* which equals:

$$\text{Conversion ratio} = \frac{\text{Par value of convertible security}}{\text{Conversion price}}$$

The *conversion price* is the effective price paid by the holder for the common stock when the conversion is effected. The conversion price and the conversion ratio are set when the convertible security is issued. The conversion price should be tied to the growth potential of the company; the greater the company's earnings potential, the higher the conversion price.

A convertible bond is considered a quasi-equity security because its market value is tied to its value if converted rather than its value as a bond. The convertible bond may be considered a delayed issue of common stock at a price above the current level.

EXAMPLE 17-5

If the conversion price of stock is $25 per share, a $1,000 convertible bond is convertible into 40 shares ($1,000/$25).

EXAMPLE 17-6

A $1,000 bond is convertible into thirty shares of stock. The conversion price is $33.33 ($1,000/30 shares).

EXAMPLE 17-7

A share of convertible preferred stock with a par value of $50 is convertible into four shares of common stock. The conversion price is $12.50 ($50/4).

EXAMPLE 17-8

A $1,000 convertible bond that entitles the holder to convert the bond into 10 shares of common stock is issued. Hence, the conversion ratio is ten shares for one bond. Since the face value of the bond is $1,000, the holder tenders this amount upon conversion. The conversion price equals $100 per share ($1,000/10 shares).

EXAMPLE 17-9

An investor holds a $1,000 convertible bond that is convertible into forty shares of common stock. Assuming the common stock is selling for $35 a share, the bondholder can convert the bond into forty shares worth $1,400. If the convertible bond is traded as a bond, it would trade at 140, or $1,400.

EXAMPLE 17-10

Y Company issued a $1,000 convertible bond at par. The conversion price is $40. The conversion ratio is:

$$\text{Conversion ratio} = \frac{\text{Par value of convertible security}}{\text{Conversion price}}$$
$$= \frac{\$1,000}{\$40}$$
$$= 25$$

The conversion value of a security is computed as follows:

$$\text{Conversion value} = \text{Common stock price} \times \text{Conversion ratio}$$

When a convertible security is issued, its percentage conversion premium is computed in the following manner:

$$\text{Percentage conversion premium} = \frac{\text{Market value} - \text{Conversion value}}{\text{Conversion value}}$$

EXAMPLE 17-11

LA Corporation issued a $1,000 convertible bond at par. The market price of the common stock at the date of issue was $48. The conversion price is $55.

$$\text{Conversion ratio} = \frac{\text{Par value of convertible security}}{\text{Conversion price}}$$

$$= \frac{\$1,000}{\$55}$$

$$= 18.18$$

Conversion value of the bond equals:

Common stock price $\times$ Conversion ratio = $48 \times 18.18 = $872

The difference between the conversion value of $872 and the issue price of $1,000 constitutes the conversion premium of $128. The conversion premium may also be expressed as a percentage of the conversion value. The percent in this case is:

Percentage conversion premium equals:

$$\frac{\text{Market value} - \text{Conversion value}}{\text{Conversion value}} = \frac{\$1,000 - \$872}{872}$$

$$= \frac{\$128}{\$872}$$

$$= 14.7\%$$

The conversion terms may not be static but may increase in steps over specified time periods. Hence, as time passes, fewer common shares will be exchanged for the bond. In some instances, the conversion option may expire after a certain time period.

Typically, convertible securities contain a clause protecting them from dilution caused by stock dividends, stock splits, and stock rights. The clause usually prevents the issuance of common stock at a price lower than the conversion price; in addition, the conversion price is reduced by the percentage amount of any stock split or stock dividend, enabling the shareholder of common stock to maintain his or her proportionate interest.

EXAMPLE 17-12

A three-for-one stock split occurs, which requires a tripling of the conversion ratio. A 20 percent stock dividend requires a 20 percent increase in the conversion ratio.

EXAMPLE 17-13

Assume the same facts as in Example 17-8 coupled with a four-for-one split. The conversion ratio now becomes 40, and the conversion price now becomes $25.

The decision whether to convert a security depends on a comparison of the interest on the bond to the dividend on the stock, the risk preference of the holder (stock has a greater risk than a bond), and the current and expected market price of the stock.

Valuation of Convertibles

A convertible security is a hybrid security, because it has attributes of both common stock and bonds. The expectation is that the holder will ultimately receive both interest yield and a capital gain. Interest yield is the coupon interest compared to the market price of the bond at purchase. The capital gain yield is the difference between the conversion price and the stock price at the issuance date and the expected growth rate in stock price.

Conversion value is the value of the stock received at conversion. As the price of the stock increases, so will its conversion value.

EXAMPLE 17-14

A $1,000 bond is convertible into eighteen shares of common stock with a market value of $52 per share. The conversion value of the bond equals:

$$\$52 \times 18 \text{ shares } = \$936$$

EXAMPLE 17-15

At the date of a $100,000 convertible bond issue, the market price of the stock is $18 a share. Each $1,000 bond is convertible into fifty shares of stock. The conversion ratio is thus 50. The number of shares the bond issue is convertible into is:

100 bonds ($100,000/$1,000) × 50 shares = 5,000 shares

The conversion value is $90,000 ($18 × 5,000 shares).

If the stock price is expected to grow at 6 percent per year, the conversion value at the end of the first year is:

Shares	5,000
Stock price ($18 × 1.06)	$19.08
Conversion value	$95,400

The conversion value at the end of year 2 is:

Shares	5,000
Stock price ($19.08 × 1.06)	$20.22
Conversion value	$101,100

Businesses that issue convertible bonds expect the value of common stock to appreciate and the bonds to be converted. If conversion does occur, the company can then issue another convertible bond. Such a financial policy is known as "leapfrog financing." If the market price of the common stock drops instead of rising, the holder will not convert the debt into equity. In this instance, the convertible security continues as debt and is termed a "hung" convertible.

A convertible security holder may prefer to hold the security instead of converting it even though the conversion value exceeds the price paid for it. First, as the price of the common stock increases, so will the price of the convertible security. Second, the holder receives regular interest payments or preferred dividends. To force conversion, companies issuing convertibles often have a call price that is higher than the face value of the bond (usually 10 to 20 percent higher). This practice in effect forces holders of convertibles to exchange them for stock as long as the stock price exceeds the conversion price, because the holder naturally prefers having common stock that is worth more than the call price he or she would receive for the bond.

The issuing company may force conversion of its convertible bond into common stock when such a move is financially advantageous, such as when the market price of the stock has dropped or when the interest rate on the convertible debt rises above prevailing market interest rates.

EXAMPLE 17-16

The conversion price on a $1,000 debenture is $40 and the call price is $1,100. Thus, upon conversion twenty-five shares ($1,000/$40) are received. In order for the conversion value of the bond to equal the call price, the market price of the stock would have to be $44 ($1,000/25). If the conversion value of the bond is 15 percent higher than the call price, the approximate market price of common stock would be $51 (1.15 × $44). At a $51 price, conversion is virtually guaranteed, since if the investor did not convert he or she would incur a material opportunity loss if the bond is called.

EXAMPLE 17-17

ABC Company's convertible bond has a conversion price of $800. The conversion ratio is 10. The market price of the stock is $140. The call price is $1,100. The bondholder would rather convert to common stock with a market value of $1,400 ($140 × 10) than have his or her convertible bond redeemed at $1,100. In this instance, the call provision forces the conversion when the bondholder might be tempted to wait longer.

Advantages and Disadvantages of Convertibles

The advantages of issuing convertible securities are:

■ It acts as a "sweetener" in a debt offering by giving the investor a chance to take part in the price appreciation of common stock.

■ The issuance of convertible debt allows for a lower interest rate on the financing compared to issuing straight debt.

■ A convertible security may be issued in a tight money market, when it is difficult for a creditworthy firm to issue a straight bond or preferred stock.

■ Convertibles usually involve fewer financing restrictions than straight debt.

■ Convertibles provide a means of issuing equity at prices higher than current market prices.

■ The call provision enables the company to force conversion whenever the market price of the stock exceeds the conversion price.

■ If the company were to issue straight debt now and common stock later to meet the debt, it would incur flotation costs twice; with convertible debt, flotation costs occur only once, at the initial issuance of the convertible bonds.

To the holder, the advantages of convertible securities are:

■ They offer the potential of a significant capital gain due to price appreciation of the common stock.

■ They offer the holder protection if corporate performance falls off.

■ The margin requirement (the amount an investor deposits when borrowing from the broker to purchase securities) for convertible bonds is lower than that for common stock. More money can be borrowed from the broker to invest in convertibles.

The disadvantages of issuing convertible securities are:

■ If the company's stock price increases appreciably in value, the company would have been better off financing through a regular common stock issue at the higher price rather than allowing conversion at the lower price.

■ The company is obligated to pay the convertible debt if the stock price does not rise.

To the holder, disadvantages of convertible securities are:
- The yield on a convertible security is lower than that on a comparable security that does not have the conversion option.
- A convertible bond is usually subordinated to other debt obligations and therefore typically has a lower bond rating.

CORPORATE FINANCING STRATEGY

When a company's stock price is depressed, it should issue convertible debt instead of common stock if the stock price is expected to rise. Establishing a conversion price above the present market price of stock will require issuing fewer shares when the bonds are converted compared to selling the shares at the current lower price. Of course, the conversion will occur only if the price of the stock rises above the conversion price. The drawback is that if the stock price does not increase and conversion does not take place, the company must face the debt burden of repaying the principal.

A convertible issuance is not recommended for a company with a modest growth rate, since it would take a long time to force conversion. During the intervening time, the company will not be able to secure additional financing easily. A long conversion interval may imply to the investing public that the stock has not done as well as expected. The company's growth rate is a prime consideration in determining whether convertibles are the best method of financing.

A company may also issue bonds that may be exchanged for the common stock of other companies. The issuer may do this if it owns a sizable stake in another company's stock, if it wants to raise cash currently, and if it intends to sell the shares at a later date because it expects the share price to rise.

In conclusion, convertibility usually allows the company to pay a lower interest rate. Since equity is the most expensive form of financing, issuing convertibles that never reach conversion might be viewed as an optimal strategy. A convertible bond is a delayed common equity financing to be used when the issuer expects its stock price to rise in the future (e.g., over the next two to four years) to stimulate conversion.

FINANCIAL STATEMENT ANALYSIS

When performing financial statement analysis, the creditor should consider a convertible bond with an attractive conversion feature as equity instead of debt since in all likelihood it will be converted into common stock and the future payment of interest and principal on the debt will not be required.

CONVERTIBLES VERSUS WARRANTS

The differences between convertibles and warrants are:

1. Exercising convertibles does not usually provide additional funds to the company, while the exercise of warrants does.

2. When conversion occurs, the company's debt ratio is reduced. However, the exercise of warrants adds to the equity position and debt remains unchanged.

3. Because of the call feature, the company has more control over its capital structure with convertibles than with warrants.

DERIVATIVES

A derivative is a contract whose value is tied to the value of an underlying asset (e.g., foreign currency, market index, stock, debt security). Derivative can be used to reduce risk exposure such as that related to foreign exchange exposure. Speculators can attempt to obtain significant profit from price level changes or simultaneous price differences in different markets. Further, derivatives may be used to hedge a position so that an unfavorable price movement in one asset is offset by a favorable price movement in another asset.

OPTIONS

An option is a contract to give the investor the right-but not an obligation-to buy or sell something. It has three main features. It allows you, as an investor, to "lock in"

- a specified number of shares of stock,
- at a fixed price per share, called strike or exercise price,
- for a limited length of time.

EXAMPLE 17-18

If you have purchased an option on a stock, you have the right to "exercise" the option at any time during the life of the option. This means that, regardless of the current market price of the stock, you have the right to buy or sell a specified number of shares of the stock at the strike price (rather than the current market price).

Calls and puts are types of options. You can buy or sell options in round lots, typically 100 shares.

When you buy a call, you are buying the right to purchase stock at a fixed price. You do this when you anticipate the price of the stock will go up. In buying a call you have the chance to make a significant gain from a small investment if the stock price increases, but you also risk the loss of your entire investment if the stock does not increase in price. Calls are in bearer-negotiable form with a life of one to nine months.

The price per share for 100 shares, which the purchaser may buy (call), is referred to as the *striking price (exercise price)*. For a put, it is the price at which the stock may be sold. The purchase or sale of the stock is to the writer of the option. The striking price is set for the life of the option on the options exchange. When stock price changes, new exercise prices are introduced for trading purposes reflecting the new value.

The option expires on the last day it can be exercised. Conventional options can expire on any business day, whereas options have a standardized expiration date.

The cost of an option is termed the *premium*. It is the price the purchaser of the call or put has to pay the writer.

PREMIUM FOR A CALL OPTION

The premium depends on the exchange on which the option is listed, prevailing interest rates, dividend trend of the related security, trading volume, market price of the stock it applies to, amount of time remaining before the expiration date, variability in the price of the related security, and width of the spread in price of the stock relative to the option's exercise price (a wider spread means a higher price).

IN-THE-MONEY AND OUT-OF-THE-MONEY

When the market price is greater than the strike price, the call is in-the-money. When the market price is less than the strike price, the call is out-of-the-money.

	A Call at a $50 Strike Price
In-the-money	Over $50
At-the-money	$50
Out-of-the-money	Under $50

Call options in-the-money have an intrinsic value equal to the difference between the market price and the strike price.

Value of call $=$ (Market price of stock $-$ Exercise price of call) $\times 100$

The market price of stock is at the current date. Of course, the market price will typically change on a stock each day. The exercise (strike) price of the call is fixed for its life. For example, the exercise (strike) price for a 3-month call is the same for the entire period.

EXAMPLE 17-19

The market price per share of a stock is $45, with a strike price of $40. Remember that one call is for 100 shares of stock. The value of the call is

$$\$45 - \$40 = \$5 \times 100 \text{ shares } = \$500$$

Recall that out-of-the-money call options have no intrinsic value.

In effect, the total premium consists of the intrinsic value plus speculative premium (time value) based on factors such as risk, variability, forecasted future prices, expiration date, leverage, and dividend.

$$\text{Total premium } = \text{ Intrinsic value } + \text{ Speculative premium}$$

The call purchaser takes the risk of losing the entire investment price for the option if a price increase does not take place.

EXAMPLE 17-20

A two-month call option allows you to buy 500 shares of ABC Company at $20 per share. Within that time period, you exercise the option when the market price is $38. Your gain is $9,000 ($38 − $20 = $18 × 500 shares). If the market price had declined from $20 you would not have exercised the call option, and you would have lost your entire investment.

By purchasing a call you can own common stock for a fraction of the cost of purchasing regular shares. Calls cost significantly less than common stock. Leverage exists because a little change in common stock price can result in a major change in the call option's price. A part of the percentage gain in the price of the call is the speculative premium attributable to the remaining life on the call.

EXAMPLE 17-21

A stock has a current market price of $35. A call can be purchased for $300 allowing the acquisition of 100 shares at $35 each. If the price of the stock increases, the call will be worth more. Assume that the stock is at $55 at the call's expiration date.

The profit is $20 ($55 − $35) on each of the 100 shares of stock in the call, or a total of $2,000 on an investment of $300. A return of 667 percent ($2,000/$3,000) is earned.

THE BLACK-SCHOLES OPTION PRICING MODEL

The Black-Scholes option pricing model (OPM) provides the relationship between call option value and the five factors that determine the premium of an option's market value over its expiration value:

▬ *Time to maturity*—The longer the option period, the greater the value of the option.

▬ *Stock price volatility*—The greater the volatility of the underlying stock's price, the greater its value.

▬ *Exercise price*—The lower the exercise price, the greater the value.

▬ *Stock price*—The higher the price of the underlying stock, the greater the value.

▬ *Risk-free rate*—The higher the risk-free rate, the higher the value.

The formula is:

$$V = P[N(d_1)] - PV(E)[N(d_2)]$$

where V = Current value of a call option

P = current stock price

$PV(E)$ = present value of exercise or strike price of the option, $E = E/e^{-rt}$

r = risk-free rate of return, continuously compounded for t time periods

e = 2.71828

t = number of time periods until the expiration date (For example, 3 months means $t = 3/12 = 1/4 = 0.25$)

n = normal

$N(d)$ = probability that the normally distributed random variable Z is less than or equal to d

σ = standard deviation per period of (continuously compounded) rate of return on the stock

$d_1 = \ln[P/PV(E)]/\sigma\sqrt{t} + \frac{\sigma\sqrt{t}}{2}$

$d_2 = d_1 - \sigma\sqrt{t}$

The formula requires readily available input data, with the exception of σ^2, or volatility. P, X, r, and t are easily obtained. The implications of the option model are as follows:

▬ The value of the option increases with the level of stock price relative to the exercise price [P/PV(E)], the time to expiration, and the time to expiration times the stock's variability ($\sigma\sqrt{t}$).

Other properties:

▬ The option price is always less than the stock price.

▬ The option price never falls below the payoff to immediate exercise (P − E or zero, whichever is larger).

▬ If the stock is worthless, the option is worthless.

■ As the stock price becomes very large, the option price approaches the stock price less the present value of the exercise price.

EXAMPLE 17-22

The current price of Sigma Corporation's common stock is $59.375 per share. A call option on this stock has a $55 exercise price. It has 3 months to expiration. If the standard deviation of continuously compounded rate of return on the stock is 0.2968 and the risk-free rate is 5 percent per year, we calculate the value of this call option as follows.

First, calculate the time until the option expires in years:

$$t \text{ in years } = 30 \text{ days}/365 \text{ days } = 0.0822$$

Second, calculate the values of the other variables:

$$
\begin{aligned}
PV(E) &= E/e^{-rt} \\
&= \$50/e^{0.05 \times 0.0822} \\
&= \$54.774
\end{aligned}
$$

$$
\begin{aligned}
d_1 &= \ln[P/PV(E)]/\sigma\sqrt{t} + \frac{\sigma\sqrt{t}}{2} \\
&= \ln[\$59.375/\$54.774]/(0.2968 \times \sqrt{0.0822}) \\
&\quad +(0.2968 \times \sqrt{0.0822})/2 \\
&= 0.9904
\end{aligned}
$$

$$
\begin{aligned}
d_2 &= d_1 - \sigma\sqrt{t} \\
&= 0.9904 - 0.2968 \times \sqrt{0.0822} \\
&= 0.9053
\end{aligned}
$$

Next, use a table for standard normal distribution (See Table 17-1) to determine $N(d_1)$ and $N(d_2)$:

$$
\begin{aligned}
N(d_1) &= N(0.9904) = 0.8389 \\
N(d_2) &= N(0.9053) = 0.8173
\end{aligned}
$$

Finally, use those values to find the option's value:

$$
\begin{aligned}
V &= P[N(d_1)] - PV(E)[N(d_2)] \\
&= \$59.375(0.8389) - \$54.774(0.8173) \\
&= \$5.05
\end{aligned}
$$

This call option is worth $5.05, a little more than its value if it is exercised immediately, $4.375 ($59.375 − $55), as one should expect.

EXAMPLE 17-23

You want to determine the value of another option on the same stock that has an exercise price of $50 and expires in 45 days. The time until the option expires in years is t in years = 45 days/365 days = 0.1233. The values of the other variables are:

$$PV(E) = E=e^{-rt}$$
$$= \$50/e^{0.05 \times 0.1233}$$
$$= \$49.6927$$

$$d_1 = \ln[P/PV(E)]/\sigma\sqrt{t} + \frac{\sigma\sqrt{t}}{2}$$
$$= \ln[\$59.375/\$49.6927]/(0.2968 \times \sqrt{0.1233})$$
$$+(0.2968 \times \sqrt{0.1233})/2$$
$$= 1.7602$$

$$d_2 = d_1 - \sigma\sqrt{t}$$
$$= 1.7602 - 0.2968 \times \sqrt{0.1233}$$
$$= 1.6560$$

Next, use a table for the standard normal distribution (see Table 17-1) to determine $N(d_1)$ and $N(d_2)$:

$$N(d_1) = N(1.7603) = 0.9608$$
$$N(d_2) = N(1.6561) = 0.9511$$

Finally, use those values to find the option's value:

$$V = P[N(d_1)] - PV(E)[N(d_2)]$$
$$= \$59.375[0.9608] - \$49.6927[0.9511]$$
$$= \$9.78$$

The call option is worth more than the other option ($9.78 versus $5.05) since it has a lower exercise price and a longer time until expiration.

FUTURES

A futures is a contract to purchase or sell a given amount of an item for a given price by a certain date (in the future—thus the name "futures market"). The seller of a futures contract agrees to deliver the item to the buyer of the contract, who agrees to purchase the item. The contract specifies the amount, valuation, method, quality, month and means of delivery, and exchange to be traded in. The month of delivery is the expiration date; in other words, the date on which the commodity or financial instrument must be delivered.

Commodity contracts are guarantees by a seller to deliver a commodity (e.g., cocoa or cotton). Financial contracts are a commitment by the seller to deliver a financial instrument (e.g., a Treasury bill) or a specific amount of foreign currency.

Future markets can be used for both hedging and speculating.

EXAMPLE 17-24

Investors use hedging to protect their position in a commodity. For example, a citrus grower (the seller) will hedge to get a higher price for his products while a processor (or buyer) of the item will hedge to obtain a lower price. By hedging an investor minimizes the risk of loss but loses the prospect of sizable profit.

CHAPTER PERSPECTIVE

A warrant and a convertible security give the holder the option to convert the security into common stock at a later date. They may act as a "sweetener" to a debt issue. A warrant may be detached or nondetached from the bond it is associated with. The two types of convertible securities are convertible bonds and convertible preferred stock. A convertible bond is a "hybrid" security because, while it is debt, it will appreciate in value with an increase in the market price of the related stock. Financial derivatives are used to hedge risk.

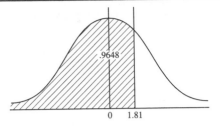

TABLE 17-1

NORMAL DISTRIBUTION TABLE

Areas under the normal curve

Z	0	1	2	3	4	5	6	7	8	9
.0	.5000	.5040	.5080	.5120	.5160	.5199	.5239	.5279	.5319	.5359
.1	.5398	.5438	.5478	.5517	.5557	.5596	.5636	.5675	.5714	.5753
.2	.5793	.5832	.5871	.5910	.5948	.5987	.6026	.6064	.6103	.6141
.3	.6179	.6217	.6255	.6293	.6331	.6368	.6406	.6443	.6480	.6517
.4	.6554	.6591	.6628	.6664	.6700	.6736	.6772	.6808	.6844	.6879
.5	.6915	.6950	.6985	.7019	.7054	.7088	.7123	.7157	.7190	.7224
.6	.7257	.7291	.7324	.7357	.7389	.7422	.7454	.7486	.7517	.7549
.7	.7580	.7611	.7642	.7673	.7703	.7734	.7764	.7794	.7823	.7852
.8	.7881	.7910	.7939	.7967	.7995	.8023	.8051	.8078	.8106	.8133
.9	.8159	.8186	.8212	.8238	.8264	.8289	.8315	.8340	.8365	.8389
1.0	.8413	.8438	.8461	.8485	.8508	.8531	.8554	.8577	.8599	.8621
1.1	.8643	.8665	.8686	.8708	.8729	.8749	.8770	.8790	.8810	.8830
1.2	.8849	.8869	.8888	.8907	.8925	.8944	.8962	.8980	.8997	.9015
1.3	.9032	.9049	.9066	.9082	.9099	.9115	.9131	.9147	.9162	.9177
1.4	.9192	.9207	.9222	.9236	.9251	.9265	.9278	.9292	.9306	.9319
1.5	.9332	.9345	.9357	.9370	.9382	.9394	.9406	.9418	.9430	.9441
1.6	.9452	.9463	.9474	.9484	.9495	.9505	.9515	.9525	.9535	.9545
1.7	.9554	.9564	.9573	.9582	.9591	.9599	.9608	.9616	.9625	.9633
1.8	.9641	.9648	.9656	.9664	.9671	.9678	.9686	.9693	.9700	.9706
1.9	.9713	.9719	.9726	.9732	.9738	.9744	.9750	.9756	.9762	.9767
2.0	.9772	.9778	.9783	.9788	.9793	.9798	.9803	.9808	.9812	.9817
2.1	.9821	.9826	.9830	.9834	.9838	.9842	.9846	.9850	.9854	.9857
2.2	.9861	.9864	.9868	.9871	.9874	.9878	.9881	.9884	.9887	.9890
2.3	.9893	.9896	.9898	.9901	.9904	.9906	.9909	.9911	.9913	.9916
2.4	.9918	.9920	.9922	.9925	.9927	.9929	.9931	.9932	.9934	.9936
2.5	.9938	.9940	.9941	.9943	.9945	.9946	.9948	.9949	.9951	.9952
2.6	.9953	.9955	.9956	.9957	.9959	.9960	.9961	.9962	.9963	.9964
2.7	.9965	.9966	.9967	.9968	.9969	.9970	.9971	.9972	.9973	.9974
2.8	.9974	.9975	.9976	.9977	.9977	.9978	.9979	.9979	.9980	.9981
2.9	.9981	.9982	.9982	.9983	.9984	.9984	.9985	.9985	.9986	.9986
3.0	.9987	.9990	.9993	.9995	.9997	.9998	.9998	.9999	.9999	1.0000

Failure and Reorganization

INTRODUCTION AND MAIN POINTS

In this chapter, we present the warning signs of potential bankruptcy. If bankruptcy can be predicted, the company may be able to do something to prevent it. We discuss the many ways to avoid liquidity and solvency problems.

When a company fails it can be reorganized or dissolved, depending on the circumstances. Business failures occur in a number of ways, including technical insolvency and bankruptcy.

In this chapter, you will learn:
- The quantitative and qualitative indicators of potential business failure.
- How the "Z score" is used.
- How future bankruptcy may be avoided.
- What bankruptcy is about.
- How extensions and compositions work.
- The implications of a Chapter 11 reorganization.
- The priority claims in bankruptcy.

SIGNS OF BANKRUPTCY

It is vital that you recognize the warning signs for impending bankruptcy and know what can be done to avoid failure.

Since bankruptcy occurs when the company is unable to meet maturing financial obligations, cash flow is one major predictor. Financial difficulties affect the P/E ratio, bond ratings, and the effective interest rate.

Many quantitative factors are used in predicting corporate failure, including:
- Low cash-flow-to-total-liabilities ratio
- High debt-to-equity ratio and high debt-to-total-assets ratio
- Low return on investment
- Low profit margin
- Low retained-earnings-to-total-assets ratio

■ Low working-capital-to-total-assets and low working-capital-to-sales ratios

■ Low fixed-assets-to-noncurrent-liabilities ratio

■ Inadequate interest-coverage ratio

■ Unstable earnings

■ Small company size measured in sales and/or total assets

■ Sharp decline in stock price, bond price, and earnings

■ A significant increase in beta (beta is the variability in the price of the company's stock relative to market index)

■ Large gap between market price per share and book value per share

■ Reduction in dividend payments

■ A significant rise in the company's weighted-average cost of capital

■ High fixed-cost-to-total-cost-structure (also called high operating leverage)

■ Failure to maintain capital assets (e.g., a decline in the ratio of repairs to fixed assets)

A comprehensive quantitative indicator used to predict failure is Altman's Z-score, which is based on a weighted-sum of financial ratios. The Z-score model has three general outcomes: likely bankruptcy, unlikely bankruptcy, and gray area.

The Z score is about 90 percent accurate in forecasting business failure one year in the future and about 80 percent accurate in forecasting it two years in the future. For a more detailed discussion of Z-score, see Edward I. Altman, "Financial Ratios, Discriminant Analysis, and the Prediction of Corporate Bankruptcy," *Journal of Finance,* September 1968.

The Z-score equals:

$$\frac{\text{Working capital}}{\text{Total assets}} \times 1.2 + \frac{\text{Retained earnings}}{\text{Total assets}} \times 1.4$$

$$+ \frac{\text{Operating income}}{\text{Total assets}} \times 3.3$$

$$+ \frac{\text{Market value of common and preferred stock}}{\text{Total liabilities}} \times 0.6$$

$$+ \frac{\text{Sales}}{\text{Total assets}} \times 1$$

The scores and the probability of failure developed by Altman follow:

Score	Probability of Failure
1.80 or less	Very high
1.81 − 2.7	High
2.8 − 2.9	Possible
3.0 or greater	Not likely

EXAMPLE 18-1

A company presents the following information:

Working capital	$280,000
Total assets	875,000
Total liabilities	320,000
Retained earnings	215,000
Sales	950,000
Operating income	130,000
Common stock	
Book value	220,000
Market value	310,000
Preferred stock	
Book value	115,000
Market value	170,000

The Z-score equals:

$$\frac{\$280,000}{\$875,000} \times 1.2 + \frac{\$215,000}{\$875,000} \times 1.4 + \frac{\$130,000}{\$875,000} \times 3.3$$
$$+ \frac{\$480,000}{\$320,000} \times 0.6 + \frac{\$950,000}{\$875,000} \times 1$$
$$= 0.384 + 0.344 + 0.490 + 0.9 + 1.0857$$
$$= 3.2037$$

The probability of failure is not likely.

The qualitative factors that predict failure include:
- Poor financial reporting system and inability to control costs
- Newness of company
- Declining industry
- High degree of competition
- Inability to obtain adequate financing and significant loan restrictions on any financing obtained
- Inability to meet past-due obligations
- Poor management
- Ventures into areas in which management lacks expertise

■ Failure of the company to keep up-to-date, especially in a techno-logically oriented business

■ High business risk, such as a positive correlation in the product line, meaning that demand for all the company's products moves up or down together, or susceptibility to strikes

■ Inadequate insurance coverage

■ Fraudulent actions (e.g., misstating inventories to avoid impending bankruptcy)

■ Cyclical business operations

■ Inability to adjust production to meet consumption needs

■ Susceptibility to stringent governmental regulation (e.g., rent control laws affecting landlords)

■ Susceptibility to energy shortages

■ Susceptibility to unreliable suppliers

■ Renegotiated debt and/or lease agreements

■ Deficient accounting and financial reporting systems

If you can predict with reasonable accuracy that the company is developing financial distress, you can better protect it and recommend corrective action.

AVOIDING BUSINESS FAILURE

Companies have many financial and quantitative ways to minimize the potential for failure. Liquidity and solvency problems may be minimized by:

■ Avoiding heavy debt. If liabilities are excessive, finance with equity.

■ Disposing of losing divisions and product lines.

■ Managing assets for maximum return and minimum risk.

■ Staggering and extending the maturity dates of debt.

■ Using quantitative techniques such as multiple regression analysis to compute the correlation between variables and the likelihood of business failure.

■ Ensuring that there is a safety buffer between actual status and compliance requirements (e.g., working capital) in connection with loan agreements.

■ Having a negative correlation in products and investments.

■ Lowering dividend payouts.

Nonfinancial factors that minimize the potential for failure include:

■ Vertical and horizontal diversification of product lines and operations.

■ Financing assets with liabilities of similar maturity (hedging).

- Diversifying geographically.
- Having adequate insurance.
- Enhancing the marketing effort.
- Engaging in cost-reduction programs.
- Improving productivity (e.g., using timely and detailed variance analysis).
- Minimizing the adverse effect of inflation and recession on the entity (e.g., price on a next-in, first-out basis).
- Investing in multi-purpose, rather than single-purpose, assets, because of their lower risks.
- Avoiding entering industries that have historically had a high failure rate.
- Having many projects, rather than only a few, that significantly affect operations.
- Introducing product lines that are only slightly affected by the business cycle and that possess stable demand.
- Avoiding going from a labor-intensive to a capital-intensive business, since the latter has a high operating leverage.
- Avoiding long-term fixed-fee contracts to customers and instead incorporating inflation adjustment and energy-cost indices in contracts.
- Avoiding markets that are on the downturn or that are already highly competitive.
- Adjusting to changes in technology.

BUSINESS FAILURE

A technically insolvent or bankrupt company may be considered a business failure.

Technical Insolvency

Technical insolvency means that the company cannot meet current obligations when due even if its total assets exceed its total liabilities. In this case, one or more creditors can petition to have a debtor judged insolvent by a court in order to obtain an orderly and equitable settlement of obligations.

Bankruptcy

In bankruptcy, liabilities exceed the fair market value of assets and the company has a negative real net worth.

According to law, a company failure can be either a technical insolvency or a bankruptcy. When credit or claims against a business are in question, the law gives creditors recourse against the company.

Some causes of business failure include poor management, an economic downturn that affects the company and/or industry, overexpansion, the end of the company's life cycle, lawsuit, and catastrophe.

VOLUNTARY SETTLEMENT

A voluntary settlement with creditors allows the company to save many of the costs that would occur in bankruptcy while enabling it to recover some of its investment. Such a settlement is reached out of court and permits the company to either continue or be liquidated.

A creditor committee may elect to permit the company to operate if it is anticipated that the company will recover. Creditors may also keep doing business with the company. To sustain the company's existence, there may be:

- An extension
- A composition
- Integration of each

Extension

In an *extension,* creditors receive the balances due them—but over an extended time period. Current purchases by the company are made with cash. Creditors may agree not only to extend the maturity date for payment but also to subordinate their claims to current debt for suppliers providing credit in the extension period. The creditors expect the debtor to be able to work out its problems.

The creditor committee may mandate certain controls, including establishing legal control over the company's assets or common stock, obtaining a security interest in assets, and obtaining the right to approve all cash payments.

If some creditors dissent from the extension agreement, they may be paid immediately to prevent their having the company declared bankrupt.

Composition

In a *composition,* creditors voluntarily reduce the amount the debtor owes them. The creditor obtains from the debtor a specified percent of the obligation in full satisfaction of the debt, regardless of how low the percent is. The agreement permits the debtor to continue to operate. The creditor may attempt to work with the debtor in handling the company's financial difficulties in hope of eventually obtaining a stable customer. The benefits of a composition are that it eliminates court costs as well as the stigma of a bankruptcy.

For an extension or composition to be practical, it should be reasonable to expect that the debtor will recover, and present business conditions must be conducive to that recovery.

Integration

In an *integrated* agreement, the company and creditors negotiate a plan involving a combination of extension and composition. For example, the agreement may provide for a 10 percent cash payment of the balance owed plus five future payments of 15 percent each, usually in notes. The total payment is thus 85 percent.

The benefits of a negotiated settlement are these:
- They cost less, particularly in legal fees.
- They are easier to implement than bankruptcy proceedings.
- They are less formal than bankruptcy.

The following drawbacks to a negotiated settlement exist:
- If the troubled debtor still has control over its business affairs, asset values may decline further. However, creditor control can provide some protection.
- Unrealistic small creditors may drain the negotiating process.

BANKRUPTCY REORGANIZATION

If no voluntary settlement is agreed upon, creditors may put the company into bankruptcy, which may either reorganize or liquidate the company.

Bankruptcy occurs when the company cannot pay its bills or when liabilities exceed the fair market value of the assets. A company may file for reorganization under which it will formulate a plan for continued life.

Chapter 11 of the Bankruptcy Reform Act of 1978 describes the steps involved in reorganizing a failed business. (Chapter 7 of the Bankruptcy Reform Act, which outlines the procedures to be followed for liquidation, applies when reorganization is not practical.)

The two kinds of reorganization petitions are:

1. *Voluntary*—In this petition the company seeks its own reorganization. The company need not be insolvent to file for voluntary reorganization.
2. *Involuntary*—Creditors file for an involuntary reorganization of the company and must establish either that the debtor firm is not meeting its debts when due or that a creditor or another party has taken control of the debtor's assets. In general, most of the creditors or claims must support the petition.

The five steps in a reorganization are:
1. A reorganization petition is filed under Chapter 11 in court.
2. A judge approves the petition and either appoints a trustee or allows the creditors to elect one to handle the disposition of the assets.
3. The trustee provides a fair plan of reorganization to the court.
4. The plan is given to the creditors and stockholders of the company for approval.
5. The debtor pays the expenses of the parties performing services in the reorganization proceedings.

The trustee in a reorganization plan is required to:
- Value the company
- Recapitalize the company
- Exchange outstanding debts for new securities

Valuation

In valuing the company, the trustee must estimate its liquidation value versus its value as a going concern. Liquidation is called for when the liquidation value exceeds the continuity value; if the company is more valuable when operating, reorganization is the answer. To determine the value of the reorganized company, the trustee must predict future earnings. The going concern value represents the present value of future earnings.

EXAMPLE 18-2

A petition for reorganization of a company was filed under Chapter 11. The trustee computed the firm's liquidation value after deducting expenses as $4.5 million. The trustee estimates that the reorganized business will generate $530,000 in annual earnings. The cost of capital is 10 percent. Assuming the earnings continue indefinitely, the value of the business is:

$$\$530,000/.10 = \$5,300,000$$

Since the company's value as a going concern ($5.3 million) exceeds its liquidation value ($4.5 million), reorganization is called for.

Recapitalization

If the trustee recommends company reorganization, a plan must be formulated by which it can meet its debts. This can be done in a number of ways. The obligations may be extended; equity securities may be issued in place of the debt; or income bonds may be given for the debentures. (Income bonds pay interest only when there are earnings.) The process of exchanging liabilities for other types of liabilities or equity securities is referred to as *recapitalization*. The objective of recapitalizing the company is to have a mixture of debt and equity that will allow the company to meet its debts and furnish a reasonable profit for the owners.

EXAMPLE 18-3

The current capital structure of Y Corporation is presented below.

Debentures	$1,500,000
Collateral bonds	3,000,000
Preferred stock	800,000
Common stock	2,500,000
Total	$7,800,000

There exists high financial leverage:

$$\frac{\text{Debt}}{\text{Equity}} = \frac{\$4,500,000}{\$3,300,000} = 1.36$$

Assuming the company is deemed to be worth $5 million as a going concern, the trustee can develop a less leveraged capital structure having a total capital of $5 million as follows:

Debentures	$1,000,000
Collateral bonds	1,000,000
Income bonds	1,500,000
Preferred stock	500,000
Common stock	1,000,000
Total	$5,000,000

It should be noted that this recapitalization has resulted in a significant loss to stockholders.

The income bond of $1.5 million is similar to equity in appraising financial leverage, since interest is not paid unless there is income. The new debt/equity ratio is safer:

$$\frac{\text{Debt } + \text{ collateral bonds}}{\text{Income bonds } + \text{ preferred stock } + \text{ common stock}}$$
$$= \frac{\$2,000,000}{\$3,000,000}$$
$$= 0.67$$

Exchange of Obligations

In exchanging obligations to arrive at the optimal capital structure, specified priorities must be followed. Senior claims are paid before junior ones, and holders of senior debt receive a claim on new capital equal to their prior claims. The lowest priority goes to common stockholders in receiving new securities. A debtholder typically receives a combination of different securities; holders of preferred and common stock may receive nothing. Typically, however, they retain some small ownership. After the exchange, the debtholders may become the company's new owners.

LIQUIDATION DUE TO BANKRUPTCY

A company that becomes bankrupt may be liquidated under Chapter 7. The major elements of liquidation are legal considerations, claim priority, and dissolution.

Legal Considerations

When a company is declared bankrupt by the court, creditors are required to meet between ten and thirty days after than declaration. A judge or referee takes charge of the meeting in which the creditors provide their claims, and a trustee is appointed by the creditors to handle the property of the defaulted firm, liquidate the business, maintain records, appraise the creditors' claims, make payments, and provide relevant information on the liquidation process.

Claim Priority

Some claims against the company take precedence over others in bankruptcy. The following rank order exists in meeting claims:

1. *Secured claims.* Secured creditors receive the value of the secured assets in support of their claims. If the value of the secured assets is inadequate to meet their claims in full, the balance reverts to general creditor status.
2. *Bankruptcy administrative costs.* These costs include any expenses of handling the bankruptcy, such as legal and trustee expenses.
3. *Unsecured salaries and commissions.* These claims are limited to a maximum specific amount per individual and must be incurred within ninety days of the bankruptcy petition.
4. *Unsecured customer deposit claims.* These claims are limited to a nominal amount each. An example is a deposit made by a customer for future goods or services.
5. *Taxes.* Tax claims are unpaid taxes due the government.
6. *General creditor claims.* These are claims made by general cred-

itors, who loaned the company money without specific collateral. Included are debentures and accounts payable.

7. *Preferred stockholders.*
8. *Common stockholders.*

Dissolution

After claims have been met in priority order and an accounting made of the proceedings, an application to *discharge* the bankrupt business may then be instituted. A discharge occurs when the court releases the company from legitimate debts in bankruptcy, with the exception of debts that are immune to discharge. As long as a debtor has not been discharged within the previous six years and was not bankrupt due to fraud, he or she may then start a new business.

EXAMPLE 18-4

The balance sheet of Ace Corporation for the year ended December 31, 20X4, follows:

Balance Sheet

Current assets	$400,000	Current liabilities	$475,000
Fixed assets	410,000	Long-term liabilities	250,000
		Common stock	175,000
		Retained earnings	(90,000)
		Total liabilities and	
Total assets	$810,000	stockholders' equity	$810,000

The company's liquidation value is $625,000. Rather than liquidate, the company could be reorganized with an investment of an additional $320,000. The reorganization is expected to generate earnings of $115,000 per year. A multiplier of 7.5 is appropriate. If the $320,000 is obtained, long-term debtholders will receive a negotiated 40 percent of the common stock in the reorganized business in substitution for their current claims.

If $320,000 of further investment is made, the business's going-concern value is $862,500 (7.5 × $115,000). The liquidation value is given at $625,000. Since the reorganization value exceeds the liquidation value, reorganization is called for.

EXAMPLE 18-5

Fixed assets with a book value of $1.5 million were sold for $1.3 million. There are mortgage bonds amounting to $1.8 million on the fixed assets. The proceeds from the collateral sale are inadequate to meet the secured claim. The unsatisfied portion of $500,000 ($1,800,000 − $1,300,000) of the claim becomes a general creditor claim.

EXAMPLE 18-6
Land having a book value of $1.2 million was sold for $800,000. Mortgage bonds on the land are $600,000. The excess of $200,000 will be returned to the trustee to pay other creditors.

EXAMPLE 18-7
Charles Company is bankrupt. The book and liquidation values follow:

	Book Value	Liquidation Value
Cash	$ 600,000	$ 600,000
Accounts receivable	1,900,000	1,500,000
Inventory	3,700,000	2,100,000
Land	5,000,000	3,200,000
Buildings	7,800,000	5,300,000
Equipment	6,700,000	2,800,000
Total assets	$25,700,000	$15,500,000

The liabilities and stockholders' equity at the date of liquidation are:

Current liabilities		
Accounts payable	$1,800,000	
Notes payable	900,000	
Accrued taxes	650,000	
Accrued salaries	450,000[a]	
Total current liabilities		$ 3,800,000
Long-term liabilities		
Mortgage on land	$3,200,000	
First mortgage—building	2,800,000	
Second mortgage—building	2,500,000	
Subordinated debentures	4,800,000	
Total long-term liabilities		13,300,000
Total liabilities		$17,100,000

[a] The salary owed each worker is below the specified amount and was incurred within 90 days of the bankruptcy petition.

Stockholders' equity		
Preferred stock	$4,700,000	
Common stock	6,800,000	
Retained earnings	(2,900,000)	
Total stockholders' equity		8,600,000
Total liabilities and		
stockholders' equity		$25,700,000

Expenses of the liquidation including legal costs were 15 percent of the proceeds. The debentures are subordinated only with regard to the two first-mortgage bonds.

The distribution of the proceeds follows:

Proceeds		$15,500,000
Mortgage on land	$3,200,000	
First mortgage—building	2,800,000	
Second mortgage—building	2,500,000	
Liquidation expenses		
(15% × $15,500,000)	2,325,000	
Accrued salaries	450,000	
Accrued taxes	650,000	
Total		11,925,000
Balance		$ 3,575,000

The percent to be paid to general creditors is:

$$\frac{\text{Proceeds balance}}{\text{Total owed}} = \frac{\$3,575,000}{\$7,500,000} = 47.66667\%$$

The balance due general creditors follows:

General Creditors	Owed	Paid
Accounts payable	$1,800,000	$ 858,000
Notes payable	900,000	429,000
Subordinated debentures	4,800,000	2,288,000
Total	$7,500,000	$3,575,000

EXAMPLE 18-8

The balance sheet of the Oakhurst Company follows:

ASSETS
Current assets

Cash	$ 9,000	
Marketable securities	6,000	
Receivables	1,100,000	
Inventory	3,000,000	
Prepaid expenses	4,000	
Total current assets		$4,119,000

Noncurrent assets

Land	$1,800,000	
Fixed assets	2,000,000	
Total noncurrent assets		3,800,000
Total assets		$7,919,000

LIABILITIES AND STOCKHOLDERS' EQUITY
Current liabilities

Accounts payable	$ 180,000	
Bank loan payable	900,000	
Accrued salaries	300,000[a]	
Employee benefits payable	70,000[b]	
Customer claims—unsecured	80,000[c]	
Taxes payable	350,000	
Total current liabilities		$1,880,000

Noncurrent liabilities

First mortgage payable	$1,600,000	
Second mortgage payable	1,100,000	
Subordinated debentures	700,000	
Total noncurrent liabilities		3,400,000
Total liabilities		$5,280,000

Stockholders' equity

Preferred stock (3,500 shares)	$ 350,000	
Common stock (8,000 shares)	480,000	
Paid-in capital	1,600,000	
Retained earnings	209,000	
Total stockholders' equity		2,639,000
Total liabilities and stockholders' equity		$7,919,000

---

[a] The salary owed to each worker is below the specified amount and was incurred within 90 days of the bankruptcy petition.

[b] Employee benefits payable have the same limitations as unsecured wages and satisfy for eligibility in bankruptcy distribution.

[c] No customer claim is greater than the nominal amount.

Additional data are as follows:

1. The mortgages apply to the company's total noncurrent assets.
2. The subordinated debentures are subordinated to the bank loan payable. Therefore, they come after the bank loan payable in liquidation.
3. The trustee has sold the company's current assets for $2.1 million and the noncurrent assets for $1.9 million. Therefore, a total of $4 million was received.
4. The business is bankrupt, since the total liabilities of $5.28 million are greater than the $4 million of the fair value of the assets.

Assume that the administration expense for handling the bankrupt company is $900,000. This liability is not reflected in the preceding balance sheet.

The allocation of the $4 million to the creditors follows:

Proceeds		$4,000,000
Available to secured creditors		
First mortgage—payable from $1,900,000 proceeds of noncurrent assets	$1,600,000	
Second mortgage—payable from balance of proceeds of noncurrent assets	300,000	1,900,000
Balance after secured creditors		$2,100,000
Next priority		
Administrative expenses	$ 900,000	
Accrued salaries	300,000	
Employee benefits payable	70,000	
Customer claims—unsecured	80,000	
Taxes payable	350,000	1,700,000
Proceeds available to general creditors		$ 400,000

Now that the claims on the proceeds from liquidation have been met, general creditors receive the balance on a pro rata basis. The distribution of the $400,000 follows:

General Creditor	Amount	Pro Rata Allocation for Balance to Be Paid[*]
Second-mortgage balance ($1,100,000 − $300,000)	$ 800,000	$124,031[1]
Accounts payable	180,000	27,907
Bank loan payable	900,000	248,062[a]
Subordinated debentures	700,000	0
Total	$2,580,000	$400,000

---

[*] $\dfrac{\text{Individual creditor amount}}{\text{Total amount}} \times$ Total to be allocated

[1] $\dfrac{\$800,000}{\$2,580,000} \times \$400,000 = \$124,031$

[a] Since the debentures are subordinated, the bank loan payable must be satisfied in full before amount can go to the subordinated debentures. The subordinated debenture holders therefore receive nothing.

CHAPTER PERSPECTIVE

There are signs of potential bankruptcy that must be noted and corrective action must be taken. Several ways exist to sustain the company's existence, including extension and composition. A voluntary or involuntary corporate reorganization may also occur. In liquidating the business, a priority order of claims has to be followed.

International Finance

INTRODUCTION AND MAIN POINTS

Multinational corporations (MNCs) have significant foreign operations deriving a high percentage of their sales overseas. Financial managers of MNCs must understand the complexities of international finance so that they can make sound financial and investment decisions. Multinational finance involves consideration of managing working capital, financing the business, assessing control of foreign exchange and political risks, and evaluating foreign direct investments. Most importantly, the financial manager must consider the value of the U.S. dollar relative to the value of the currency of the foreign country in which business activities are being conducted.

In this chapter you will learn:
- Special features of an MNC.
- The foreign exchange market and how it works.
- How to manage foreign currency risk.
- The impact of changes in foreign exchange rates.
- Theorems associated with interest rates, inflation, and exchange rates.
- How to analyze foreign investments.
- International sources of financing.

SPECIAL PROBLEMS OF A MULTINATIONAL CORPORATION

- *Multiple-currency problem.* Sales revenues may be collected in one currency, while assets are denominated in another, and profits measured in a third.
- *Various legal, institutional, and economic constraints.* There are variations in such things as tax laws, labor practices, balance of payment policies, and government controls with respect to the types and sizes of investments, types and amount of capital raised, and repatriation of profits.
- *Internal control problem.* When the parent office of an MNC and its affiliates are widely located, internal organizational difficulties arise.

FOREIGN EXCHANGE MARKET

Except in a few European centers, there is no central marketplace for the foreign exchange market. Rather, business is carried out over telephone, telex, or the Internet. The major dealers are large banks. A company that wants to buy or sell currency typically uses a commercial bank. International transactions and investments involve more than one currency. For example, when a U.S. company sells merchandise to a Japanese firm, the former wants to be paid in dollars, but the Japanese company typically expects to receive yen. Because of the foreign exchange market, the buyer may pay in one currency, but the seller receives payment in another currency.

SPOT AND FORWARD FOREIGN EXCHANGE RATES

An exchange rate is the ratio of one unit of currency to another. An exchange rate is established between the different currencies. The conversion rate between currencies depends on the demand/supply relationship. Because of the change in exchange rates, companies are susceptible to exchange rate fluctuation risks because of a net asset or net liability position in a foreign currency.

Exchange rates may be in terms of dollars per foreign currency unit (called a *direct quote*) or units of foreign currency per dollar (called an *indirect quote*). Therefore, an indirect quote is the reciprocal of a direct quote and vice versa.

$$\text{Indirect quote} = 1/\text{Direct quote}$$
$$\text{Pound/\$} = 1/(\$/\text{pound})$$

Figure 19.1 presents a sample of indirect and direct quotes for selected currencies.

EXAMPLE 19-1

A rate of 1.617/British pound means each pound costs the U.S. company $0.6184. In other words, the U.S. company gets $1/1.617 = 0.6184$ pounds for each U.S. dollar.

The spot rate is the exchange rate for immediate delivery of currencies exchanged, whereas the forward rate is the exchange rate for later delivery of currencies exchanged. For example, there may be a 90-day exchange rate. The forward exchange rate of a currency will be slightly different from the spot rate at the current date because of future expectations and uncertainties.

Forward rates may be greater than the current spot rate (premium) or less than the current spot rate (discount).

Country	Contract	U.S. Dollar Equivalent	Currency per U.S. $
Britain	Spot	1.6170	0.6184
(Pound)	30-day future	1.6153	0.6191
	90-day future	1.6130	0.6200
	180-day future	1.6089	0.6215
Germany	Spot	0.7282	1.3733
(Mark)	30-day future	0.7290	1.3716
	90-day future	0.7311	1.3677
	180-day future	0.7342	1.3620
Japan	Spot	0.011955	83.65
(Yen)	30-day future	0.012003	83.31
	90-day future	0.012100	82.64
	180-day future	0.012247	81.65

Figure 19.1 *Foreign Exchange Rates (October 31, 20X0)*

Cross Rates

A cross rate is the indirect calculation of the exchange rate of one currency from the exchange rates of two other currencies.

EXAMPLE 19-2

The dollar per pound and the yen per dollar rates are given in Figure 19.1. From this information, you can determine the yen per pound (or pound per yen) exchanges rates. For example, you see that

$$(\$/pound) \times (yen/\$) = (yen/pound)$$
$$1.6170 \times 83.65 = 135.26 \text{ yen/pound}$$

Thus, the pound per yen exchange rate is:

$$1/135.26 = 0.00739 \text{ pound per yen}$$

Figure 19.2 displays the cross rates among key currencies.

EXAMPLE 19-3

On February 1, 20X8, forward rates on the British pound were at a premium in relation to the spot rate, whereas the forward rates for the Japanese yen were at a discount from the spot rate. This means that

	Britain	Germany	Japan	U.S.
Britain	—	0.45032	0.00739	0.61843
Germany	2.2206	—	0.01642	1.3733
Japan	135.26	60.912	—	83.65
U.S.	1.6170	0.72817	0.01195	—

Figure 19.2 *Key Currency Cross Rates (March 15, 20X0)*

participants in the foreign exchange market anticipated that the British pound would appreciate relative to the U.S. dollar in the future but the Japanese yen would depreciate against the dollar.

The percentage premium (P) or discount (D) is computed as follows:

$$P \ (orD) = \frac{F - S}{S} \times \frac{12 \text{ months}}{n} \times 100$$

where F, S = the forward and spot rates respectively and n = length of the forward contract in months.

If P > S, the result is the annualized premium in percent; otherwise, it is the annualized discount in percent.

EXAMPLE 19-4

On May 3, 20X1, a 30-day forward contract in Japanese yen was selling at a 4.8 percent discount:

$$\frac{0.012003 - 0.011955}{0.011955} \times \frac{12 \text{ months}}{1 \text{ month}} \times 100 = 4.82\%$$

CURRENCY RISK MANAGEMENT

Foreign exchange rate risk exists when the contract is written in terms of the foreign currency or denominated in the foreign currency. The exchange rate fluctuations increase the riskiness of the investment and incur cash losses. The financial manager not only must seek the highest return on temporary investments but also must be concerned about changing values of the currencies invested. You do not necessarily eliminate foreign exchange risk. You may only try to contain it. Some financial strategies follow.

In countries where currency values are likely to drop, financial managers of the subsidiaries should:

■ Avoid paying advances on purchase orders unless the seller pays interest on the advances sufficient to cover the loss of purchasing power.

■ Not have excess idle cash. Excess cash can be used to buy inventory or other real assets.

■ Buy materials and supplies on credit in the country in which the foreign subsidiary is operating, extending the final payment date as long as possible.

■ Avoid giving excessive trade credit. If accounts receivable balances are outstanding for an extended time period, interest should be charged to absorb the loss in purchasing power.

■ Borrow local currency funds when the interest rate charged does not exceed U.S. rates after taking into account expected devaluation in the foreign country.

Types of Foreign Exchange Exposure

Financial managers of MNCs are faced with the dilemma of three different types of foreign exchange risk. They are:

■ *Translation exposure,* often called *accounting exposure,* measures the impact of an exchange rate change on the firm's financial statements. An example would be the impact of a French franc devaluation on a U.S. firm's reported income statement and balance sheet.

■ *Transaction exposure* measures potential gains or losses on the future settlement of outstanding obligations that are denominated in a foreign currency. An example would be a U.S. dollar loss after the franc devalues, on payments received for an export invoiced in francs before that devaluation.

■ *Operating exposure,* often called *economic exposure,* is the potential for the change in the present value of future cash flows due to an unexpected change in the exchange rate.

Ways to Neutralize Foreign Exchange Risk

Foreign exchange risk can be neutralized or hedged by a change in the asset and liability position in the foreign currency. Here are some ways to control exchange risk.

Entering a Money-market Hedge. Here the exposed position in a foreign currency is offset by borrowing or lending in the money market.

EXAMPLE 19-5

XYZ, an American importer, enters into a contract with a British supplier to buy merchandise for 4,000 pounds. The amount is payable on the delivery of the goods, 30 days from today. The company knows the exact amount of its pound liability in 30 days. However, it does not know the payable in dollars. Assume that the 30-day money-market rates for both lending and borrowing in the United States and United Kingdom are 0.5% and 1%, respectively. Assume further that today's foreign exchange rate is $1.50 per pound.

In a money-market hedge, XYZ can take the following steps:

1. Buy a one-month U.K. money market security, worth $4,000/(1 + 0.005) = 3,980$ pounds. This investment will compound to exactly 4,000 pounds in one month.

2. Exchange dollars on today's spot (cash) market to obtain the 3,980 pounds. The dollar amount needed today is

$$3,980 \text{ pounds} \times \$1.7350 \text{ per pound} = \$6,905.30$$

3. If XYZ does not have this amount, it can borrow it from the U.S. money market at the going rate of 1%. In 30 days, XYZ will need to repay $\$6,905.30 \times (1 + 0.1) = \$7,595.83$.

Note: XYZ need not wait for the future exchange rate to be available. On today's date, the future dollar amount of the contract is known with certainty. The British supplier will receive 4,000 pounds, and the cost of XYZ to make the payment is $7,595.83.

Hedging by Purchasing Forward (or Futures) Exchange Contracts. A forward exchange contract is a commitment to buy or sell, at a specified future date, one currency for a specified amount of another currency (at a specified exchange rate). This can be a hedge against changes in exchange rates during a period of contract or exposure to risk from such changes. More specifically, do the following: (1) Buy foreign exchange forward contracts to cover payables denominated in a foreign currency and (2) sell foreign exchange forward contracts to cover receivables denominated in a foreign currency. This way, any gain or loss on the foreign receivables or payables due to changes in exchange rates is offset by the gain or loss on the forward exchange contract.

EXAMPLE 19-6

In the previous example, assume that the 30-day forward exchange rate is $1.6153. XYZ may take the following steps to cover its payable.

1. Buy a forward contract today to purchase 4,000 pounds in 30 days.

2. On the 30th day pay the foreign exchange dealer 4,000 pounds × $1.6153 per pound = $6,461.20 and collect 4,000 pounds. Pay this amount to the British supplier. Using the forward contract XYZ knows the exact worth of the future payment in dollars ($6,461.20).

Note: The basic difference between futures contracts and forward contracts is that futures contracts are for specified amounts and maturities, whereas forward contracts are for any size and maturity.

Hedging by Foreign Currency Options. Foreign currency options can be purchased or sold in three different types of markets: (a) Options on the physical currency, purchased on the over-the- counter (interbank) market, (b) options on the physical currency, on organized exchanges such as the Philadelphia Stock Exchange and the Chicago Mercantile Exchange, and (c) options on futures contracts, purchased on the International Monetary Market (IMM) of the Chicago Mercantile Exchange.

Repositioning Cash. Financial managers can reposition cash by *leading* and *lagging* the time at which an MNC makes operational or financial payments. Often, money- and forward-market hedges are not available to eliminate exchange risk. Under such circumstances, leading (accelerating) and lagging (decelerating) may be used to *reduce* risk.

Maintaining Balance Between Receivables and Payables. A balance must be maintained between receivables and payables denominated in a foreign currency. MNCs typically set up "multilateral netting centers" as a special department to settle the outstanding balances of affiliates of an MNC with each other on a net basis. It is the development of a "clearinghouse" for payments by the firm's affiliates. If there are amounts due among affiliates, they are offset insofar as possible. The net amount would be paid in the currency of the transaction. The total amounts owed need not be paid in the currency of the transaction; thus, a much lower quantity of the currency must be acquired.

Positioning of Funds. Transfer pricing can be used to position funds. A transfer price is the price at which an MNC sells goods and services to its foreign affiliates or, alternatively, the price at which an affiliate sells to the parent. For example, a parent that wishes to transfer funds from an affiliate in a depreciating-currency country may charge a higher price on the goods and services sold to this affiliate by the parent or by affiliates from strong-currency countries. Transfer pricing affects not only transfer of funds from one entity to another but also the income taxes paid by both entities.

Key Questions to Ask That Help to Identify Foreign Exchange Risk

A systematic approach to identifying an MNC's exposure to foreign exchange risk is to ask a series of questions regarding the net effects on profits of changes in foreign currency revenues and costs. The questions are:

- Where is the MNC selling? (domestic vs. foreign sales share)
- Who are the firm's major competitors? (domestic vs. foreign)
- Where is the firm producing? (domestic vs. foreign)
- Where are the firm's inputs coming from? (domestic vs. foreign)

Currency	Weak Currency (Depreciation)	Strong (Appreciation)
Imports	More expensive	Cheaper
Exports	Cheaper	More expensive
Payables	More expensive	Cheaper
Receivables	Cheaper	More expensive

Figure 19.3 *The Impact of Changes in Foreign Exchange Rates*

■ How sensitive is quantity demanded to price? (elastic vs. inelastic)
■ How are the firm's inputs or outputs priced? (domestic market vs. global market; the currency of denomination)

IMPACT OF CHANGES IN FOREIGN EXCHANGE RATES

Figure 19.3 summarizes the impact of changes in foreign exchange rates on the company's products and financial transactions.

INTEREST RATES

Interest rates have an important influence on exchange rates. In fact, there is an important economic relationship between any two nations' spot rates, forward rates, and interest rates. This relationship is called the *interest rate parity theorem* (IRPT). The IRPT states that the ratio of the forward and spot rates is directly related to the two interest rates. Specifically, the premium or discount should be:

$$P \text{ (or D)} = -\frac{r_f - r_d}{1 + r_f}$$

where r_f and r_d = foreign and domestic interest rates.

When interest rates are relatively low, this equation can be approximated by $P \text{ (or D)} = -(r_f - r_d)$.

The IRPT implies that the P (or D) calculated by the equation should be the same as the P (or D) calculated by:

$$P \text{ (or D)} = \frac{F - S}{S} \times \frac{12 \text{ months}}{n} \times 100$$

EXAMPLE 19-7

On May 3, 20X1, a 30-day forward contract in Japanese yen was selling at a 4.82 percent premium:

$$\frac{0.012003 - 0.011955}{0.011955} \times \frac{12 \text{ months}}{1 \text{ month}} \times 100 = 4.82\%$$

The 30-day U.S. T-bill rate is 8 percent annualized. What is the 30-day Japanese rate?

Using the equation:

$$P \text{ (or D)} = -\frac{r_f - r_d}{1 + r_f}$$

$$0.0482 = \frac{0.08 - r_f}{1 + r_f}$$

$$-0.0318 = -1.0482 r_f$$

$$r_f = 0.0303$$

$$- 3.03\%$$

The 30-day Japanese rate should be 3.03 percent.

INFLATION

Inflation, which is a change in price levels, also affects future exchange rates. The mathematical relationship that links changes in exchange rates and changes in price level is called the *purchasing power parity theorem* (PPPT). The PPPT states that the ratio of the forward and spot rates is directly related to the two inflation rates:

$$\frac{F}{S} = \frac{1 + P_d}{1 + P_f}$$

where F = forward exchange rate (e.g., $/foreign currency)
  S = spot exchange rate (e.g., $/foreign currency)
  P_d = domestic inflation rate
  P_f = foreign inflation rate

EXAMPLE 19-8

Assume the following data for the United States and France:

> Expected U.S. inflation rate = 5%
> Expected French inflation rate = 10%
> S = $0.220/franc

Then,

$$\frac{F}{0.220} = \frac{1.05}{1.10}$$

So

$$F = \$0.210/\text{franc}$$

Note: If France has the higher inflation rate, then the purchasing power of the franc is declining faster than that of the dollar. This will lead to a forward discount on the franc relative to the dollar.

ANALYSIS OF FOREIGN INVESTMENTS

Foreign investment decisions are basically capital budgeting decisions at the international level. The decision requires three major components:

▬ *The estimation of the relevant future cash flows.* Cash flows are the dividends and possible future sales price of the investment. The estimation depends on the sales forecast, the effects on exchange rate changes, the risk in cash flows, and the actions of foreign governments.

▬ *The choice of the proper discount rate (cost of capital).* The cost of capital in foreign investment projects is higher due to the increased risks of:

• Currency risk (or foreign exchange risk)—changes in exchange rates. This risk may adversely affect sales by making competing imported goods cheaper.

• Political risk (or sovereignty risk)—possibility of nationalization or other restrictions with net losses to the parent company.

INTERNATIONAL SOURCES OF FINANCING

A company may finance its activities abroad, especially in countries it is operating in. A successful company in domestic markets is more likely to be able to attract financing for international expansion.

The most important international sources of funds are the Eurocurrency market and the Eurobond market. Also, MNCs often have access to national capital markets in which their subsidiaries are located.

The Eurocurrency market is a largely short-term (usually less than one year of maturity) market for bank deposits and loans denominated in any currency except the currency of the country where the market is located. For example, in London, the Eurocurrency market is a market for bank deposits and loans denominated in dollars, yen, francs, marks, and any other currency except British pounds. The main instruments used in this market are CDs and time deposits, and bank loans.

Note: The term "market" in this context is not a physical marketplace, but a set of bank deposits and loans.

The Eurobond market is a long-term market for bonds denominated in any currency except the currency of the country where the market is located. Eurobonds may be of different types such as straight, convertible, and with warrants. Although most Eurobonds are fixed rate, variable rate bonds also exist. Maturities vary, but 10–12 years is typical.

Although Eurobonds are issued in many currencies, you wish to select a stable, fully convertible, and actively traded currency. In some cases, if a Eurobond is denominated in a weak currency, the holder has the option of requesting payment in another currency.

Sometimes, large MNCs establish wholly owned offshore finance subsidiaries. These subsidiaries issue Eurobond debt, and the proceeds are given to the parent or to overseas operating subsidiaries. Debt service goes back to bondholders through the finance subsidiaries.

If the Eurobond was issued by the parent directly, the United States would require a withholding tax on interest. There may also be an estate tax when the bondholder dies. These tax problems do not arise when a bond is issued by a finance subsidiary incorporated in a tax haven. Hence, the subsidiary may borrow at less cost than the parent.

In summary, the Euromarkets offers borrowers and investors in one country the opportunity to deal with borrowers and investors from many other countries, buying and selling bank deposits, bonds, and loans denominated in many currencies.

CHAPTER PERSPECTIVE

Financial managers of MNCs require an understanding of the complexities of international finance to make sound financial and investment decisions. Multinational finance involves consideration of managing working capital, financing the business, assessing control of foreign exchange and political risks, and evaluating foreign direct investments. Especially, the financial manager has to understand how changes in foreign exchange rates affect not only receivables and payables but also imports and exports of the MNC in its multinational operations.

Online Internet Resources

Government Statistical Data on the Internet

Department of Labor-Bureau of Labor Statistics	http://www.bls.gov
Government statistics in general	http://www.fedstats.gov

Financial and Investment Information

EDGAR SEC database	http://www.sec.gov
Morningstar, Inc.	http://www.morningstar.net
Bridge Information Systems	http://www.bridge.com/front
American Association for Individual Investors	http://www.aaii.com
Amex: American Stock Exchange	http://www.amex.com
Money Radio	http://www.roadtosuccess.com
Bloomberg Online	http://www.bloomberg.com/welcome.html
Microsoft Investor	http://investor.msn.com
Investor's Business Daily	http://www.investors.com
Wall Street Journal	http://www.wsj.com
The Motley Fool	http://www.motleyfool.com
Barron's Magazine	http://www.barrons.com
Zacks Investment Research	http://www.zacks.com
Bank Rate Monitor	http://www.bankrate.com/brm/default.asp
Mutual Funds Interactive	http://www.fundsinteractive.com
CBS MarketWatch	http://cbs.marketwatch.com
S&P Personal Wealth	http://www.personalwealth.com

Excel Financial and Investment Functions

<u>ACCRINT</u>	Returns the accrued interest for a security that pays periodic interest
<u>ACCRINTM</u>	Returns the accrued interest for a security that pays interest at maturity
<u>AMORDEGRC</u>	Returns the depreciation for each accounting period
<u>AMORLINC</u>	Returns the depreciation for each accounting period
<u>COUPDAYBS</u>	Returns the number of days from the beginning of the coupon period to the settlement date
<u>COUPDAYS</u>	Returns the number of days in the coupon period that contains the settlement date
<u>COUPDAYSNC</u>	Returns the number of days from the settlement date to the next coupon date
<u>COUPNCD</u>	Returns the next coupon date after the settlement date
<u>COUPNUM</u>	Returns the number of coupons payable between the settlement date and maturity date
<u>COUPPCD</u>	Returns the previous coupon date before the settlement date
<u>CUMIPMT</u>	Returns the cumulative interest paid between two periods
<u>CUMPRINC</u>	Returns the cumulative principal paid on a loan between two periods
<u>DB</u>	Returns the depreciation of an asset for a specified period using the fixed-declining-balance method
<u>DDB</u>	Returns the depreciation of an asset for a specified period using the double-declining-balance method or some other method you specify
<u>DISC</u>	Returns the discount rate for a security
<u>DOLLARDE</u>	Converts a dollar price, expressed as a fraction, into a dollar price, expressed as a decimal number

DOLLARFR	Converts a dollar price, expressed as a decimal number, into a dollar price, expressed as a fraction
DURATION	Returns the annual duration of a security with periodic interest payments
EFFECT	Returns the effective annual interest rate
FV	Returns the future value of an investment
FVSCHEDULE	Returns the future value of an initial principal after applying a series of compound interest rates
INTRATE	Returns the interest rate for a fully invested security
IPMT	Returns the interest payment for an investment for a given period
IRR	Returns the internal rate of return for a series of cash flows
MDURATION	Returns the Macauley modified duration for a security with an assumed par value of $100
MIRR	Returns the internal rate of return where positive and negative cash flows are financed at different rates
NOMINAL	Returns the annual nominal interest rate
NPER	Returns the number of periods for an investment
NPV	Returns the net present value of an investment based on a series of periodic cash flows and a discount rate
ODDFPRICE	Returns the price per $100 face value of a security with an odd first period
ODDFYIELD	Returns the yield of a security with an odd first period
ODDLPRICE	Returns the price per $100 face value of a security with an odd last period
ODDLYIELD	Returns the yield of a security with an odd last period
PMT	Returns the periodic payment for an annuity
PPMT	Returns the payment on the principal for an investment for a given period
PRICE	Returns the price per $100 face value of a security that pays periodic interest
PRICEDISC	Returns the price per $100 face value of a discounted security
PRICEMAT	Returns the price per $100 face value of a security that pays interest at maturity
PV	Returns the present value of an investment

<u>RATE</u>	Returns the interest rate per period of an annuity
<u>RECEIVED</u>	Returns the amount received at maturity for a fully invested security
<u>SLN</u>	Returns the straight-line depreciation of an asset for one period
<u>SYD</u>	Returns the sum-of-years' digits depreciation of an asset for a specified period
<u>TBILLEQ</u>	Returns the bond-equivalent yield for a Treasury bill
<u>TBILLPRICE</u>	Returns the price per $100 face value for a Treasury bill
<u>TBILLYIELD</u>	Returns the yield for a Treasury bill
<u>VDB</u>	Returns the depreciation of an asset for a specified or partial period using a declining balance method
<u>XIRR</u>	Returns the internal rate of return for a schedule of cash flows that is not necessarily periodic
<u>XNPV</u>	Returns the net present value for a schedule of cash flows that is not necessarily periodic
<u>YIELD</u>	Returns the yield on a security that pays periodic interest
<u>YIELDDISC</u>	Returns the annual yield for a discounted security (e.g., a Treasury bill)
<u>YIELDMAT</u>	Returns the annual yield of a security that pays interest at maturity

Index